LEADERSHIP
Dynamics and Wellbeing

ENDORSEMENTS

Leadership is not a static concept, especially in a disruptive and connected world. It is complex and multi-dimensional. It needs to be understood and applied at contextual, operational and micro levels. Certainly it is much more than a set of competencies.

More has probably been written and spoken about leadership than almost any other topic throughout history. However, to understand leadership is to understand the concept from multiple perspectives. That is what this very comprehensive book provides. There is no single approach to leadership and the variety of perspectives provided in this book will further enhance our understanding and practice of leadership.

An important book with highly qualified and insightful contributors which will add to the conversations about leadership for a long time to come. An essential read for leaders and those responsible for leadership in their organisations now and in the future.

Terry Meyer, Strategy & Leadership Consultant, Leadership SA

Truly a standout book that packs a real punch in the sea of books on leadership. This extraordinary book has to be the most updated, and most comprehensive and definitive compendium on leaders and leadership, written by an impressive array of prominent and respected experts in the field.

Understanding the "what" and "how" of leadership is something that most organisations continue to grapple with in these volatile, complex, uncertain and ambiguous times. This book offers advice on the toughest challenges leaders are facing in business today.

This is compulsory reading for anyone seeking to understand and distil powerful perspectives on leadership and how to become a better leader.

The book provides robust perspectives on leadership fundamentals ranging from leadership theory, models and frameworks on leadership, leadership principles and philosophy, and, in addition, offers authentic, actionable examples. It is bursting with great tips and advice that are immediately applicable and anchored in research.

An indispensable and essential resource for leaders and aspiring leaders at all levels.

Shirley Zinn, Professor Shirley Zinn, Group HR Director, Woolworths

This book is rooted in the challenges facing leaders today, and offers current and future leaders a perspective to help them lead in a VUCA world. The authors take a unique view of leadership from a "value chain" perspective. They provide executives and those in the leadership development business a framework and insight into both being and building better leaders for tomorrow. I believe this book – a product of frontline leaders – will prove to be a great handbook for those who regard leadership as both an interest and a passion.

Paul Norman, MTN Group: Group Human Resources and Corporate Affairs Officer

I have read dozens of books on leadership but none of them has tackled this complex topic in the way that *Leadership Dynamics and Wellbeing* has done. This book tackles the real issues of leadership from understanding the foundations of leadership; to examining leadership within its unfolding context; to leadership identification, growth and development to issues of leadership transitions and leadership wellbeing. The insights and models are based on research and on real experiences and I particularly enjoyed the section on leadership articles and stories – real-life leadership experiences as told by the leaders themselves.

This book is that rare mix of a treasure house of up-to-date knowledge about every aspect of leadership and at the same time full of insights and suggestions for practical implementation. It is both thought-provoking and enlightening, and a must-read for anyone trying to understand the complex issues surrounding leadership. This is one of the best books on the topic of leadership I have been privileged to read.

Italia Boninelli, HR Strategist, Executive Coach and Author, (recent past Executive Vice-president: People and Organizational Development, AngloGold Ashanti)

The seminal guide to the kind of transformational leadership required in the 21ˢᵗ century and beyond.

S'ne Mkhize, Senior Vice President, Human Resources – Sasol

What a phenomenal work!

This is the most comprehensive, insightful and well-grounded work on leadership ever published in South Africa.

It unpacks leadership in its many facets and perspectives – from individual to organisational and global leadership.

The authors are thought leaders, scientists and subject-matter experts; they ask the difficult questions and reveal the essence of leadership as an art and science.

This book is a must for everybody in leadership positions – be it the business sector, public sector, religious organisations, education, or community organisations.

An ideal reference work for the consultant or business science practitioner.

Dr Johan de Beer, Human Capital Executive, Africa Division, Imperial Logistics

Leadership Dynamics and Wellbeing is a feast for scholars, students and practitioners alike who will find a comprehensive reference book on leadership theories, a diversity of the schools of thought that have influenced and continue to shape the evolution of leadership as a fully fledged discipline that is applied to complex and changing contexts. As someone trying to master the leadership discipline and as an aspirant leadership expert myself, I was pleasantly surprised at how much there is still to know and learn about this enthralling subject called leadership.

Dudu Msomi, Chief Executive Officer, Busara Leadership Partners

Given the plethora of books on Leadership, one is tempted to think, "What else can be written about leadership?"

This masterful creation crushes that thought. It is a call to choose to be a different and better leader, to stand up and … lead.

I recommend that current and future leaders, young and old, study this gem and weave the learnings into their approach to leading our most precious asset, people.

Leon Steyn, Group Human Resources Executive, Bidvest

First published in 2017

ISBN: 978-1-86922-694-7 (Printed)
ISBN: 978-1-86922-695-4 (ePDF)

Published by KR Publishing
P O Box 3954
Randburg
2125
Republic of South Africa

Tel: (011) 706-6009
Fax: (011) 706-1127
E-mail: orders@knowres.co.za
Website: www.kr.co.za

Printed and bound: HartWood Digital Printing, 243 Alexandra Avenue, Halfway House, Midrand
Typesetting, layout and design: Cia Joubert, cia@knowres.co.za
Cover design: Marlene de'Lorme, marlene@knowres.co.za and Cia Joubert, cia@knowres.co.za
Editing: Adrienne Pretorius, pretorii@mweb.co.za
Proofreading: Valda Strauss, valda@global.co.za
Project management: Cia Joubert, cia@knowres.co.za

LEADERSHIP

Leadership Dynamics and Wellbeing

Edited by

Andrew J Johnson and Theo H Veldsman

kr
publishing

2017

ACKNOWLEDGEMENTS

What a pleasure to work with authors who see the unquestionable criticality of leadership, and are passionate about the difference leadership must make in assuring a desirable, sustainable future for all. It was wonderful to have worked with each and every one of our 69 authors over such an extended period of time. Your wisdom, expertise, suggestions and time willingly shared in crafting your invaluable contribution in making *Leadership Dynamics and Wellbeing* the outstanding and trend-setting Thought Leadership Book it has turned out to be is gratefully acknowledged.

A warm word of thanks is due to:

- All of our Peer Reviewers for your valuable input and time.
- To all our Endorsees for your time given, to offer our book the cachet it deserves.
- Wilhelm Crous, Managing Director of KR, for your constant stretch and guidance; constructive criticism; ongoing encouragement; infectious enthusiasm; and advice and help in working around and through barriers, that made it such a pleasure to work on our book.
- Joann Hill for organising the peer reviews and endorsements.
- Cia Joubert, for your excellent project management of our book that was mission critical in ensuring that the right things happened at the right time and in the right way so that our book became a reality.
- Adrienne Pretorius, our technical editor, for ensuring the technical quality excellence of our book.
- Valda Strauss, for the excellent proofreading of our book after layout.

Last but not least, a warm, appreciative "Thank you" to our families for their understanding, support and sacrifices throughout the painful birth process of the book which took two years from initiation, through conceptualisation and production, to final delivery.

TABLE OF CONTENTS

FOREWORD BY PEARL MAPHOSHE

To be a leader today is a tough challenge. Operating in a fast-changing context, leaders face increased uncertainty, ambiguity and complexity. In addition, the rise of digital and social media means leaders, and their actions, are entirely exposed to public opinion. As a result, distrust of leaders is increasingly common. On top of that, leading in a country that has been rated as the second most stressed in the world is even more difficult. It is no wonder many of South Africa's leaders are highly stressed, burnt-out, derailed and, in many cases, toxic.

In *Leadership Dynamics and Wellbeing,* the editors alongside the contributors, show how it is possible for leaders to lead in *and thrive under* these challenging times. This book does so in tackling the following themes in Sections Two and Three:

In the first place, it is suggested that a leadership transformation from leading individually to building a *leadership community* in the organisation is required, engendering shared leadership. The transition implies movement from 'I' to 'We' leadership. In pursuit of the common good.

In the second place it is argued that in order to find a stable anchor in the hyper-turbulent and hyper-fluid context, leaders in the first instance have to look inward to find at their core who they are as individuals – i.e., their *identity* – and how their central identity finds expression in their respective social, work and role identities; uncover the identity transition they are facing; and make the adaptations they need to make in order to manage the transition.

In the third place, it is argued that *leadership transitions* are inherent to and form critical passages in the career of any leader when he/she has to take up and engage with a new set of accountabilities, responsibilities and/or authority. By all accounts the frequency of these transitions is on the increase because of the emerging context with its correspondingly significant and radical impact on organisations as they seek to respond appropriately, and these responses in turn having an impact on leaders in their roles. Organisations invest hundreds of hours and billions of rands into leadership development, but pay scant attention to probably the most regularly occurring, highest-risk event in the career of leaders when this investment is significantly endangered: Leadership Transitions.

In the fourth place, it is asserted that *leadership failure*, particularly during these turbulent times, seems to be more common than success. Deep insight into the role of *stress* and *burnout* in leadership, as well as the possible ways in which leaders *derail*, can go far in mitigating the risk of leadership failure that these factors pose for organisations. Understanding this risk should, however, go hand in hand with building and maintaining the resilience of individuals and organisations.

In the fifth place, in the over-demanding context, with its over-emphasis on reaching near impossible (short-term) profit targets, which often results in the deterioration of ethics, and values being ignored in many organisations, the prevalence of *toxic leadership* and *toxic organisations* is on the rise. A comprehensive framework to help tease out toxic leadership and a toxic organisational landscape is provided. This includes identifying toxic preconditions, potential toxic leadership conduct, toxic leadership archetypes as well as the toxic organisation and archetypes.

In the sixth place, a stern warning is sounded to readers not to be readily seduced by the 'romance' of what leadership and leaders is all about. The question 'what is the hard, real everyday reality of leadership and leaders at the front line that truly happens?' is addressed. The author is of the firm conviction that leaders are the custodians of their organisations' souls. The author most skilfully – based on his coaching of close on 18 000 managers over his career – aims to bring the 'brutal' reality of leadership creating soulless organisations into the open as a real-life encounter in stark contrast to the often over-romanticised picture of leadership in the academic and packaged personal advice literature. In this way he demonstrates the actual gap between 'Should be' and 'Is' leadership at the front line.

In the last instance, it is argued that future leadership challenges, and the growing leadership crisis, demand more than the mere enhancement and/or addition of new leadership competencies and behaviours. Future leadership-fit for the radically changing and more demanding world of work – requires a far greater insight into the inner, deeper dynamics of leaders, relative to themselves and others. In particular, how to grow more advanced psychosocial maturity in leaders. Greater psychosocial maturity would result in a lowered likelihood of the manifestation of signs of failed leadership, like underperformance, mistrust, derailment and burnout.

Against this background … is there a way out? Definitely! Being a leader in South Africa, and in the world at large, will not become any easier. Socio-economic demands, political volatility, and increased competition will persist for many years to come, if not increase. However, the research and insights shared in **Leadership Dynamics and Wellbeing** will provide current and aspiring leaders with a wealth of knowledge, ideas and tools on how not only to cope but also *thrive* in this world.

Pearl Maphoshe, Group Executive Head Resources, Pick n Pay

ABOUT THE EDITORS

Dr Andrew J Johnson

Andrew is the Chief Learning Officer at Eskom's Academy of Learning. An Industrial Psychologist by profession, he holds an MSc in Occupational Psychology (Nottingham) and a PhD in Industrial Psychology from the University of Johannesburg (UJ). He has also completed formal philosophical, theological and exegetical studies at Sts. Peter & John Vianney Seminaries and St Joseph's Scholasticate.

A seasoned HR executive, his special interests are HR strategy consulting, leadership development, talent and succession management, organisational transformation, and change management. His career in Organisational Effectiveness in the private sector has seen him working for Edcon, MTN, Avmin, JSE and Liberty in senior positions, and he has consulted to other state-owned entities, private companies, and African and BRICS (Brazil, Russia, India, China and South Africa) utilities.

He held non-executive roles in FASSET, the NEF, the COJ Property Company, Transparency SA, NSFAS, & King II; currently he serves on the Advisory Committee of the Industrial Psychology Department of UJ (where he is an occasional lecturer), and the HR (Staffing) Committee of the University of KwaZulu-Natal (UKZN). Andrew is involved in the Society for Industrial & Organisational Psychology of South Africa (SIOPSA) (president in 2011/12), and the Global Forum on Executive Development and Business Driven Action Learning. He is the winner of the prestigious IPM HR Director of the Year (2014), and the recipient of the SABPP Lifetime Achievement Award (2014) and of SIOPSA's Honorary Life Membership (2012).

He is in high demand as a speaker, coach and mentor. At his core he is a deeply passionate student of human behaviour in the context of work, and how this can create a better self, team, organisation and society.

Prof Theo H Veldsman

Theo, who is regarded as a thought leader in South Africa with respect to people management and the psychology of work, has demonstrated his ability to proactively identify emerging people and leadership needs and arrive at fit-for-purpose, innovative solutions that are theoretically and practically sound.

Theo holds a PhD in Industrial Psychology and is a registered Industrial Psychologist and Research Psychologist and accredited HRM Practitioner. He prefers to call himself a Work Psychologist. He has extensive research and development, as well as consulting experience gained over the past 35 years in strategy formulation and implementation; strategic organisational change; organisational (re)design; team building; leadership/management and strategic people/talent management. He consults with many leading South African companies as well as organisations overseas, in the roles of advisor, expert and coach/mentor.

In addition to being the author of nearly 200 technical/consulting reports/articles, he has done numerous management and professional presentations and attended seminars at a national and international level. He is the author of two books, and has contributed nine book chapters.

Up to the end of 2016, when he retired, he was Professor and Head of the Department of Industrial Psychology and People Management, Faculty of Management, University of Johannesburg. Since the beginning of 2017 he is a Visiting Professor at the sam eDepartment. He has led the profession of Psychology and Industrial Psychology nationally as president on several occasions. He has been awarded fellowship status by the Society of Industrial and Organisational Psychology of South Africa (SIOPSA), and is the 2012 recipient of a Life-Long Achievement Award from the South African Board for People Practices (SABPP).

ABOUT THE CONTRIBUTORS

Jopie de Beer

Jopie is CEO of the JvR Africa Group and MD of JvR Psychometrics. The JvR Africa group of companies (JvR Psychometrics, JvR Consulting Psychologists, JvR Academy and JvR Safety) practically apply the vast body of knowledge developed in Psychology to make a difference in the lives of people, teams, departments, organisations and society. The journey with clients includes validating and developing assessments, sculpting context-appropriate interventions and monitoring the effectiveness thereof by collating and analysing the people metrics obtained in the process.

Jopie, who is passionate about people development, has taken up the challenge to do everything possible to make a difference in the lives of the people of Africa. As a qualified psychologist and entrepreneur, she works hard to create an enabling business environment where employees and clients alike benefit from having access to modern technology and professional learning. Teams of excellent and ethical people, a culture of customer service, exceptional products and very hard work all add to making the dream come true.

Danie du Toit

Danie, who holds a DCom, is a registered Industrial Psychologist and senior lecturer at North-West University where he teaches postgraduate students and gives study guidance to Master's and doctoral candidates. He is the co-author of peer-reviewed articles, and has contributed chapters in specialist books, in addition to presenting at numerous national and international conferences. He divides his time between academic work, consulting to organisations on leadership development and individual growth interventions. He spent 20 years in business organisations in various human resource management (HRM) and development positions, before joining the consulting and academic worlds.

In 2011, he received the award for best paper based on a doctoral study at the 7th European Conference on Management, Leadership and Governance in Nice, at Skema Business School. He is also the recipient of awards for research excellence at North-West University in 2012, 2013 and 2014. E-mail: danie.dutoit@nwu.ac.za

Ilka Dunn

llka is an organisational and people developer who believes education will solve all our problems. She holds a BA Dramatic Art (Hons) (University of the Witwatersrand), an MEd (University of Johannesburg [UJ]) and a PhD in Personal, Interpersonal and Professional Leadership (UJ).

Her diverse career began in an educational theatre company before she moved into teaching at the ORT-STEP Institute, an international technology education NGO. This provided great foundational skills for starting her own educational consultancy: Actions Speak Educational Design. At Actions Speak she wrote a handful of textbooks, created over 700 online lessons, developed over 250 teachers and principals, researched a number of NGOs across South Africa, worked with local government and universities to design training for outcomes-based teacher development, wrote a variety of educational film scripts, offered development programmes to corporates, and designed and delivered a number of conferences.

In 2006 Ilka re-joined the corporate world full time and has since worked in organisational development and learning for Rand Merchant Bank (RMB). Here she leads the learning architecture team, heads up young talent marketing and development initiatives, handles internal conference design and development, designs and supports leadership and management development, and helps to drive business-wide culture and change initiatives.

Ilka is an accredited internal meta-coach with the Meta-coach Foundation and the International Society for Neuro-Semantics. She sits on the RMB fund board and helps run the RMB NGO Leadership Network. When she has a spare moment she mentors arts organisations through Business Arts South Africa (BASA) and serves on the board of the South African Graduate Employers Association (SAGEA). She has presented and published on arts-based methods, teacher development, leadership, identity transitions, diversity, gender and graduate identity development in South Africa.

Ina Rothmann

Ina is Managing Director of Afriforte (Pty) Ltd and Extraordinary Associate Professor at the WorkWell Research Unit. Afriforte (Pty) Ltd is the commercial arm of the WorkWell Research Unit, Faculty of Economic and Management Sciences, North-West University (Potchefstroom Campus), whose primary focus is to provide executives and managers with the tools to assess, quantify and profile human factor and workplace risks in support of sustainable development and capability to act on strategic intent. Ina is passionate about research, innovation and technology, and is very excited about the possibilities that the Fourth Industrial Revolution offers. She believes that the future of workplaces lies in the blending of technologies that will muddle the lines between the physical, digital and biological spheres.

Renate Scherrer

Renate is the Managing Director of JvR Consulting Psychologists, a premier psychological consulting firm that applies the principles and methods of psychology to support people in dealing with the demands of organisational life. She is a registered Clinical Psychologist with the Health Professions Council of South Africa and holds a PhD in Clinical Psychology.

Renate mainly consults in the field of leadership and engagement, focusing on optimising human potential in the organisational context. She is passionate about the assessment and development of people, i.e., individual coaching; enhancing team synergy through facilitated discussion, awareness and growth; succession planning and executive on-boarding. From a clinical perspective, she has a specific interest in leadership derailment, psychopathy in the workplace, toxic leadership and conflict mediation. She is an internationally accredited user of various psychometric assessments and a regular speaker at conferences, as well as an international affiliate member of the American Psychological Association (APA).

Deon van Zyl

Deon, who holds a DPhil, has 26 years' experience as Management Development Consultant within a wide range of organisations. He is also a Clinical Psychologist and a former Associate Professor of Psychology at the University of Pretoria, where he lectured and practised for 13 years. He is past Chairperson of the South African Institute for Clinical Psychology, a member of the International Association for Jungian Studies, and the African representative of the International Association for the Study of Dreams. He completed two summer intensive continuing education study programmes at the CG Jung Institute and the International School for Analytical Psychology in Zurich, Switzerland. Recently he delivered papers at international conferences in Kyoto (Japan) and Chicago, Asheville, New York and Burlington (in the USA), as well as in the Netherlands. He has 46 scientific and popular publications to his name, including four book chapters, both locally and overseas.

SECTION 1

SETTING THE SCENE

Chapter 1

ORIENTATION

Theo H Veldsman and Andrew J Johnson

On many fronts, and in many ways, our insight into and the exercise of leadership is under severe scrutiny because of a radically changing and significantly different world; reinventing organisations; and working persons with significantly different, or significantly shifting, needs, expectations and aspirations. Without doubt, leadership is in the overheating crucible of a reframed/reframing world that is in the throes of fundamental and radical transformation.

The current fierce debate about leadership and leadership excellence (or lack thereof) may be one of the most important issues of our present time, alongside issues such as demographic shifts, the distribution of economic prosperity, food and water security, world peace, global warming, and sustainability. It could even be argued that these issues in and of themselves are but symptomatic of poor leadership; or, at worst, of the inability and/or a lack in the commitment to lead.

The clarion call is clear and unequivocal. At this critical juncture in our history, the search is on for better *and* different leadership. Leaders and leadership have to reinvent themselves if they wish to be successful in the unfolding world of tomorrow. Old recipes and conventional ways of leading will no longer suffice. They may even be detrimental and destructive. It can be argued that those nations, societies, communities and organisations that are able to demonstrate leadership excellence consistently will dominate and inherit the future, in particular in the case of emerging countries in Africa. Our very future is predicated on the quality of our current and future leadership who will either make us architects or victims of the future.

Without any doubt leadership is *the* critical strategic capability of nations, societies, communities and organisations, making them sustainably future-fit. The primary trigger for *Leadership Dynamics and Wellbeing* is therefore to be found in the snowballing crisis around leadership, and the consequential imperative for better and different leadership.

The Strategic Leadership Value Chain Perspective: A Meta-framework From Which to View Leadership

Leadership is a critical organisational capability and intervention. To the best of our knowledge no overall, systemic, integrated and holistic perspective is available in the literature viewing leadership from a Strategic Leadership Value Chain perspective. Such a perspective would provide a meta-framework from which to look at leadership systemically and holistically as an organisational intervention. Such a perspective would assist one not only in bringing order to the overwhelming, exploding leadership literature, but also serve as an overall, integrative map for organisations in engaging with leadership. At best numerous, piecemeal treatises are available dealing with specialised leadership intervention topics, e.g. leadership assessment, leadership development, or leadership Wellbeing but no overarching meta-framework exists.

Figure 1.1 provides our take on the make-up of the Strategic Leadership Value Chain in terms of which leadership as a mission-critical, strategic organisational capability and intervention can be viewed.

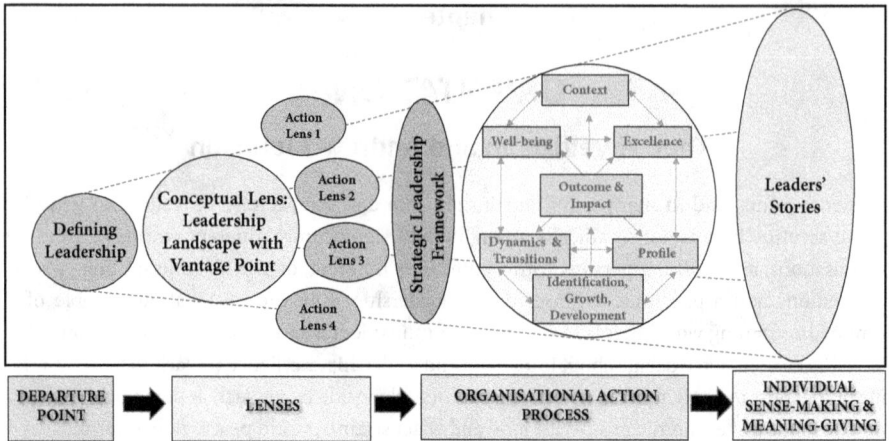

Figure 1.1 A Strategic Leadership Value Chain Perspective on leadership as an organisational capability and intervention

The make-up of the Strategic Leadership Value Chain

With reference to Figure 1.1, the Strategic Leadership Value Chain is composed of the following elements:

- **Departure point: Defining leadership**

  In crafting an organisation-specific leadership thinking framework, the organisation as a starting point must formulate explicitly and intentionally what they understand "leadership" as a phenomenon to be conceptually, in order to correctly demarcate the territory called "leadership". An incorrect definition of leadership can delineate the phenomenon either too narrowly, consequently excluding essential elements of leadership; or too broadly, resulting in the inclusion of unrelated elements ("noise") in its definition.

- **Lenses**

  Having demarcated the territory called "leadership" by defining it, the organisation must next construct and/or select the lenses it will use to map, make sense of, and give meaning to the demarcated leadership territory. The lenses represent the "toolbox" the organisation will use in engaging with the leadership territory. Three types of lenses can be discerned:

  o **Conceptual lens:** This represents the organisation's meta-view – its "Google map" - of what building blocks (= "towns with their suburbs") with their interdependencies (= "roads") make up the demarcated leadership territory. We call this meta-conceptual view the *"Leadership Landscape"*.

    The value of the Leadership Landscape as meta-conceptual view of the leadership territory is three-fold:
    - *to simplify*, organise and integrate at a meta-level the complexity of the field of leadership with its ever-expanding and overwhelming literature;
    - *to provide* a common meta-language for an all-inclusive, coherent leadership dialogue about leadership, for example in teaching, or in an organisation; and
    - *to structure* an organisation's conversation about leadership, enabling it to arrive at a customised Strategic Leadership Framework (see below) for the organisation that

will direct and guide its thinking, decisions and actions regarding leadership as a strategic organisational capability and intervention.

o   ***Interpretative Lens:*** A Vantage Point next must be chosen by which the Leadership Landscape with its building blocks will be interpreted. For example, Appreciative Inquiry or Critical Management Theory.

o   ***Action Lenses:*** Having mapped the leadership territory, and having chosen a Vantage Point, the Action Lenses serve as enabling tools selected by the organisation to deal and work with the various building blocks making up the Leadership Landscape. Action tools represent various disciplines and theoretical/practical approaches that can be used to engage with the leadership territory in order to make sense of it. Examples of such action tools are neuroscience, action science, psychodynamics, narratives, and psychobiographical profiling.

- ***Strategic leadership framework***

In proceeding along the Strategic Leadership Value Chain (see Figure 1.1), the organisation next has to make choices regarding its specific position on each of the building blocks making up the Leadership Landscape as Conceptual Lens, based on how it strategically wants to position leadership in its organisation.

For example with respect to some of the building blocks of the Leadership Landscape (given in italics), the choices are:

o   Its chosen *Leadership Stance* regarding leadership for the organisation: Does leadership need to be task- and/or people-centric? Must leadership be present and/or future focused?

o   Its desired *Leadership Style(s)*: Tell, Consultative, Co-determination and/ or Self-Governance?

o   Its repertoire of expected *Leadership Roles*: Resources, Coach, Guide, Networker?

o   *Leadership Talent Management*: its make-up; strategic talent timeframe; and talent pools.

The Strategic Leadership Framework therefore forms the reference point and basis regarding all the organisation's decisions and actions with respect to leadership. Its sits as a bridge between the organisation's Leadership Thinking Framework on the one hand, being part of the Thinking Framework itself. And, on the other hand, the Framework directs and guides how "things" must happen in the organisation with respect to leadership.

- ***Organisational action processes***

The organisational action process refers to the frontline decisions and actions the organisation has to take on a daily basis regarding leadership. This process is made up of an integrated, reciprocally interdependent, set of organisational actions, embedded in an organisational change navigation process (represented in Figure 1.1 by the circle in which these actions are contained). The actions are as follows:

o   ***Action 1:*** Understanding the unfolding *Leadership Context* with its leadership challenges, demands and requirements;

o   ***Action 2:*** Formulating a context-relevant *Leadership Excellence* model;

o   ***Action 3:*** Generating a future-fit *Leadership Brand and Profile*;

o   ***Action 4:*** *Identifying, Growing and Developing* the organisation's leadership talent;

o   ***Action 5:*** Managing the ongoing, everyday *Leadership Dynamics and Transitions* in the organisation;

o   ***Action 6:*** Ensuring and enhancing *Leadership Wellbeing* (and countering leadership mal-being); and

o   ***Action 7:*** Monitoring and tracking *Leadership Outcomes and Impact*

- ***Individual sense-making and meaning-giving: Leadership stories***

    In the final instance, leaders have to be prolific, enticing storytellers. Through the stories they construct and share, leaders make sense of and give meaning to their leadership experiences, for themselves and others. Hopefully and ideally speaking, leadership experiences are transformed into information; information into knowledge; and knowledge into wisdom. In turn, the distilled wisdom can be applied to ground, enhance and enrich in a recursive fashion the preceding Strategic Leadership Value Chain elements as elucidated above.

This book – *Leadership Dynamics and Wellbeing* – forms part of a five book series covering the respective elements of the Strategic Leadership Value Chain. The accompanying box gives a list of the books in the series, and what portion of the Strategic Value Chain they address.

Book	Portion of Strategic Leadership Value Chain Addressed (Refer back to Figure 1.1)
Book 1: Understanding Leadership	Departure Point: Defining Leadership Lenses: Conceptual, Interpretive, Action Strategic Leadership Framework
Book 2: Leadership in Context	Organisational Action Process • *Action 1: Understanding the unfolding Leadership Context with its leadership challenges, demands and requirements*
Book 3: Leadership Excellence	Organisational Action Process • *Action 2: Formulating a context relevant, Leadership Excellence Model* • *Action 3: Generating a future-fit, Leadership Brand and Profile* • *Action 7: Monitoring and tracking Leadership Outcomes and Impact*
Book 4: Building Leadership Talent	Organisational Action Process • *Action 4: Identifying, growing and developing the organisation's leadership talent*
Book 5: Leadership Dynamics and Well Being (This book)	Organisational Action Process • *Action 5: Managing the ongoing, everyday Leadership Dynamics and Transitions in the organisation* • *Action 6: Ensuring and enhancing leadership Wellbeing (and countering leadership mal-being)*

Book	Portion of Strategic Leadership Value Chain Addressed (Refer back to Figure 1.1)
Leadership Stories	Throughout the above five books stories by prominent SA leaders are given to illustrate how they have made sense of and given meaning to leadership

Purpose and Structure of *Leadership Dynamics and Wellbeing*

The purpose of *Leadership Dynamics and Wellbeing* is to address *Leadership Identification, Growth* and *Development* as action domain in the Organisational Action Process, premised on the desired Leadership Excellence, Brand and Profile as formulated within the other action domains. (To note: all of the actions making up the Organisational Action Process are encapsulated in an organisational change navigation process, represented in Figure 1.2 by the circle enclosing these actions).

The location of the Organisational Action Process within the Strategic Leadership Value Chain, and the action domain of Identification, Growth and Development, are indicated by arrows in Figure 1.2.

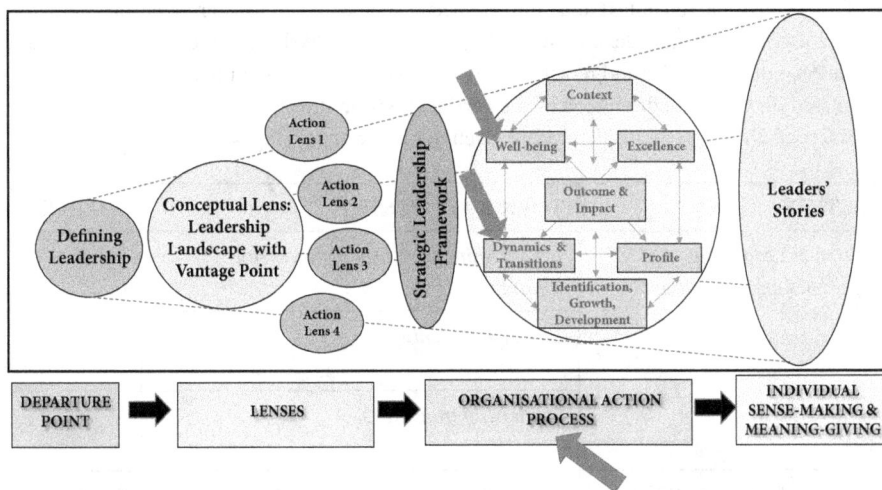

Figure 1.2 Organisational Action Process of the Strategic Leadership Value Chain: Dynamics and Wellbeing

The action domain of *Dynamics and Transitions* deals with the day-to-day working together of the organisation's leadership; changes occurring in their ways of working together; and the transition they have to make.

Throughout the Organisational Action Process, the organisation has to pay careful attention on a continuing basis to *Leadership Wellbeing* in order to protect and sustain leadership as a critical organisational capability. Figure 1.3 depicts the respective elements making up the Leadership Wellbeing action domain.

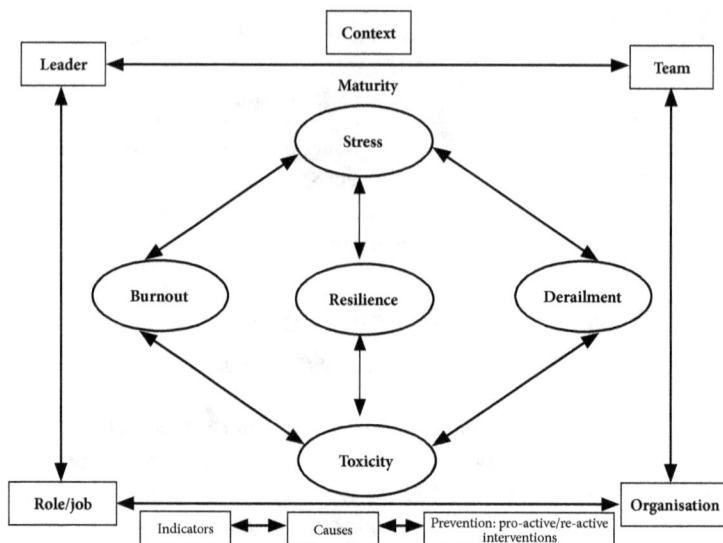

Figure 1.3 The make-up of the Leadership Wellbeing action domain

According to Figure 1.3 the organisation has to pay attention to the interdependent Wellbeing destructive categories of stress, burnout, derailment and toxicity, and the constructive Wellbeing categories of resilience and maturity. These categories are embedded in a certain context made up of the overall macro context and context-specific elements – the leader, role/ job, team and organisation – affecting leadership Wellbeing. Process wise, Wellbeing indicators, causes and prevention, both pro-active and re-active, have to receive ongoing attention.

Based on the above discussion of the pertinent Action Process Steps, the topics addressed in *Leadership Dynamics and Wellbeing* are given in the accompanying box.

SECTION	TOPICS ADDRESSED	CHAPTER
Section 2: Leadership Dynamics and Transitions	*A flourishing and thriving leadership community*	2
	Leadership identity	3
	Leadership transitions	4
Section 3: Leadership Wellbeing	*Leadership stress, burnout, derailment and resilience*	5
	Toxic leadership and organisations	6
	A leadership lament: A counter-view	7
	Leadership maturity	8

Leadership Stories (Section 4: Chapter 9)

In this section prominent leaders express their personal views on leadership from the front line where it is happening for them, illustrating many of the topics discussed in *Leadership Dynamics and Wellbeing*.

The future of leadership (Section 5: Chapter 10)

In this chapter we would like to gaze into the crystal ball by answering the question: Is there is a need for better and different leadership going into the future? If yes, and what would it look like with the conditions attached to such future-fit leadership?

Our intention with and aspirations for *Leadership Dynamics and Wellbeing* – ambitious and bold, but humble

Our intention with and aspiration for *Leadership Dynamics and Wellbeing* is for it to be a thought-leadership book on leadership at the front line in four ways. *Firstly,* by providing cutting edge, present-into-the-future, and future-into-the-present, thinking with respect to leadership lenses, leveraged from the best currently available insights and informed views about the expected probable future to be faced by leadership. *Secondly,* by providing actionable knowledge and theory-informed practice about leadership lenses where it matters at the organisational front line.

We realise we may be overly ambitious and bold both in our intention and aspiration by making the total Strategic Leadership Value Chain the focal point of *Leadership Dynamics and Wellbeing*. Also, in covering in the comprehensive menu of topics what we believe are the most critical topics related to each element of the chain, while applying the Pareto principle of the 20% telling 80% of the story. Simultaneously, however, we are fortuitously humbled by the depth, richness and diversity of the overwhelming, exploding body of knowledge regarding leadership. In no way can we claim, or wish to claim, that at a topic level a high degree of seamless conceptual and practical integration within an element or across the total Strategic Leadership Value Chain exists. That would be arrogant.

The Intended Audience of *Leadership Dynamics and Wellbeing*

In the first place, *Leadership Dynamics and Wellbeing* intends to assist executives and leadership specialists within organisations, whether public or private, to direct, guide and build – confidently and with well-grounded insight – leadership as a mission critical organisational capability and intervention in their organisations, using a Strategic Leadership Value Chain perspective. In this way we hope that they will be able to ensure a future-fit organisation and leadership who are able and willing to be architects of the future they so ardently desire.

In the second place, *Leadership Dynamics and Wellbeing* aims to assist academics and their students in the teaching and studying of leadership as a critically important subject. In the third place, the topics covered in *Leadership Dynamics and Wellbeing* may also provide creative triggers to future leadership research.

The Intended Use of *Leadership Dynamics and Wellbeing*

The intended use of *Leadership Dynamics and Wellbeing* is to serve as a handy daily "desktop" reference book on leadership lenses to our intended audience:

- for ongoing referral as and when ways of understanding leadership matters arise in an organisation, and
- where input from a thought leadership source is desired and necessary on available leadership lenses.

Thus *Leadership Dynamics and Wellbeing* is not intended to "Rest in Peace" on the bookshelf but to be a "Working Manual" by being an ever-present companion for continuous, daily consulting, referral and advice. Also in a similar fashion assist as a reference for teaching on and research into leadership.

The Expected Value-add of *Leadership Dynamics and Wellbeing*

We hope *Leadership Dynamics and Wellbeing* will provide you as the reader with seven overriding insights (or Lessons-to-be-Learnt):

Leadership Dynamics and Transitions

- The unfolding Leadership Context has resulted in a shift from THE leader: the sole, supposedly all-knowing and all-powerful individual at the top of the organisation exercising leadership to *shared (or distributed) leadership*: simultaneously, interdependent leadership at all organisational levels and functions. The constellation of leaders of an organisation thus has to viewed as a *Leadership Community,* operating seamlessly beyond hierarchy and function in the organisation.
- The emerging hyperturbulent and hyperfluid Leadership Context requires leaders to find and have clarity on the core of who they are as persons: their *social, work and role identities*. Additionally, being able to deal on a continuous basis with identity transitions, and the adaptations they need to make if they are to manage their identity transitions successfully.
- *Leadership transitions* – taking charge of a new role as a leader – are inherent, critical and recurring passages in the career of leaders. As a high-risk organisational occurrence, the nature and dynamics of Leadership Transitions need to be an openly discussed event in the organisation and have to be carefully and deliberately managed.

Leadership Wellbeing

- Leadership failure, particularly during turbulent times as at present, seems to be more common than success. Understanding the role of *stress and burnout* in leadership, as well as the possible ways in which leaders *derail*, can go far in mitigating the risks that these factors pose for organisations. However, understanding and mitigating these risks should go hand in hand with building and maintaining the resilience of leadership and organisations.
- There is a worrying, accelerating increase in *toxic leadership* in organisations endangering people and organisational Wellbeing, as well as sustainable organisational performance and success. Organisations must understand, and be able to identify and counter toxic leadership and organisations.

- At the front line in organisations most frequently a significant gap exists between the *'Should Be'* and the *'As Is' of leadership*. The organisation must make this gap visible and have the courage and perseverance to address it in order to ensure the long-term Wellbeing and viability of its people and the organisation.
- Future leadership challenges, and the growing leadership crisis, will require a far greater insight into the inner, deeper dynamics of leaders, relative to themselves and others, in particular their levels of *psychosocial maturity*. A higher degree of leadership psychosocial maturity will result in a lowered likelihood of failed leadership, manifested in underperformance, mistrust, derailment, and burnout, and heighten leaders' resilience.

We wish you a stimulating, enriching and capacitating journey through *Leadership Dynamics and Wellbeing*

SECTION 2

LEADERSHIP DYNAMICS
AND TRANSITIONS

Chapter 2

A FLOURISHING AND THRIVING
LEADERSHIP COMMUNITY

Theo H Veldsman

In recent years the organisational context has transformed from being relatively uniform, independent, simple, orderly, stable, predictable and localised to one of increasing variety, interdependency (that is, connectivity), complexity, change, ambiguity, and seamlessness, typified as the VICCAS context. These contextual shifts have resulted in the growing need in organisations to move from THE leader – the sole, supposedly all-knowing and all-powerful individual at the top of the organisation exercising leadership – to SHARED (or distributed) leadership – simultaneously interdependent leadership at all organisational levels and functions – to deal effectively with the more demanding, constantly changing and radically different context, both internally and externally.[1]

Shared leadership implies among other things viewing the constellation of leaders in an organisation as a potential community of practice, a Leadership Community. "Potential", because a community of practice, in this case a Leadership Community, has to be deliberately thought through and set up. It goes beyond the typical organisational hierarchy and function, not to replace but complement it in addressing organisation-wide challenges, issues and problems spanning across hierarchy and function.[2]

The purpose of this chapter is to discuss – given the imperative in the emerging new order for *shared* organisational leadership – the transformation of the organisation's leadership group into a genuine Leadership Community. To this end the chapter unfolds by addressing the following topics regarding the Leadership Community: what is a leadership community?; its make-up, dynamics and evolution as elucidated in terms of its constituent building blocks; the features of a flourishing and thriving Leadership Community; and its critical success factors.

What is a Leadership Community?

In general a community of practice is a social, relational, learning network of persons in an organisation[3] who: occupy similar roles (in this case, the role of leadership); intentionally congregate to build support for an overarching cause and/or direction; are guided and driven by a common passion, challenge, concern and/or profile; are tied together by a shared identity, ideology and code of practice; interact frequently in an interdependent fashion with one another through joint learning to deepen their knowledge, expertise, and wisdom around their shared role and/or area of concern/interest; aspire to act in concert in order to acquire access to, mobilise and/or grow resources, such as opportunities and information; take up challenges; and deal with issues, problems, and counter-threats.[i]

Against this backdrop, a Leadership Community more specifically refers to the purposely created collective of leadership in the organisation working together collaboratively and in concert in order to deliver jointly on the strategic intent of the organisation – strategically,

---

i   Global, or worldwide, communities of practice also exist, for example, a worldwide community of scientists working jointly in finding cures for diseases such as HIV/AIDS, SARS. For local, national and international civic communities of practice, see Snyders & Wenger (2010). This chapter focuses on communities of practice in organisations only.

tactically and operationally – within a selected operating arena, and infusing the intent with an organisationally shared purpose and meaning. This implies a deliberate movement in the organisation:[4]

- From "I" to "We" leadership;
- From an individualistic to a collective identity for leadership;
- From leading by oneself single-handedly to leading in concert with others as a synergistic unit;
- From pursuing "narrow" personal, individual or parochial interests to a shared, common good, agenda;
- From singularised to shared responsibility and accountability;
- From one-on-one relationships to being bound together by multiple, reciprocal relationships, in this way acting as a seamless whole in the pursuit of a shared pursuit and cause; and
- Acknowledging that none of us as individual leaders are as clever and wise as all of us as leaders together.

From this description of a Leadership Community it must be patently clear that a Community does not equate to a meeting, team, task force, working group or forum. Inversely, constituting a Community does not of necessity replace the former.

A Leadership Community is the concrete manifestation and endorsement that the very essence of an organisation in the final instance is to be found in relationships, and in particular among the organisation's leadership. The quality of these relationships results in the amount of available social capital within the organisation, and externally with stakeholders.[5] As has been stated above, turning the leadership group of the organisation into a genuine Leadership Community is moving the group beyond hierarchy and function to direct and guide the organisation as a collective "Us". The implementation of answers arrived at and solutions crafted by the Community still has to occur through hierarchy and function.

Based on the above it can be readily posited that the presence and quality of the Leadership Community of an organisation constitute and significantly affect the leadership capital of an organisation. As an intangible asset it represents the organisation's strategic leadership capability.[6] The overall leadership excellence of the organisation therefore is also to a large measure a function of the real presence of a flourishing and thriving Leadership Community in the organisation, working across hierarchy and function.

It is therefore mission critical that the nature, dynamics and evolution of Leadership Communities are not only clearly understood but that the conversion of the leadership group of the organisation into a genuine Leadership Community is deliberately conceived, designed, directed, guided, and assessed. Typically an organisation will set up only a single Leadership Community, and not multiple Communities, for reasons that will become clearer as the discussion unfolds.

Building Blocks of the Leadership Community

Given that a Leadership Community has to be intentionally created by transforming the leadership group into such, it must be clearly stated as a departure point that a Leadership Community forms a dynamic, organic whole with somewhat "fuzzy" boundaries, that reconfigures itself in self-organising and fluid ways on an ongoing basis through time, in the process settling into a pattern of interaction for shorter or longer durations. Described in this manner, a Leadership Community is a concrete example in practice of the chaos/complexity world view at work.

The decomposition of the Leadership Community into building blocks is merely a convenient aid when discussing it. In the final instance, a Community is far greater than the mere sum total of its building blocks because it forms a synergistic, organic whole in the manner described above. Figure 2.1 depicts the building blocks of a Leadership Community that will be elucidated in subsequent sections of this chapter.[7]

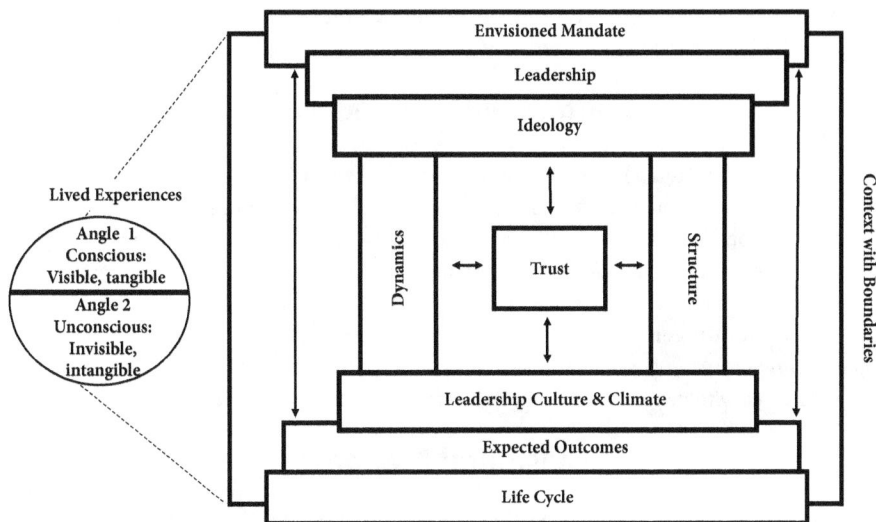

Figure 2.1: The make-up of a Leadership Community

Each of the building blocks making up the Leadership Community – as depicted in Figure 2.1 – is discussed next, starting with Lived Experiences dealing with angle(s) from which the Community can be viewed; moving onto the Context with its Boundaries that encloses the other building blocks; and then dealing with the "internal" building blocks, starting with Envisioned Mandate through to Life Cycle.

Given that the Leadership Community is a dynamic, organic whole, it must be understood at all times that the discussion of one building block must be seen against the backdrop of all other building blocks. That is, each building block is encapsulated in the other, so to speak, and one cannot be understood without the other (in other words, this is a holographic approach to viewing the building blocks). For example, when Context with Boundaries is discussed, the Envisioned Mandate and Leadership of the Community are also indirectly already implicated. Inversely, when the latter two are discussed, the former two are also implicated.

Lived Experiences: The Choice of an Angle

The Leadership Community comes to life through an unfolding dynamic, real-time collective of shared lived experiences through time of the organisation's leadership, individually and severally: how they make sense of and give meaning to the world – in this case as a Community – and then enact their sense-making and meaning-giving though their conduct, the decisions they make, and the actions they take with regard to the building blocks constituting the Leadership Community.

In understanding the lived experiences of members and stakeholders of the Leadership Community, one or two angles can be used (see Figure 2.1):

- *Angle 1 – Conscious: visible, tangible.* This is the observable, "above-the-water" acting out by the Community of all of the above building blocks.
- *Angle 2 – Sub/unconscious: invisible, intangible.* This is the "under-the-water" adoption of and dynamics affecting the sense-making and meaning-giving – for example, beliefs, assumptions, mindsets, personal history, organisational politics – regarding the above building blocks that affect the concrete enactment and observable manifestations of the blocks. The changing mindset and psychodynamic lenses are useful ways of understanding to adopt for this angle of the Leadership Community.

Context with Boundaries

The Context (see Figure 2.1) specifies the space-time in which Community will be active – its sphere of influence and action – and by implication the demarcation of its boundaries: what is in and what is out?[8] The Context with its boundaries is set by the tripartite of the Envisioned Mandate, Expected Outcomes and Leadership membership of the Leadership Community. The Leadership Community's Context is embedded in the organisation's Operating arena with its associated contextual complexity. In turn the Envisioned Mandate, Expected Outcomes and Leadership membership have to take account of and fit the demands and requirements of the Operating arena with its contextual complexity if the Community is to be effective.

Envisioned Mandate

The Mandate (put differently, intent or purpose) (see Figure 2.1) spells out why the Leadership Community exists. It provides the raison d'être for and terms of reference for the Community, in this way supplying the Community with a clear and coherent identity, and a delineated workspace-time. The Mandate embraces the actions to be facilitated, enabled and undertaken by the Community.

A menu of such possible actions is given in Table 2.1 from which a Leadership Community can formulate its Mandate.[9]

Table 2.1: Menu of actions from which a leadership community's mandate can be formulated

Possible Actions Forming Part of a Leadership Community's Mandate
• Nurture and entrench a shared engagement mode as an interpretative framework with the resultant, agreed-upon approach(es) to deal coherently with the Operating Arena.
• Jointly crystallise and strengthen the identity and philosophy (including core values) of the organisation.
• Re-interpret the organisation's strategic intent with its commensurate initiatives in real time as the Operating Arena changes dynamically.
• Collectively address and solve ("wicked) challenges, issues and problems faced by the organisation in its Operating Arena.
• Engender cross-functional co-ordination and integration in order to arrive at synergistic organisational answers and solutions instead of siloed, functional solutions.
• Accelerate information-sharing, decision-making, problem-solving and conflict resolution across the organisational landscape, especially in the white spaces between hierarchy and function.

Possible Actions Forming Part of a Leadership Community's Mandate
• Build core organisational capabilities and competences.
• (Re-)deploy critical resources as and when circumstances demand.
• Exchange best/leading practices and expertise.
• Make joint learning happen, and share lessons learnt.
• Mentor, coach and develop experientially critical talent.
• All in all, strengthen, deepen and sustain the organisational memory by making it a lasting common property.

The listed actions in Table 2.1 can be grouped into the following categories: (i) *Delivery (including People and Resources)*: How will we deliver value to our stakeholders? What people and resources do we need, and how must they be deployed? (ii) *Policies and Standards*: What are the guidelines for our decisions and actions, and the levels of expected excellence? (iii) *Direction*: where is the organisation going, and how is it going to get there? (iv) *Identity and Philosophy*: Who and what the organisation are, and what does it stand for? And (v) *Interpretative Framework*: How do we see, think and act with regard to the world, our engagement mode?

Relative to its crafted Mandate, the Community must craft a vision (or dream): what difference will the Community want to make? In other words, the Mandate must be turned into an Envisioned Mandate.

Finally, it must also be clearly specified with what autonomy – what degree of freedom – the Community can pursue its Envisioned Mandate, and the power base from which the Community will leverage this pursuit.[10] The power base can include positional, expertise, reputational, resources and/or relationship power. Without an Envisioned Mandate, an agreed-upon workspace-time, and clearly specified autonomy and power, a Leadership Community will be directionless and disempowered.

Leadership

The Leadership building block (see Figure 2.1) encompasses the depth, breadth and profile of leadership being members of the Community. "Depth" refers to organisational levels included in the Community: all or only some. "Breadth" entails the range of organisational functions forming part of the Community: from all to only a few organisational functions. "Profile" relates to the make-up of organisational members in terms of their diversity (for example, age, personality, behavioural styles, skills, experience, expertise, race, gender, nationality) who can and will belong to the Community. A potentially powerful, high-impact, genuine Leadership Community would be deep, broad and diverse in its endeavour to operate beyond hierarchy and function.[11]

As the Leadership Context in terms of its Operating Arena becomes more complex, seamless, interdependent and unpredictable, and as an organisation operates across more countries with more products/services in many markets/customers, the globalised/globalising organisation needs to create and sustain a Leadership Community that has a high diversity of leadership types, and many of each type, if it wishes to be successful in a sustainable way.

Ideology

The Ideology building block (see Figure 2.1) encompasses the belief and value system that will frame and inform the Leadership Community's engagement with its Envisioned Mandate, and through the Envisioned Mandate, the Context in which the Community is embedded. The *belief system* embraces the agreed-upon lens which the Community will use when looking at the Operating Arena, and by implication its Context, in addressing its Envisioned Mandate.[12] In other words, its adopted Interpretative Framework encompasses a certain engagement mode made up of a worldview, a decision-making framework, and value orientation.

The *value system* pertains to the core values guiding the conduct of and interactions between the leaders making up the Community. Those values can be operationalised into a Leadership Charter that specifies what is acceptable and unacceptable leadership behaviour.[13] Table 2.2 gives an example of what such a Charter could look like.

Table 2.2: Example of a Leadership Charter

Sample Leadership Charter
As the Leadership of Organisation ABC, we uncompromisingly commit ourselves to the principles listed below.
We will:
• Value others and treat them with respect and dignity at all times.
• Act with integrity and transparency.
• Lead by example.
• Enable and empower others.
• Act as good corporate citizens by promoting sustainability.
• Enjoy passionately what we do.
• Challenge the *status quo* and seek out calculated innovation.
• Deliver in a trustworthy way in respect of what we commit to, regardless of circumstances and challenges.
• Recognise and reward performance fairly, equitably and timeously.
• Keep others informed at all times through continuous communication.
• Be accountable for our decisions and actions.
• Build and sustain the resilience of ourselves and of others.
• Aspire to leave behind a lasting, worthy legacy for this generation, and generations to come.

Dynamics

The Dynamics building block (see Figure 2.1) entails the "software" of the Community: the intense, real-time, interpersonal interactions between leaders making up the Community; the prevalent interpersonal styles in handling critical Community processes (for example, information gathering and processing, decision-making, problem-solving, conflict handling, creative and innovative thinking); the taking up and exercise of authority and responsibility; and emerging process roles as Community members interact and evolve.

The very essence of the Community is dialogue (conversation, narrative or communication)[14ii] within an action-learning frame of reference, made up of exploration, discovery, action, reflection and learning. Dialogue is the centrepiece of shared leadership: the art of shared seeing, interpreting, thinking, acting through co-creation. Even more so if it is accepted that an organisation equates in the final instance to relationships.

The dialogue cannot be static but needs to unfold and evolve to deeper, more honest and open sharing not only about Us but also about Me in our joint endeavour to realise a shared desired future dream and lasting, worthy legacy for the organisation and stakeholders though intense ongoing, real time conversations, informed by a learning attitude (see also later the discussion of the Life Cycle building block). In this way a synergistic, intimate and empathetic feeling of a cohesive 'Us', an inclusive collective consciousness, a shared intentionality, and a common destiny will emerge, transcending the Me as single leader since We will be acting in concert, singly and collectively.[15]

Against this backdrop it must be understood that in the case of the Leadership Community, Structure serves Dynamics. The Structure must be flexible and fit-for-purpose to enable the emergence of the desired Dynamics within the Community in its endeavour to go beyond hierarchy and function in order to mould organisational solutions. This is not the other way round: Dynamics serving Structure. This is why Dynamics as a building block of the Community is discussed before Structure.

Structure

The Structure building block (see Figure 2.1) covers the "hardware" of the Community: the dynamically emergent pattern of interaction within the Community that configures and re-configures itself in real time as an organic whole on an ongoing basis while real-time dialogue unfolds and evolves.[16] Put differently, the Community's structure is driven by the unfolding, dialogical process of working together, and not by set, formalised, standardised and rigid roles, structures, procedures and rules.

However, in time, the self-designing structure of the Community will include, *inter alia*, work roles with their respective responsibilities; the needed member abilities to deliver on its Envisioned Mandate; an agreed-upon action learning mode and rhythm of working; a typical agenda; a specified frequency of get-togethers; communication platforms and channels to be accessed; any enabling technology required to assist the Community to get its work done; and the generally accepted leadership style to be used. (This style typically would be highly participative and democratic.) But all of these will be driven by the dynamics requirements of the Leadership Community.

Leadership Culture and Climate

The Leadership Community is significantly influenced and shaped by the shared ways of seeing, believing, interpreting and being active within the Leadership Community – for example, views such as scarcity versus abundance; co-operation versus competition; and an inside-out versus an outside-in perspective – which consequently inform and frame the Leadership Community's dialogue. These shared ways within the leadership community, which can be explicit and/

---

ii The word "community" derives from the Old French "comuneté", which comes from the Latin "communitas", from Latin "communis", things held in common. The words "community" and "communication" come from the same root word. The word "dialogue" stems from two Greek roots, "dia" and "logos", jointly suggesting the meaning of "meaning flowing through". "Dialogue" stands in stark contrast to the word "debate" or even "discussion", meaning in Greek "to break [things] up".

or implicit, visible/tangible and/or invisible/intangible, form the Leadership Culture as a building block of the Community (see Figure 2.1). They are the "glue" that keeps the Leadership Community together, and gives it a certain personality as a Community.[17]

Leadership culture – similarly to organisational culture, which correlates at 70% with leadership – therefore provides leadership with:[18] (i) an *identity*: "Leadership in our organisation means to walk in front and to know all that there is to know."; (ii) a *place in the world*: "Our top leaders are the only true leaders in our organisation."; (iii) a *way of interacting*: "Do not create surprises for fellow leaders."; (iv) an *explanation and understanding of how things work*: "Any change to the *status quo* is a threat to be eliminated as quickly as possible."; and (v) *power*: "Respect the authority of leadership unquestionably, regardless of competence and conduct."

Whereas Leadership Culture relates to the shared ways of seeing, believing, interpreting and doing present within the Leadership Community, Leadership Climate as a building block of the Community (see Figure 2.1) refers to the general "vibe" (or atmosphere) that infuses everything and everyone within the Leadership Community. It entails the shared meanings leadership give to their daily experiences, resulting in certain shared feelings: a specific, "touchable" atmosphere within the Leadership Community. This atmosphere can be comfortable and bearable or uncomfortable and unbearable.[19]

Leadership Climate can be profiled in terms of contrasting climate poles on various dimensions of Leadership Climate: (i) **Worldview:** Inclusive, open minded versus Exclusive, closed minded; (ii) **Attitudinal:** Optimistic, confident versus Pessimistic, anxious; (iii) **Relationship:** Warm, personal, close, inclusive, comfortable versus Cold, impersonal, distant, exclusive, stressful; (iv) **Power:** Empowering, enabling versus Controlling, disabling; (v) **Action building:** Risk taking, experimenting, creative versus Risk avoidance, mistake minimisation, more-of-the-same; and (vi) **Outcomes:** Fair, fulfilled, satisfied versus Discriminatory, unfulfilled, dissatisfied.

The ruling Leadership Culture and Climate infect the total Leadership Landscape populated by the Leadership Community, and consequently the total organisational culture and climate.

Trust

The quality of the Dynamics within the Leadership Community – and consequently the likelihood of its delivering on its Envisioned Mandate – arises out of the level of trust that exists among the leaders making up the Leadership Community. Trust as a building block is therefore pivotal to the effectiveness and efficiency of the Community. Because trust permeates the whole Community Landscape, it is placed centrally in the Landscape (see Figure 2.1).

Trust refers to positive expectations, validated progressively and consistently over time, about others' motives and conduct ("I know what to expect of him/her/them").[20] The components of trust are shown in Figure 2.2.

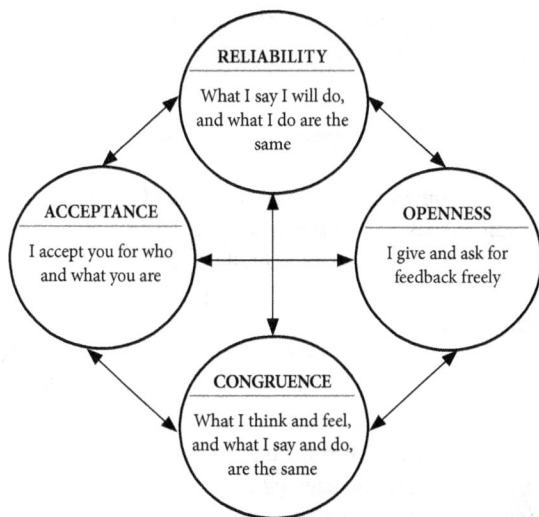

Figure 2.2: The components of trust

From one angle, trust is the resultant outcome of positive, constructive interactions in terms of the meeting of expectations among the leaders making up the Leadership Community. From another angle, trust, or more correctly increasing levels of trust, acts as probably the most critical enabler in creating conducive conditions under which a Leadership Community can flourish and thrive in a sustainable manner, particularly if a VICCAS Context prevails. Trust grows out of increasing levels of Understanding ("Head") and Acceptance ("Heart") among the members of a Leadership Community. Figure 2.3 depicts this relationship.

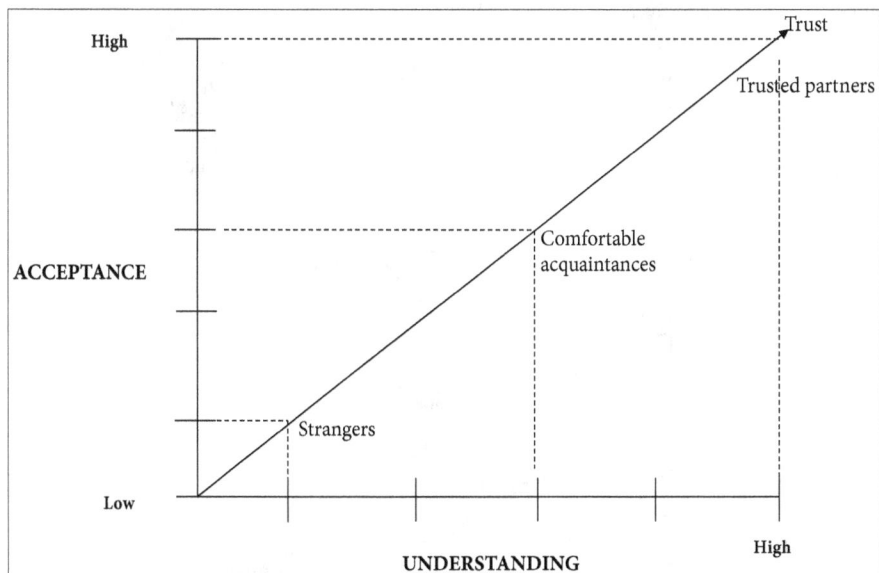

Figure 2.3: Trust within a leadership community as a function of mutual understanding and acceptance

According to Figure 2.3 leaders making up a Leadership Community can become Trusted Partners only if there are high levels of Understanding and Acceptance of one another. The higher the diversity in the Leadership Community, the greater the challenge to build mutual Understanding and Acceptance among the leaders making up the Leadership Community. Without high levels of trust, that is, leaders seeing one another as Trusted Partners, the Leadership Community cannot function effectively.

Expected Outcomes

What value-add must the Community generate in terms of its Envisioned Mandate? What contributions does it want to make? In what way will the organisation – and for that matter the world – look different when the Community has fulfilled its Envisioned Mandate regarding its stakeholders? All of these questions pertain to the Expected Outcomes building block of the Community (see Figure 2.1).

Five types of outcomes can be distinguished: (i) *Tuning*: Enhance the Existing, for example, better operational delivery; (ii) *Adaptation*: Extend the Existing by adding the New, for example new products/services added to existing portfolio; (iii) *Re-direction*: Taking the Existing in a New direction and/or context, for example, turning the organisation into a virtual entity delivering anywhere, at any time, to anyone, in any way; (iv) *Re-invention*: Transform the Existing into the completely New, for example reconceiving cellphones as smart phones; and (v) *Ideation*: Bring the New completely into being, for example, time travel.[21]

As one moves from (i) to (iv) – from earlier to later Expected Outcomes – the challenges to and dynamics in the Community intensify significantly, requiring significantly greater ownership, involvement, personal investment and resources.

Life Cycle

During its existence the Leadership Community goes through a certain Life Cycle (see Figure 2.1) – the diagonal axis – relative to its Envisioned Mandate and Intended Outcomes, the horizontal and vertical axes respectively as depicted in Figure 2.4.

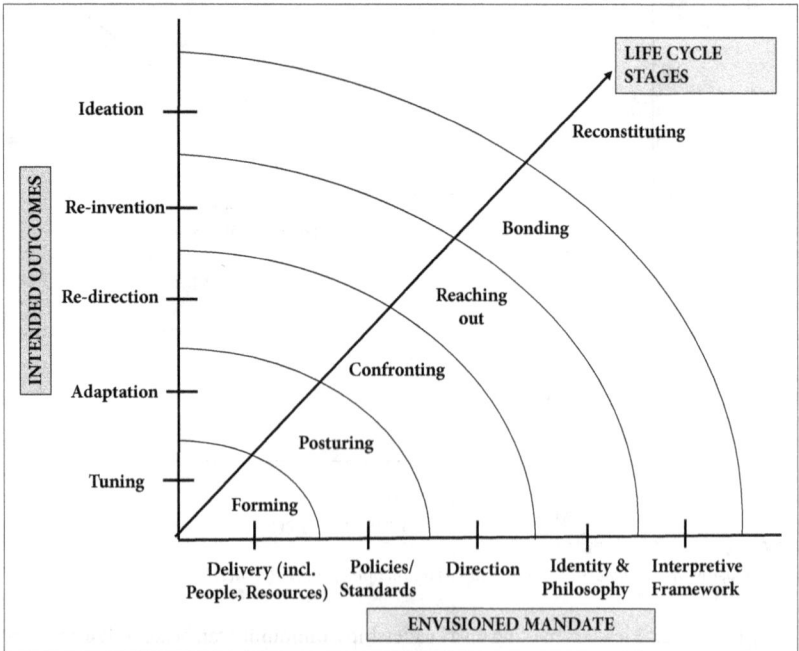

Figure 2.4: Life cycle of the leadership community

The focus of the discussion will be on the Life Cycle itself because the ingredients making up the Envisioned Mandate and Expected Outcomes have already been discussed. Suffice it to state that the intensity of the evolution process to be described below becomes more intense and demanding as the Envisioned Mandate shifts from Delivery to Interpretative Framework and the Intended Outcomes move from Tuning to Ideation.

According to Figure 2.4, the Life Cycle of the Leadership Community is made up of six sequential stages, starting with Forming and advancing to Re-constituting. If the very essence of the Community is dialogue as discussed above, then the Life Cycle is reflective of a movement from an initially superficial and narrow conversation towards a deep, wide and genuine dialogue critical in establishing a true Community. In short, the Life Cycle reflects an unfolding, dialogical evolution.[22] Movement from one stage to another is not automatic but has to be guided and facilitated. Regression to an earlier stage is also possible when, for example, a critical number of key members leave and/or join the Community:

- *Forming:* The leadership group sees the need to turn itself into a Leadership Community. It formally constitutes a Community by specifying the kick-off basic requirements with regard to the building blocks (see Figure 2.1), for example, Envisioned Mandate, Expected Outcomes, Leadership, Ideology, and Structure.
- *Posturing:* The conversation within the Community commences but is all about the superficial, narrow exchange of personal opinions and views around the selected Envisioned Mandate, being shared in the politest possible ways so as not to offend anyone. "Being nice" is the crux of this stage.
- *Confronting:* During this stage in addressing the Envisioned Mandate, members take definitive, opposing positions in Me vs. Them or an Us vs. Them camps manifested in ferocious, rigorous judgemental and advocacy debates infused by a parochial win-lose attitude. 'Talking tough' typifies this stage: 'My/Our view is by far the better/the best.' By implication, 'I am/We are better than you'. Frequently an appeal is made to having more authority and rank, and hence having better/weightier opinions and views.
- *Reaching out:* During this stage members let go of their entrenched views and opinions. They are driven by the empathic desire to listen and truly understand others' positions and the rationales for the positions adopted. A shared exchange, "Us" space is emerging, infused by a win–win attitude.
- *Bonding:* During this stage authentic dialogue emerges, engendering the co-creation of answers to jointly agreed-upon questions regarding a collectively interpreted and owned Envisioned Mandate, enabled by an open-ended, inclusive, fluid and dynamic learning process. Wholeness, We, Commonality, Equality, Mutual respect and Reciprocity characterise this stage.
- *Reconstituting:* At this stage the Community agrees it has delivered on its set Envisioned Mandate, and has to reconstitute itself in order to address a new Envisioned Mandate. If the Community remains essentially unchanged, then it can re-launch itself at the Bonding stage. However, if its composition needs to change significantly, it will be pushed back to an earlier stage. How far back, cannot be predicted up front.

Recognising a Flourishing and Thriving Leadership Community

A truly flourishing and thriving Leadership Community will be recognisable by a visible and tangible *sense of community*. Table 2.3 (below) gives the typical manifestations of a sense of community.[23]

Table 2.3: Manifestations of a sense of community

A Sense of Belonging to a Leadership Community
We know we are part of a community when we experience high levels of:
• Belonging: strong personal identification with and commitment to the community
• Reciprocal influence and support
• Cohesion: a strong "we-ness"
• Fulfilment and pride in achievements: we are making a real difference
• Authenticity reflected, *inter alia*, in healthy, constructive processes
• Enablement and empowerment
• Psychosocial capital: hope, efficacy, resilience, optimism, courage
• Caring for each other's wellbeing
• Diversity: friendliness across the full spectrum of diversity
• Growth through learning, continuous improvement and innovation

Critical Success Factors for a Flourishing and Thriving Leadership Community

The critical success factors for a flourishing and thriving Leadership Community are given in Table 2.4.[24]

Table 2.4: Critical success factors for a flourishing and thriving Leadership Community

Critical Success Factors
• Genuinely shared leadership
• An inspiring Envisioned Mandate with the appropriate degree of authority/power
• Adequate space-time with expandable, permeable boundaries, allowing evolution to higher levels of functioning and dialogue
• The right members with the right abilities
• Mutual trust and openness
• A safe dialogical space-time: anything and anybody can be questioned at any time
• Ongoing learning and growth
• Dynamics typified by fluidity, responsiveness, agility
• Adequate resources, for example, time, information
• Authentic, deepening, unfolding dialogue

Conclusion

An imperative of the emerging new order of tomorrow is Shared Leadership. A concrete manifestation of such leadership is a flourishing and thriving Leadership Community in the organisation, enabling the leadership group of the organisation to move beyond mere hierarchical and primitive functions as a mode of functioning. In this way, organisation-wide challenges, issues and problems can be addressed expeditiously and innovatively because the collective expertise, experience and wisdom of the total leadership group have been mobilised effectively and efficiently.

Endnotes

1   Avolio, Walumbwa & Weber, 2009; Bennis, 2007; Currie, Lockett & Suhomlinova, 2009; DeRue, 2011; Fletcher & Käufer, 2003; McGuire et al, 2009; McGuire & Rhodes, 2009; Osborn, Hunt & Jauch, 2002; Pearce & Conger, 2003; Ramthun & Matkin, 2012; Veldsman, 2013.

2   Wenger, 2010a; Wenger, 2010b.

3   Bardon, & Borzillo, 2016; Iaquinto, Ison & Faggian, 2011; Mirvis & Gunning, 2006; Nikolova & Devinney, 2008; Wenger & Snyder, 2000; Wenger-Trayner & Wenger-Trayner, 2015.

4   Balkundi & Kilduff, 2005; Currie, Lockett & Suhomlinova, 2009; Mirvis & Gunning, 2006; Veldsman, 2013; Van der Merwe & Verwey, 2016; Veenswijk & Chisalita, 2007.

5   Balkundi & Kilduff, 2005; Mirvis & Gunning, 2006.

6   Saint-Onge & Wallace, 2003; Van der Merwe & Verwey, 2016; Veldsman, 2013.

7   *cf.* Balkundi & Kilduff, 2005; Bardon, & Borzillo, 2016; Currie, Lockett & Suhomlinova, 2009; Iaquinto, Ison & Faggian, 2011; Koortzen, 2016; Mirvis & Gunning, 2006; Nikolova & Devinney, 2008; Ramthun & Matkin, 2012; Scarso, Bolisani & Salvador, 2009; Snyders & Wenger, 2010; Veldsman, 2013; Van der Merwe & Verwey, 2016; Veenswijk & Chisalita, 2007; Wenger, 2010a, 2010b.

8   For example, Wenger, 2010a, 2010b.

9   Hernandez, 2012; Iaquinto, Ison & Faggian, 2011; Nikolova & Devinney, 2008; Pearce & Conger, 2003; Saint-Onge & Wallace, 2003; Scarso, Bolisani & Salvador, 2009; Van der Merwe & Verwey, 2016; Veenswijk & Chisalita, 2007; Wenger & Snyder, 2000; Wenger, 2010a, 2010b.

10   For example, Wenger, 2010a, 2010b.

11   Wenger, 2010a, 2010b.

12   For example, Wenger, 2010a, 2010b.

13   Veenswijk & Chisalita, 2007.

14   Fletcher & Käufer, 2003; Mirvis & Gunning, 2006; Nikolova & Devinney, 2008.

15   Fletcher & Käufer, 2003; Groysberg & Slind, 2012; Mirvis & Gunning, 2006.

16   For example, Wenger, 2010a, 2010b.

17   Veldsman, 2013 . See also McGuire et al, 2009; McGuire & Rhodes, 2009; Obholzer & Roberts, 1994; Osburn, Hunt & Jaunch, 2002; Porter & McLaughlin, 2006; Ramthun & Matkin, 2012; Stapley, 1996; Veldsman, 2002; Vroom & Jago, 2007.

18   De Jager, Cilliers & Veldsman, 2003; McGuire et al, 2009; Northhouse, 2007; Pierce & Newstrom, 1994; Veenswijk & Chisalita, 2007.

19   Veldsman, 2013.

20   *cf.* Reynolds, 1997.

21   Adapted and expanded from Nadler & Tushman, 1995.

22   Scharmer, 2009 . See also Fletcher & Käufer, 2003.

23   Fletcher & Käufer, 2003; Iaquinto, Ison & Faggian, 2011; McMillan & Chavis, 1986; Mirvis & Gunning, 2006; Wenger, 2010a, 2010b.

24   Fletcher & Käufer, 2003; Iaquinto, Ison & Faggian, 2011; McMillan & Chavis, 1986; Mirvis & Gunning, 2006; Scarso Bolisani & Salvador, 2009; Wenger, 2010a, 2010b.

References

Avolio, BJ, Walumbwa, FO & Weber, TJ. 2009. 'Leadership: Current theories, research, and future directions'. *Annual Review of Psychology*, 60:421–449.

Balkundi, P & Kilduff, M. 2005. 'The ties that lead: A social network approach to leadership'. *The Leadership Quarterly*, 16:941–961.

Bardon, T & Borzillo, S. 2016. 'Communities of practice: Control or autonomy?' *Journal of Business Strategy*, 37(1):11-18.

Bennis, W. 20077. 'The challenge of leadership in the modern world: Introduction to the special issue'. *American Psychologist*, 62(1):2-5.

Currie, G, Lockett, A & Suhomlinova, O. 2009. 'The institutionalisation of distributed leadership: A "catch-22" in English public services'. *Human Relations*, 20(10):1–27.

De Jager, W, Cilliers, F & Veldsman, TH. 2003. 'Leadership development from a systems psychodynamic consultancy stance'. *SA Journal of Human Resource Management*, 1(3):85–92.

DeRue, DS. 2011. 'Adaptive leadership theory: Leading and following as a complex adaptive process'. *Research in Organisational Behavior*, 31:125–150.

Fletcher, JK & Käufer, K. 2003. 'Shared leadership: Paradox and possibility' (Ch. 2). In CLPearce & JA Conger (eds). *Shared leadership. Reframing the hows and whys of leadership.* Thousand Oaks, CA: Sage Publications. 21–47.

Groysberg, B & Slind, M. 2012. 'Leadership is a conversation'. *Harvard Business Review*, 76–84, June.

Hernandez, M. 2012. 'Toward an understanding of the psychology of stewardship'. *Academy of Management Review*, 37(2):172–193. [Online]. Available: http://dx.doi.org/10.5465/amr.2010.0363. [Accessed 25 April 2016].

Iaquinto, B, Ison, R & Faggian, R. 2011. 'Creating communities of practice: Scoping purposeful design'. *Journal of Knowledge Management*, 15(1):4–21.

Koortzen 2016. 'Leadership dynamics' (Ch. 9). In TH Veldsman & AJ Johnson (eds). *Leadership: Perspectives from the front line.* Johannesburg, ZA: Knowledge Resources.

McGuire, JB, Palus, CJ, Pasmore, W & Rhodes, GB. 2009. *Transforming your organisation. Global organisational development.* White paper series Greensboro, NC: Center for Creative Leadership.

McGuire, JB & Rhodes, GB. 2009. *Transforming your leadership culture.* San Francisco, CA: Jossey-Bass.

McMillan, DW & Chavis, DM. 1986. 'Sense of community: A definition and theory'. *Journal of Community Psychology*, 14(1):6–23.

Mirvis, P & Gunning, LT. 2006. 'Creating a community of leaders'. *Organisational Dynamics*, 35 (1):69–82.

Nadler, DA & Tushman, ML. 1995. 'Types of organisational change: From incremental improvement to discontinuous transformation'. In DA Nadler, RB Shaw, AE Walton & Associates (eds.). *Discontinuous change: Leading organisational transformation.* San Francisco, CA, Jossey-Bass. 15–34.

Nikolova, N & Devinney, T. 2008. 'Building community'. In D Barry & H Hansen (eds). *The Sage Handbook of new approaches in management and organisation.* Los Angeles, CA: Sage. 503–513.

Nohria, N & Khurana, R (eds). 2010. *Handbook of leadership theory and practice.* Boston, MA: Harvard Business Press.

Northouse, P.G. 2007. *Leadership. Theory and practice,* Thousand Oaks, CA: Sage.

Obholzer, A & Roberts, VZ. 1994. *The unconscious at work. Individual and organisational stress in the human services.* London, UK: Routledge.

Osburn, RN, Hunt, JG & Jaunch, LR. 2002. 'Toward a contextual theory of leadership'. *The Leadership Quarterly*, 13:797–837.

Pearce, CL & Conger, JA (eds). 2003. *Shared leadership. Reframing the Hows and Whys of leadership.* Thousand Oaks, CA: Sage.

Pierce, JL & Newstrom, JW. 2003. *Leaders and the leadership process.* Boston, MA: McGraw-Hill.

Porter, LW & McLaughlin, GB. 2006. 'Leadership and the context: Like the weather?' *The Leadership Quarterly*, 17:559–576.

Ramthun, AJ & Matkin, GS. 2012. 'Multicultural shared leadership: a conceptual model of shared leadership in culturally diverse teams'. *Journal of Leadership and Organisational Studies*, 19(3):303–314.

Reynolds, L. 1997. *The trust effect. Creating the high trust, high performance organisation.* London, UK: Nicholas Brealey.

Saint-Onge, H & Wallace, D. 2003. *Leveraging communities of practice for strategic advantage.* Amsterdam, NL: Butterworth Heinemann.

Scarso, E, Bolisani, E & Salvador, L. 2009. 'A systematic framework for analysing the critical success factors of communities of practice'. *Journal of Knowledge Management*, 13(6):431–447.

Scharmer, CC. 2009. *Theory U: Leading from the future as it emerges.* San Francisco, CA: Berrett-Koehler.

Snyders, WM & Wenger, E. 2010. 'Our world as a learning system: A communities-of-practice approach'. In C Blackmore (ed). *Social learning systems and communities of practice.* London, UK: Springer. 107–124.

Stapley, L. 1996. *The personality of the organisation. A psycho-dynamic explanation of culture and change.* London, UK: Free Association Books.

Van der Merwe, L & Verwey, AM. 2016. *Building the corporate leadership community.* Johannesburg, ZA: KR Publishing.

Veenswijk, M & Chisalita, CM. 2007. 'The importance of power and ideology in communities of practice. The case of a de-marginalised user interface design team in a failing multi-national design company'. *Information Technology & People,* 20(1):32–52.

Veldsman TH. 2013. *Leadership culture and climate – Enhancing or destroying leadership excellence within the leadership community? Towards a typology of different leadership cultures and climates infusing leadership communities with their consequential effect on the leadership building blocks and excellence.* Paper presented at 16th Congress of 2013 European Association Work and Organisational Psychology 22–25 May, Münster, Germany.

Vroom, VH. & Jago, AJ. 2007. 'The role of the situation in leadership'. *American Psychologist*, 62(1):17–24.

Wenger, E. 2010a. 'Conceptual tools for COPs as social learning systems: Boundaries, identity, trajectories and participation'. In C Blackmore (ed). *Social learning systems and communities of practice*. London, UK: Springer. 125–143.

Wenger, E. 2010b. 'Communities of practice and social learning systems: The career of a concept'. In C Blackmore (ed). *Social learning systems and communities of practice*. London, UK: Springer. 179–198.

Wenger, EC & Snyder, EC. 2000. 'Communities of practice. The organisational frontier'. *Harvard Business Review*, 139–145, January-February.

Wenger-Trayner, E & Wenger-Trayner, B. 2015. *Communities of practice: A brief introduction*. 15 April. [Online]. Available: http://wenger-trayner.com/introduction-to-communities of practice/. [Accessed 17 April 2016].

Chapter 3

LEADERSHIP IDENTITY

Ilka Dunne

How often have you heard the complaints: "So-and-so seemed to be the perfect candidate for the leadership role and yet just isn't performing."; "Since so-and-so took over the team they're just not delivering the same results."; "Why does so-and-so seem so out of sorts in the new leadership role?"; "Why does the leadership team seem so uncertain?" Despite years of research into leadership and management, organisations still struggle to understand why new leaders and managers seem to go backwards before they go forwards. Employees promoted for their fantastic technical skillsets; then trained in all the people skills such as how to work with Emotional Intelligence (EQ), listening with intent, holding coaching conversations, and so forth, still seem to flounder when faced with transitioning into a leadership or management role. Even long-term leaders who have successfully managed entire business units seem to struggle when given the opportunity to make the transition into a business-wide leadership role. How is this possible? And why does it seem so much more prolific today than in years gone by?

There is little doubt that the world has speeded up. Open any business magazine or newspaper and you will be bombarded with stories about the pace of change in our increasingly networked and connected world. You will find stories about the impact of the VUCA (= **V**olatile, **U**ncertain, **C**haotic and **A**mbiguous) world on companies struggling to find ways to adapt more quickly. You will come across data that highlights how the average lifespan of a company listed in the S&P 500 has significantly decreased – in the 1920s companies lasted an average of 67 years, yet today they average 15 years. You will read advice on how to future-proof your organisation through growing employee agility, a fail-fast mindset, and greater mindfulness. You will learn that today's workforce no longer wants the 8–5 working hours role, tied to a desk, but rather looks for flexibility and wants a career that looks more like a jungle gym than a corporate ladder. Add to this the extended life expectancy of the workforce, the increasing influx of millennials, and the complexity of coping with a multigenerational workforce. Finally, consider the fact that the global economy is redefining what it means to be successful. Developing nations, many in Africa, with smart tech are able to leapfrog the traditional global powerhouses because they're not bogged down with century-old mindsets reminding them that "this is the way it's always been done".

This also changes our beliefs around who can become leaders in our organisations. Gone are the days of leaders needing the obligatory grey hair and the years of experience that this represents. Nowadays many of the fastest growing organisations in the world are created in their parents' garages by people in their early twenties. How is it possible for someone who is in Levinson's "entering the adult world"-stage to be successful as a leader, leading a multibillion dollar corporation? I would challenge that these very linear notions of life in clearly depicted and categorised stages are somewhat outdated, particularly when considering the complexity of growing up in a developing world, where one needs to take on the burdens of adulthood far earlier, where education is continually challenging young adults to become more individualised and individualistic, and where millennials are known to have quarter-life crises well before the standard mid-life crisis.

All our focus on the future may also lead us to believe that all our leaders need to do is get future fit, ensure that they are more agile, better able to fall fast and pick themselves up again. While these are useful considerations, all of these skills and abilities are outward looking while in fact what is needed is a far deeper inward look. But in this high-paced, ever-changing world, leaders strain under the knowledge that they do not have the time their forefathers had to find their feet in new roles. They need to adapt quickly and make a transition into new positions. This again means that traditional linear models of managerial and leadership development are rather blunt tools with which to engage in the current leadership debate.

Despite our rapidly changing world, the best organisations are still known for their great leaders. These leaders are able to bring all of themselves to the boardroom table and are able to manage their own state of mind in times of stress, disruption and chaos. What leaders need to do is to go back to the fundamentals, to find the core of who they are. Identity studies seek to understand exactly this: who are you as an individual, and what are the social, work and role identities you wish to be part of? What is the identity transition you are facing, and what are the adaptations you need to make in order to manage the transition?

Getting to Grips with Identity

The notion of identity has puzzled humankind since the birth of humanity. From those early days when scientists first sought to understand the laws of science and physics, they were also exploring what it meant to be human and what impact this had on our relationship with the world and others around us.

Over time, different domains have applied the study of identity research in many similar but also many different ways, and have evolved differing, although not entirely dissimilar, insights into the nature of the self. This has meant bodies of research exploring personal, role, social, and work identity (among other fields) as if they are disparate entities.

Recently, however, within the fields of both sociology and social psychology, there have been calls to find ways to collapse some of the traditional boundaries between these studies. The anthropologist Geertz argues that:

> "The Western conception of the person as a bounded, unique, more or less integrated motivational and cognitive universe, a dynamic centre of awareness, emotion, judgement and action, organised into a distinctive whole and set contrastively against such wholes and against a social and natural background is, however incorrigible it may seem to us, a rather peculiar idea within the context of the world's cultures." [1]

This opens up new avenues for insight as it is often the tensions between identities that cause the most discomfort during periods of identity transition.

It is therefore useful to examine personal, social, role and work identities where they intersect, considering how a leader may balance the need for personal and role identity, within the work identity in which they function and their need to be accepted into the social identities of their team and colleagues.

In this chapter we will define personal, role, social, and work identities in order to understand how these identities form the basis for how we engage with the world. We will explore how these multiple identities interrelate, align and compete, and how this is particularly heightened when experiencing periods of transition.

We will examine the notion of liminality (the often heightened emotional sensation of being between identities during periods of transition) and help you, as a leader, to understand how you can use warrants (behaviours which may be either verbal or physical) in order to assess and test aspects of identity, or acceptance into new identities, so that the transition is effected more rapidly.

This insight will help you, as a leader, to understand your experiences better during periods of identity transition, how you can best prepare for these transitions, and what you can do to make sense of your experiences during the transition. It will also help you to understand what others may be experiencing while you and they are making the transition into new roles.

Let us pause here to define the varying identities a bit more clearly before meeting a few leaders and learning about their identity transitions into leadership.

Identity Studies: A Brief Reader

In this section we will discuss personal, role, social, and work identities.

Personal identity

On a highly simplified level, personal identity can be said to be an amalgamation of personal elements, such as your values, beliefs, attitudes, skills, and personality traits that develop throughout your life, and are therefore fairly fixed.[i] A personal identity could be said to be how you define yourself in the present, which displays the stability between how you understand yourself as you were in the past, and how you understand yourself as you wish to be in the future.[2]

The term "*the looking glass self*" explains how you develop a self-concept through interpreting how others react to you.[3] Your self-concept can be either improved or diminished by the conclusions you reach based on the reactions from people around you. Identity is therefore not static. It is characterised by a reflexive process that takes place through language. Based on your engagements with others, you work to understand yourself through an internal conversation between your sense of *me*, the person you have always been with all your past experiences and *I*, your dialogue with yourself, in the present, which will evolve to become the *you* of the future.[4]

This presupposes an inner psychological structure of your own being that, although shaped and modified by interaction with society, maintains a core of sameness and continuity, unless a crisis of some sort has an impact on it.[5] This is commonly termed *personal identity*.

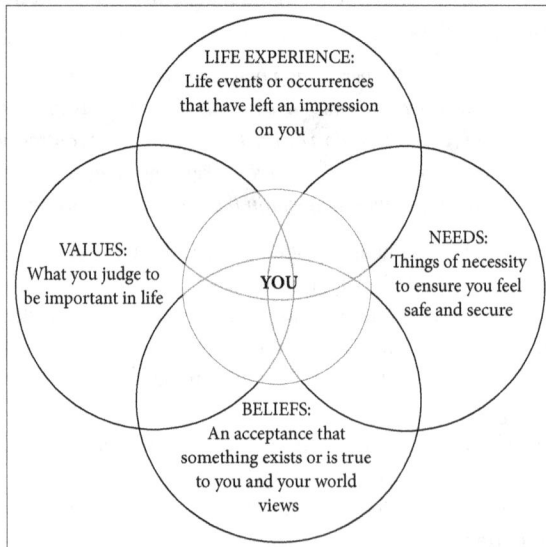

Figure 3.1: Personal Identity Map

---

i   Personal identity theories stem from sociological work by, among others, Cooley (1902) and Mead (1934), and psychological theories, many of which were first proposed by Erik Erikson (1980).

> **Take time to consider:** *Using the Personal Identity Map above, **complete a map for your own life**. Be as detailed as you can. Use this map as the basis for a discussion with a good friend, a spouse, a personal coach or a colleague as this can be very useful in deepening your thinking around what is core to you on a personal identity level.*

Role identity

Role identity theory is concerned with the roles you play in social contexts. Role theory proposes that a large part of your everyday activities is the acting out of socially defined roles, such as mother, scholar, teacher. Roles have boundaries that have been defined by society over time in order to help simplify the world. You are therefore better able to make sense of your own behaviour and understand the behaviour of others.[6] This also helps you to know which behaviours are appropriate in which context, and minimises the cognitive load you may feel when taking on a new role identity.[7] The role of leader is one such role identity, and as a new leader you will use what you know about leadership and what you have seen from other leaders as the basis for taking on this role.

We choose which roles to take on based both on what society needs of us and our own idealised and individual identity hierarchy.[ii] The role of leader has been given great prominence in society. This means that being successful as a leader will be critically important to you when taking on this role and will often lead to lowered levels of self-esteem when you are not immediately successful.

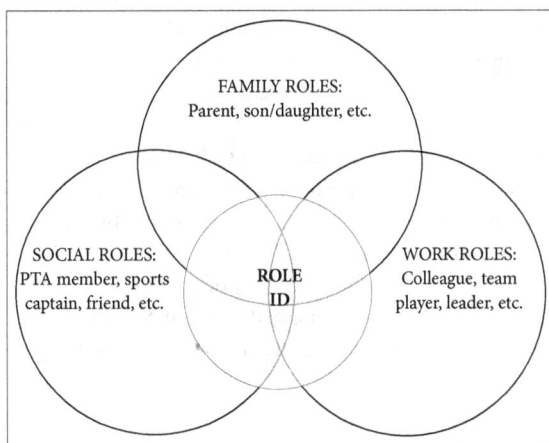

Figure 3.2: Role Identity Map

> **Take time to consider:** *Using the map above and what you now know about yourself as based on your personal identity map, **create your own role identity map.***

---

ii Termed a hierarchy of prominence by McCall and Simmons (1978) and, similarly, a salience hierarchy by Stryker (1980).

Social identity

At its simplest level, social identities are identities you take on in order to be accepted into social groups. You choose these groups carefully as they enable you to bolster your self-esteem. Social groups may include sports teams, business chapters, community bodies, or even school governing bodies (SGBs). In each of these you are able to prove your self-worth in that particular context. For example, becoming a member of a school governing body may help you to prove that you are a really good administrator, with strong financial skills. A business chapter may equally enable you to highlight your consummate business skills in your role as a businessperson.

We all focus on our individuality in order to emphasise our distinctiveness *vis-à-vis* others. We do this through a relational process in which we act the role, in order to see how others react to us, before selecting which group is the best source for our self-esteem.[8]

Maintaining self-esteem or a positive and secure self-concept is critical to all individuals. Termed the *self-esteem hypothesis*,[9] this is cited as the reason you may seek to leave a group or distance yourself from a group, if you perceive the group to be of a lower status. When it is not possible to move away from a low-status group, you will engage in a *social creativity strategy* or *social competition*. Social competition involves competing with other groups (out-groups), in order to improve the status of the current group (in-group). A social creativity strategy involves making the in-group look better by focusing on aspects of the group that are positive, downplaying aspects that reflect poorly on the group, or choosing a new out-group for comparison. As a leader you will engage in both *social creativity* and *social competition strategies* in order to improve the social standing of your team, thereby helping you to improve your personal levels of self-esteem.

Entitativity is defined in the online Psychology Dictionary as meaning "the consideration of something as pure entity".[10] As a subset of Social Categorisation Theory,[iii] it further seeks to understand why some groups are accepted as a group while others are seen to be merely a cluster of individuals. Groups that are valued as important by their members interact regularly, and share common goals and outcomes, are seen to be entities and therefore generally have higher Entitativity.[11]

Entitativity is desirable to the group, and members of a highly entitative group will find ways to exclude members of the group who detract from the entitative behaviours of the group, thereby maintaining the high entitativity status of the group.[12] By increasing the entitativity of a group, members will identify more greatly with the group and wish to be a part of it.[13] As a leader you are continually seeking to build the entitativity of your team and will work hard to maintain this status. This can be useful to a highly engaged team but can equally lead to in-group and out-group politics if not all the members of your team feel accepted by the group.

---

iii Where SIT sought to explain individual and intergroup engagement and how people choose to be part of or remove themselves from a group (Tajfel & Turner, 1979), Social Categorisation Theory (SCT) seeks to explain intragroup categorisation more deeply (Hogg, 1992; Turner, 1982; Turner et al., 1987).

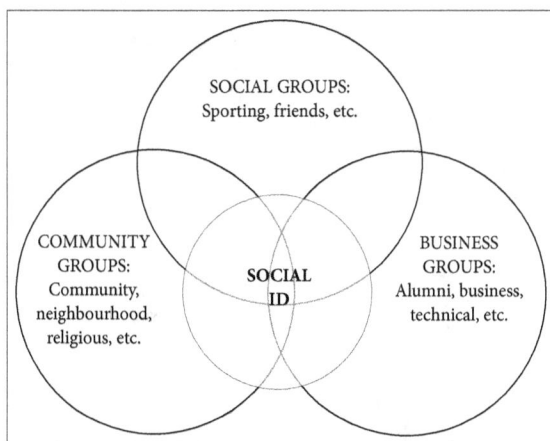

Figure 3.3: Social Identity Map

Take time to consider: *Using the map above and what you now know about yourself as based on both your personal identity map and your role identities, create your own social identity map.*

Work identity

Work is central to adult life, and it is the way in which we achieve success, status, and power. Work, therefore, is a cornerstone of your identity, and identification in the workplace promotes a sense of belonging and acceptance that will bring you a sense of comfort, thereby increasing your self-esteem.[14]

In the South African context, work identity is defined as "a multi-identity, multi-faceted and multi-layered construction of the self (in which the self-concept fulfils a core, integrative function), that shapes the roles that individuals are involved in, in their employment context".[15]

Work identity is therefore dynamic, interpretive, and ongoing as it involves you seeking to identify with aspects of your job, your work environment, and your employer, and this has an impact on the roles you choose to take on, and the way in which you perform when completing your work.[16]

Work identity relates closely to the culture of an organisation. As a leader you will therefore need to feel congruence with the work culture because you become the custodian of this culture when you take on a leadership role.

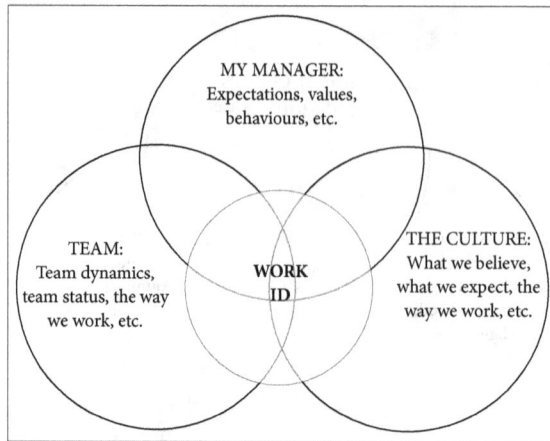

Figure 3.4: Work Identity Map

Take time to consider: *Using the map above and everything you now understand about yourself,* **create your own work identity map**. *Then imagine overlaying these maps of all your identities. Where are the overlaps? How do these identities relate to or potentially conflict with each other?*

Identity Transitions

Although we are continually making small adaptations to our identities, there will often be times in our lives when we find ourselves undergoing a more intense identity change. These are transitional periods and they are generally brought on by a major shift in our circumstances: the birth of a child, a marriage, the acceptance of a new job role, or a change in one's organisation are all examples of these. These are periods in our lives when we are left feeling uncertain about who we are, what we stand for, and whether we fit in. This heightened emotional time in an identity transition is called "liminality".

Liminality: the sensation of being betwixt and between, and warranting: affirming your leadership identity

The term *liminal* is the moment in a rite of passage where a person is betwixt and between one identity and another, and not quite either.[17] It is a moment of being "in and out of time".[18] Liminality is a therefore the phase in which identity is reconstructed, and this happens through engagement with others.

The term *emergent identity* is used to describe this period. Emergent identity "arise[s] from the interaction between claim/disclaim by the individual, and affirmation/disaffirmation by significant others",[19] so it is both what is claimed by you as your identity and the affirmation of others that leads to an agreed social and role identity being formed. These claims and affirmations are made through the process of warranting.[iv]

---

iv A warrant (Draper, 1988; Gergen, 1985, 1989; Holmes, 2000; Toulmin, 1958) is a discourse (including, in its broadest sense, behaviour) that is used to seek acceptance and therefore entry into a social context or grouping.

Warranting is a process in which you affirm your leadership identity by behaving in a manner that you deem appropriate of being a leader. Those around you will then affirm or disaffirm your warrant and this will lead to further identity adaptation and further warrants. If you quickly learn the "conventions of warrant,"[20] or legitimate modes of discourse, you are more likely to be readily accepted into the social context. If you aren't immediately accepted you may experience identity threat, begin to doubt your power and identity, and may even choose to disengage. Identity transition is therefore a period of great personal uncertainty filled with emotional ups and downs. During this transition you will seek to find equilibrium between your own personal identity and your role identity (your view of what it means to be a leader), within the context of the work environment (your work identity). This is a constant process in which you will try on facets of an identity in order to decide whether it aligns with your own self-concept. This process, referred to as *identity work,* involves ongoing reflexivity and adaptation in order to achieve the required identity. Ibarra and Petriglieri (2010) remind us that "[a] primary objective of identity work … is acting and looking the part, so as to be granted the claimed identity".[21] However, this identity needs to be congruent with your own sense of self. Identity dissatisfaction will ensue if you feel trapped within a role that you may be able to fulfil, but with which you feel no personal alignment. This sense of feeling trapped leads, in turn, to further identity work. You will continually seek equilibrium through your identity work in order to "fit in" and feel salience within the in-group.[22]

Identity work, identity dissatisfaction, and identity threat during periods of transition

At an extreme, identity dissatisfaction may lead to identity threat.[v] When your attempts to be accepted within an identity group fail, you are likely to perceive this as an identity threat. When you are unable to balance old and new selves, you will be left feeling inauthentic, and this, in turn, will lead to heightened levels of insecurity and emotion.[23] The more recurrent a negative experience, the higher the likelihood will be that you will perceive it as threatening.

Both identity threat and identity dissatisfaction and, at an extreme, identity disengagement, lead to lowered levels of self-esteem and have an impact on your personal agency. It is therefore valuable to consider how these may relate to each other and where possible tensions may play out for you during times of transition.

Holmes's *Claim-affirmation model of emergent identity* in Figure 3.5 (below) provides a visual tool illustrating what you may experience during this identity transition.

---

v Petriglieri (2011: 644) defines identity threats as "experiences appraised as indicating potential harm to the values, meanings or enactment of an identity".

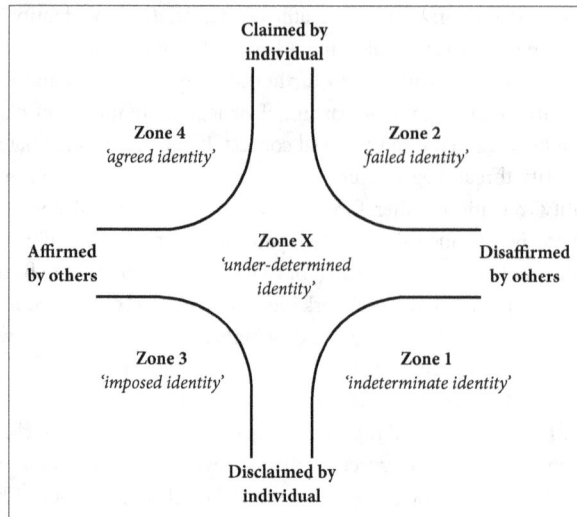

Figure 3.5: The claim-affirmation model of emergent identity (Holmes (2001))[24]

As can be seen from the Claim-affirmation model above, the results of warranting can place you in one of four quadrants: Zone 1: "indeterminate identity"; Zone 2: "failed identity"; Zone 3: "imposed identity"; or Zone 4: "claimed identity".

During an identity transition, while you are still trying to find your feet, you could be said to be in *Zone X: "under-determined identity"*. During the period of identity transition you will find yourself putting yourself forward through warrants and watching to see how these are accepted in the context. Transitions always take a while, and you may have some warrants affirmed while others are disaffirmed during this process. You may therefore find yourself moving backwards and forwards through these zones as you test and adapt to find the fit.

If in order to fit in you find yourself doing things that are contrary to your usual behaviour, and not in alignment with your identities, and these actions are disaffirmed by those around you, then you are likely to find yourself in *Zone 1: "indeterminate identity"*. If your usual behaviours, as aligned to your identities, are disaffirmed by others, you will find yourself in *Zone 2: "failed identity"*. If you can be affirmed by others only when you display behaviours out of alignment with your identities, you will find yourself in *Zone 3: "imposed identity"*. So it is only when your usual behaviours, as aligned to your identities, are accepted by others that you will find yourself in *Zone 4: "claimed identity"*.

Keeping this in mind, let us now go on to see how these may play out in some leadership identity transitions.

Let us Meet Some Leaders

Meet Thandi

Sithandiwe (Thandi to her friends and colleagues) is a 32-year-old Xhosa woman who has worked as a key member of the marketing team in a successful advertising agency over the last four years. Having grown up in a small town where she always managed to come top of the class, with a mother who is a teacher and a younger brother who is currently studying to be an accountant, she knows the value of hard work.

On a personal level she believes that hard work will always pay off. She has high ideals around attention to detail and is very responsible, so she often puts herself second when completing a project or task, working until late at night if necessary to ensure that her high standards are met.

She is a sociable young woman who quickly makes friends with those around her. She very soon feels responsible to these people, and goes out of her way to help members of the team when they are having a bad day, have broken up with a boyfriend, or just need an ear.

She has a great deal in common with her teammates as they are all young, up-and-coming professionals who are in new relationships, with common goals and ambitions for their careers. She and her teammates often work late together, sharing jokes and gossiping while they work.

Thandi feels great personal and social identity congruence working in this team as she is able to satisfy her personal identity needs of making friends and having fun, delivering high-quality work, and taking responsibility within the team. The work identity of the organisation she is in suits her too, as it is a young and lively advertising agency with a very entrepreneurial culture that celebrates hard work and fun equally. There is always an atmosphere of buzz and activity.

She has had fantastic performance reviews year on year, and the business enjoys the fact that she is a safe pair of hands for any task. Recently, the head of this team has resigned and the business has, after careful consideration, asked Thandi if she would be willing to step into the team leader role. Her new manager is a hands-off type which Thandi enjoys as she likes to be trusted and will always deliver on her promises.

Thandi starts her new role with a great sense of enthusiasm because it shows her career is progressing in a positive direction and that her hard work and long hours have paid off. She is sure that the team will be equally excited, particularly since this is something they have all been chatting about when they have hung out together in the evenings.

The first few weeks seem okay as Thandi starts to hand over her old tasks to team members in order to free herself up from the day-to-day work so that she has more time to manage the team. One Tuesday, Susan delivers the work Thandi has been waiting for. It doesn't quite meet Thandi's expectations but she doesn't want to hurt Susan's feelings and wants to keep the social camaraderie among them alive and well, so she accepts the work as is.

That evening Thandi stays later than usual to redo Susan's piece of work. This is the first instance of many where Thandi will stay behind to finish tasks others have not finished to her liking. Slowly Thandi's team, knowing she will just redo their work, become more and more sloppy with regard to what they hand in, and Thandi is soon carrying not only her managerial duties but also a large amount of the team's work.

Thandi feels totally torn. Not only is she not coping with the immense workload of carrying out her managerial duties and the workload for a number of team members, the team around her is no longer the fun-loving space it used to be. She doesn't feel accepted by the team and this puts her high personal identity need for friends and fun under pressure. Thandi is no longer able to balance her personal, social, and now even her work identities. She feels, despite working longer hours than ever before, that she is failing everyone, in particular her manager, who she knows trusts her implicitly.

Thandi's identity transition highlights a few things. Thandi feels tension in maintaining congruence within her personal identity during the period of transition. Her personal identity values high delivery, attention to detail, and responsibility. As a team member she has control over the quality of her output, but as a leader she needs to trust others to deliver, and this means that the end result may not always look exactly the way she would have done it.

As Thandi's team's delivery standards deteriorate, its social identity becomes less and less of an entity in her eyes. This means that the team is no longer quite as desirable as a social group. Thandi is potentially left wondering whether she even wants to be their leader. Finally, the social and work identities of the team as being a fun-loving group towards whom she feels responsibility are also tarnished, and so she no longer feels the same level of congruence with the team. She therefore finds herself moving between Zone 2: "imposed identity" and Zone 3: "failed identity".

This state of affairs is unsustainable as on the simplest level Thandi cannot maintain the continued workload, but even more so she cannot continue to handle the sense of inadequacy she feels which now has an impact on her self-esteem.

Meet Niven

Niven has been the Head of Technology in a thriving FMCG company for the past three years. Historically, Niven has not been a member of the management board of the organisation, but as a result of recent restructuring, a new seat has been created with the aim of helping the organisation to develop its technology footprint better as part of its expansion into Africa.

As she comes from a large family, Niven's personal identity is driven by a need always to feel part of a community, and her social identity mirrors this. She plays on various sports teams, is a member of her neighbourhood community watch project, and keeps in touch with a broad range of old and new friends. She feels inspired when she is working together with others to find creative solutions to complex problems, and loves the fact that her IT team is recognised for its innovative solutions. These solutions are created by using her community spirit to bring together multiple ideas, particularly since she believes that many voices lead to better solutions. She is also always willing to take a chance on a project, knowing that sometimes it's important to break a few rules because this may lead to the most creative and exciting solution.

The management board is a high-entitativity group for Niven, because it shows that she has broken through with regard to seniority. She is hopeful that she will be able to bring all her skills and abilities to the table. The management board is a predominantly male group, has been together for a number of years, and the team has some tried and tested ways of making decisions. When Niven first attends board meetings, she is struck by the fact that it often feels as though decisions have been made before she even enters the room. The board members, many of whom are personal friends, seem not to need to discuss things to the depth and at the level Niven prefers, so she is not able to hear all the voices and thereafter find the creative solutions she so loves. This is highly frustrating as she can often see solutions that may be better than what has been decided on.

The management board also seems quite risk averse, so although she feels a need to bring her team's voice into the room, she is regularly challenged to think about things from a business-wide perspective and not based on her own more agile business-unit view. This too is frustrating, because she has always felt immense pride in being associated with her business unit. After all, they are recognised for their ability to find creative solutions, and now, in comparison to the management board's entitativity, it feels as if they are no longer the high-entitativity grouping she had always thought them to be.

Niven's identity transition again highlights the tensions in maintaining congruence between one's personal identity and the requirements of the social identity during a period of transition. Feeling as if she is not accepted as an equal partner in the management board social identity and not wishing to endanger her role in this high-entitativity team, she slowly withdraws her contributions to the team, sometimes allowing the team to go ahead with decisions that she is well aware are not ideal. In addition, although she has always felt congruence with the work identity of the organisation, which is a dynamic consumer goods company with radical and forward-thinking strategies about its growth into Africa, she now feels that this is not the full story, and struggles to find alignment with a revised view of her work identity.

As her attempts to be accepted as a fellow leader on the management board fail, she starts to feel identity threat and is unable to balance her previous self with her new self. She therefore finds herself, like Thandi, moving between Zone 2: "imposed identity" and Zone 3: "failed identity". She begins to doubt her ability to come up with creative solutions, and this has an impact on her personal identity, leaving her feeling inauthentic.

Meet Herman

Herman is a 47-year-old engineer who has worked on many mining projects in his 20-something years with a large mining company. He has grown up in the company and so has experienced a slow and steady career progression through the ranks. He has some traditional values around respect for authority and experience, and looks up to his leaders as role models. He believes slow and steady is the best way to make decisions and so will often sit with a problem for a while before reaching a conclusion.

As a result of Herman's years of experience, he is parachuted into playing a temporary leadership role for a young mining team who have been working on setting up the infrastructure for a new mine. The mining team is predominantly made up of young engineers who have worked together for the last two years on this project. They have established processes and ways of working together and have formed a strong social identity. They work well together as a team and don't feel the need to conform to traditional hierarchical norms. They therefore make group decisions easily and quickly.

Herman arrives expecting acceptance into the group immediately because of his advanced years and level of experience. The team, however, do not value his experience in the same way, so he does not feel welcomed into the group. The team continue to make rapid and agile decisions, and he begins to feel immensely frustrated at not having the extended periods of time he has traditionally enjoyed in which to make careful, considered decisions. The longer this continues, the more dictatorial Herman becomes, while the team around him slowly withdraw from him and respect him less and less. He feels unwelcome in the team and so, although his domineering behaviour enables him to maintain his need for careful consideration with regard to decisions, he loses the respect and the position that is so important to him.

Herman's identity transition highlights the difficulties a leader may experience when being asked to transfer into an established social identity, particularly when the social identity does not follow the norms and values of one's work and personal identities. This is likely to leave him in Zone 2: "imposed identity" for extended periods of time. Generally, in this sort of situation, a leader would need either to adapt aspects of their personal identity or to share more openly why they value or believe in certain things, in order to be accepted into the already established social identity. This attitude is more likely to lead to his feeling successful in the leadership role. If Herman had been more willing to adapt to the social identity, he would have been more likely to have gained the respect that his personal identity required. At the moment he feels that his leadership role is under threat.

Learning from the Above Leaders About Identity Transition

Identity work is ongoing

Firstly, during times of transition you have an emergent identity; in other words, identity **work is ongoing**. This identity is relational in that you use warrants to test your identity within the new context. You then monitor reactions to your warrants and adapt according to these reactions. Understanding this process makes you better prepared for the identity work you will need to do, and even potentially enables you to have a more playful attitude towards identity transition.

There is a difference between identity work and play. "Whereas, identity work fundamentally seeks the preservation of existing identities or compliance with externally imposed image requirements, identity play is concerned with inventing and reinventing oneself."[25] We play because we want "... enjoyment and discovery rather than goal and objectives".[26] In identity work, the pressure is to get from A to B as quickly as possible, while in identity play, a person is open to taking a circuitous route, which can be likened to taking the scenic route. Being more aware of the experience of identity transition can help you more consciously take the scenic route, thereby alleviating some of the emotional trauma of identity transition.

> **Take time to consider:** *What warrants have you tried in testing your identity during the transitional period? How have others reacted to these warrants? How did this make you feel? What warrants might you use next time?*

Growing your personal insight

Secondly, **the primary tools for identity transition involve growing your personal insight**. It is critical for you to develop a heightened self-awareness. Self-awareness involves a deepening sense of your personal identity: *"Who am I? What do I stand for? What do I believe about the world? What do I value? Why am I here?"* It also involves a realisation of the tension between your need for social acceptance: *"Why is it important that I am accepted by this group?"*, and your need to stand out as an individual; and finally a sense of what you appreciate about your work identity and a flexible sense of leadership role identity: *"What kind of leader might I be in this role? And how might I adapt to create this?"* Ongoing reflection on these questions will help you to become more self-aware of the identity transition you are experiencing, and also to avoid Zones 1 to 3 of Holmes's (2001) *Claim affirmation model of emergent identity.*[27]

> **Take time to consider:** *How deeply do you understand your own reasons for certain behaviours? What would help you to become more reflective during times of identity transition?*

Finding alignment

Finally, **identity transition is about alignment**. You need to understand that it is natural to feel tension between personal, social, work and leadership role identity during periods of emergent identity. This enables you to become more reflective and therefore cognisant of the dynamics playing out at different times. This allows you to become more mindful of your choices, making better-qualified decisions that you can explain to others, and slowly leading to a place of alignment. If alignment is not possible, you will feel identity threat and disengagement which will have an impact on your self-esteem and levels of agency.

> **Take time to consider:** *How does your understanding of your own identity transitions help you to understand how your team might cope during their own transitions? How could you better help them during these times? And how could this help all of you to find alignment?*

Conclusion

In seeking to develop great leaders, able to cope in a rapidly changing and complex world, it is valuable to consider how identity studies may be used as a lens to help us understand the nature of leadership identity transition. Leaders armed with an understanding of identity transitions, able to look deeply inwards, be more reflective about their experiences, and take a more playful attitude towards the identity transition, are far better equipped to make the transition into their new role more seamlessly.

Endnotes

1   Geertz 1973, 1979, in Sampson, 1989, p. 1.
2   Weinreich, 1986.
3   Cooley, 1902, p. 184.
4   Mead, 1934.
5   Eriksen, 1980.
6   Ashforth, 2001.
7   Stryker & Serpe, 1982.
8   Goffman, 1959; Tajfel & Turner, 1986.
9   Tajfel & Turner, 1986.
10   Psychology Dictionary, nd.
11   Lickel et al., 2000.
12   Yzerbyt et al., 2000.
13   Castano et al., 2002.
14   Buche, 2006.
15   Lloyd, Roodt & Odendaal, 2011, p. 65.
16   Walsh & Gordon, 2008.
17   Van Gennep, 1960.
18   Turner, 2008, p. 35.
19   Holmes, 2001, p. 115.
20   Gergen, 1989, p. 74.
21   Ibarra & Petriglieri, 2010, p. 12.
22   Turner, Oakes, Haslam & McGarty, 1994.
23   Ibarra, 1999.
24   Holmes, 2001.
25   Ibarra & Petriglieri, 2010, p. 14.
26   Ibarra & Petriglieri, 2010, p. 12.
27   Holmes, 2001.

References

Ashforth, BE. 2001. *Role transitions in organizational life: An identity-based perspective*. Mahwah, NJ: Lawrence Erlbaum.

Buche, MW. 2006. 'Gender and IT professional work identity'. In EM Trauth (ed). *Encyclopedia of gender and information technology*. Covent Garden, London, UK: Idea Group Inc. 434–439.

Castano, E, Yzerbyt, V, Paladino, MP & Sacchi, S. 2002. 'I belong, therefore I exist: Ingroup identification, ingroup entitativity, and ingroup bias'. *Personality and Social Psychology Bulletin*, 28(2):135–143.

Cooley, CH. 1902. *Human nature and the social order*. Rev. ed. New York, NY: Charles Scribner's Sons.

Draper, S. 1988. What's going on in everyday explanation? In C. Antaki (Ed.), *Analysing everyday explanation*. London, UK: Sage.

Erikson, EH. 1980. *Identity and the life cycle*. New York, NY: WW Norton & Co.

Gergen, KJ. 1985. 'The social constructionist movement in modern psychology'. *American Psychologist*, 40(3): 266–275.

Gergen, KJ. 1989. 'Warranting voice and the elaboration of self'. In J Shotter & KJ Gergen (eds). *Texts of identity*. London, UK: Sage.

Goffman, E. 1959. *The presentation of self in everyday life*. New York, NY: Doubleday.

Hogg, MA. 1992. *The social psychology of group cohesiveness: From attraction to social identity*. New York, NY: Harvester Wheatsheaf.

Holmes, L. 2000. *Reframing learning: Performance, identity and practice*. Conference paper presented at Critical Contributions to Managing and Learning: Second Connecting Learning and Critique Conference, Lancaster University. [Online]. Available: http://www.re-skill.org.uk/papers/lanc00.html. [Accessed 1 July 2016].

Holmes, L. 2001. 'Reconsidering graduate employability: The "graduate identity" approach'. *Quality in Higher Education*, 7(2):111–119.

Ibarra, H. 1999. 'Provisional selves: Experimenting with image and identity in professional adaptation'. *Administrative Science Quarterly*, 44(4):764–791.

Ibarra, H & Pertriglieri, JL. 2010. 'Identity work and play'. *Journal of Organizational Change Management*, 23(1):10–25.

Lickel, B, Hamilton, DL, Wieczorkowska, G, Lewis, A, Sherman, SJ, & Uhles, AN. 2000. 'Varieties of groups and the perception of group entitativity'. *Journal of Personality and Social Psychology*, 78(2):223–246.

Lloyd, S, Roodt, G & Odendaal, A. 2011. 'Critical elements in defining work-based identity in post-apartheid South Africa'. *SA Journal of Industrial Psychology/SA Tydskrif vir Bedryfsielkunde*, 37(1), Art. #894, 15 pages.

McCall, GJ & Simmons, J Holmes, 2001.L. 1978. 'Identities and interactions'. New York, NY: Free Press.

Mead, GH. 1934. *Mind, self and society: From the standpoint of a social behaviorist*. Chicago, IL: University of Chicago Press.

Petriglieri, JL. 2011. 'Under threat: Responses to and the consequences of threats to individuals' identities'. *Academy of Management Review, 36*(4):641–662.

Psychology Dictionary. nd. Definition of 'entitavity'. *Psychology Dictionary*.

Stets, JE & Burke, PJ. 2003. 'A sociological approach to self and identity'. In M Leary & J Tangney (eds). *Handbook of self and identity*. New York, NY: Guilford Press.

Stryker, S. 1980. *Symbolic interactionism: A social structural version*. Menlo Park, CA: Benjamin/Cummings Publishing Company.

Stryker, S & Serpe, RT. 1982. 'Commitment, identity salience, and role behavior: Theory and research example'. In W Ickes & ES Knowles (eds). *Personality, roles, and social behavior*. New York, NY: Springer. 199–218.

Tajfel, H & Turner, JC. 1979. 'An integrative theory of intergroup conflict'. In S Worchel & LW Austin (eds). *The social psychology of intergroup relations*. Belmont, CA: Brooks/Cole Publishing Company. 33–47.

Tajfel, H & Turner, JC. 1986. 'The social identity theory of inter-group behavior'. In S Worchel and LW Austin (eds). *Psychology of intergroup relations*. 2nd ed. Chicago, IL: Nelson-Hall. 7–24.

Turner, E. 2008. 'Exploring the work of Victor Turner: Liminality and its later implications'. *Suomen Antropologi: Journal of the Finnish Anthropological Society*, 33(4):26–44.

Turner, JC, Oakes, PJ, Haslam, SA & McGarty, C. 1994. 'Self and collective: Cognition and social context'. *Personality and Social Psychology Bulletin*, 20(5):454–463.

van Gennep, A. 1909. *Les rites de passage*. Paris: Nourry. Trans. by MB Vizedom & GL Caffee. 1960. *The rites of passage*. Chicago, IL: University of Chicago Press.

Weinreich, P. 1986. 'The operationalisation of identity theory in racial and ethnic relations'. In J Rex & D Mason. *Theories of race and ethnic relations*. Cambridge, MA: Cambridge University Press. 299–320.

Yzerbyt, V, Castano, E, Leyens, JP & Paladino, MP. 2000. 'The primacy of the ingroup: The interplay of entitativity and identification'. *European Review of Social Psychology*, 11(1):257–295.

CHAPTER 4

LEADERSHIP TRANSITIONS
Theo H Veldsman

Leadership transitions (LTs) are inherent to and form critical passages in the career of any leader, for example, from one requisite Level of Work to another; from one type of position/role to another; or from one organisational function to another. An LT can be defined as the taking up of and engagement with a new set of accountabilities, responsibilities and/or authority by a leader in a leadership role. By implication, it may also be defined as the disengagement from an existing role.[1] Simply put, an LT is about taking charge of a new role as a leader.[i]

During his/her career, a leader will make many of these transitions with varying degrees of risk of success (or failure). By all accounts the frequency of these transitions are on the increase because of the VICCAS world with its correspondingly significant and radical impact on organisations as they seek to respond appropriately, and these responses in turn having an impact on leaders in their roles.[2]

By their very nature, LTs are at best disruptive. At worst, they are highly costly and draining for the leader involved, his/her direct team, and the organisation(s) and stakeholders concerned as the leader is moving into and through the transition. For example, it has been estimated that 75% of leaders experience moderate to significant adjustment during transitions.[3] Organisations invest hundreds of hours and billions of rands into leadership development, but pay scant attention to probably the most regularly occurring, highest-risk event in the career of leaders when this investment is significantly endangered: transitions.[4] It appears that leaders who are effective at handling transitions are more likely to be effective throughout their careers.[5]

Openly addressing, and formally dealing with, LTs is hampered by the view that they are a "No Go" area. Why? Firstly, it is believed that the intimate details of the process of moving through an LT must be kept as secret as possible in order to protect and enhance the image of the infallible, invincible, all-knowing leader able to overcome any challenge, *inter alia* a transition, effortlessly and with confident ease. Secondly, it is an undiscussable experience because it possibly will incapacitate and undermine the incoming leader's confidence as he/she is endeavouring to find his/her feet during the "vulnerable" period. Thirdly, the unpreparedness of all parties for the LT results in nobody knowing what roles they are expected to play, and contributions they are expected to make, in assisting with and enabling the LT, which results in a "hands off" attitude because of this ambiguity.[6]

The purpose of this chapter is to discuss the nature and dynamics of LTs in depth in order to bring LTs into the public domain of the organisation as openly discussed, critically high-risk organisational occurrences that have to be mitigated. The following topics are addressed: debunking some of the myths associated with LT; providing a basic map of the LT Landscape; unpacking the LT Landscape in terms of its constituent elements; and LT critical success factors.

---

i   This definition implies that more general, non-leadership-related, work transitions are excluded from the discussion, such as a person's initial entry into the world of work; career switches between professions; and retirement.

Debunking Myths Associated with Leadership Transitions

At the outset some of the myths that distort the true reality of LTs must be debunked. In this way, leaders and organisations will be enabled to consider the "genuine and true" nature of LTs. Some of the more dominant LT myths to be brought into the open and destroyed are:[7]

- *Myth 1: "All LTs are created equal."* Truth: Each LT has its own unique features and dynamics, and therefore has to be looked at every time with fresh eyes. The same recipe cannot be applied automatically to each and every LT, regardless of how many LTs the leader concerned has gone through.
- *Myth 2: "LTs are a 'plug-and-play event'. The leader leaves his/her existing role today, and takes up his/her new role tomorrow, and is up and running virtually immediately."* Truth: LT is a change process of short or long duration, requiring all round adjustments – not only concretely and objectively, but also intangibly and subjectively – over time in multiple Domains (to be discussed below). The more Domains affected, and the more boundaries crossed, the longer and more intense the adjustment process and period.
- *Myth 3: "The New Role as espoused upfront, and the actual new Role being bought into, are the same."* Truth: Typically, only formal Role accountabilities and duties are shared upfront: the espoused Role. The invisible, intangible role requirements as well as the dynamics and factors surrounding and affecting the Role are not shared at all, or are near impossible to share down to the finest detail: the actual Role. If shared at all, they are at most covered superficially.
- *Myth 4: "You are essentially 100% ability-wise ready for the new Role, except for maybe some minor tweaks. Otherwise, you would not have been approached to take up the new Role."* Truth: There is never a 100% ability-wise and readiness match between the leader and the new Role. Until the transitioned leader fully understands his/her new Role, he/she has to accept that he/she is unconsciously incompetent with regard to the Role. Past success recipes or habits from the previous Role(s) also cannot be applied uncritically and indiscriminately to the new Role.
- *Myth 5: "We expect you to take charge immediately and be effective from the word 'Go'. We would like to see a (comprehensive) action plan as soon as possible."* Truth: This is the typical "first 90 days" syndrome associated with the incoming leader as the healer, fixer, saviour and knight on a white horse, especially when the new leader is brought in to rectify a bad or deteriorating set-up. This myth builds on Myth 2 of LT being an event, and Myth 4 of a 100% match with the new Role. (See also Myth 6 below.). However, before a leader can become truly effective in his/her new Role, he/she has to have a good understanding of the new Role, and all the factors affecting his/her new Role, now and going into the future.
- *Myth 6: "Given that you are the right person for the Role, and that you have an excellent track record, you will have automatic and unconditional credibility and legitimacy with all of your new stakeholders, especially with your new team. If not, use your authority and power to get them in line and on your side."* Truth: Credibility, legitimacy and trust have to be earned. This takes time. Credibility, legitimacy and trust also affect the initial full disclosure and open sharing of essential information with the incoming leader, especially the undiscussables that are present in all settings. Until the leader is able to bring these into the open, he/she will not have been fully accepted, and cannot be fully effective.
- *Myth 7: "Making a transition is a solo flying act for the leader in transition. He/she must make it work."* Truth: This myth also builds on Myth 2: LT being an event. Without a proactively conceived, formalised, organisationally supported transition process to support and enable the leader in transition, the risk of his/her failure is significantly increased. It is

also not a sign of weakness on the side of such a leader to request, and even insist on, such support; or, from the organisational side, to indicate a sign of doubting the ability of the leader in transition by offering and even enforcing such support.

We are now ready to consider the "genuine and true" nature of LTs. Firstly, I would like to draw a basic map of the LT Landscape.

A Basic Map of the Leadership Transition Landscape

Figure 4.1 provides a basic map of the LT Landscape with its constituent elements.[8]

According to Figure 4.1, LT is a process, the transition, occurring between two points in time: *Time 1: Current* and *Time 2: New*. The transition has an impact on five interdependent Domains: Role, Person, Relationships, Organisation, and Immediate Context. When the terms 'Current' or 'New' are used in the discussion below, they apply to all five Domains in combination.

In the introduction, a *Role* was defined as a set of set of accountabilities, responsibilities and/or authority allocated to a leader, together with the associated expected conduct and performance. *Person* relates to the leader affected by the transition. *Relationships* encompass the stakeholders related to the Role: immediate stakeholders, such as superior, peers, and team; and more remote stakeholders, such as suppliers, clients, regulators, the community, and society. *Organisation* is the entity affected by the LT. *Immediate context* entails the micro setting in which the Role is embedded and the LT will occur, such as the organisational department/ function and contextual location of the Role.

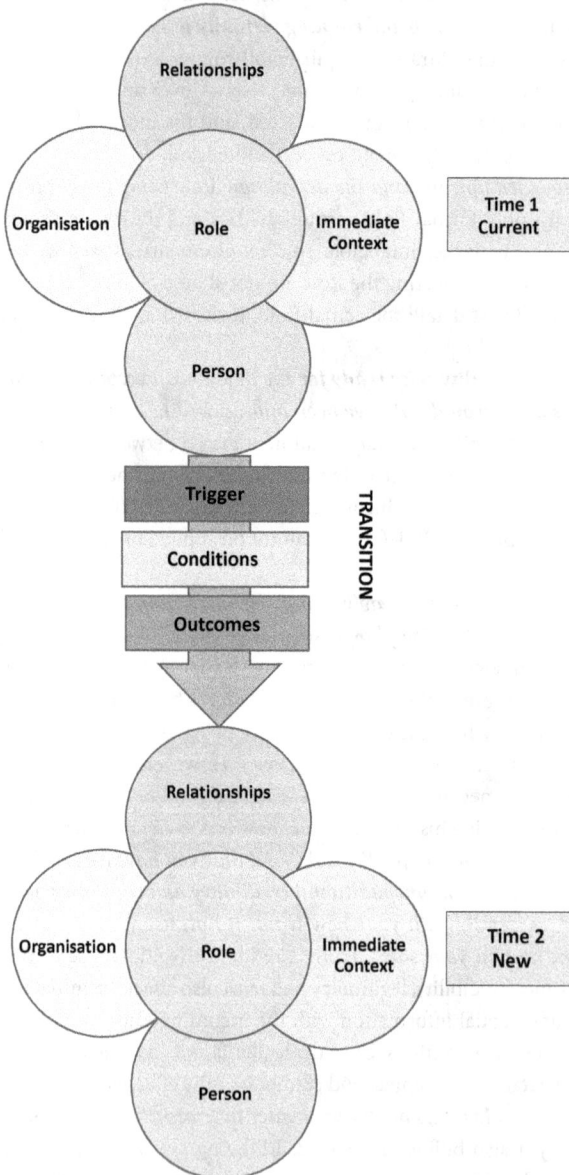

Figure 4.1: A basic map of the LT Landscape

An LT may affect only two or more or up to all five of the Domains simultaneously. Because the Role is the centrepiece of an LT, it is located as the middle circle among the Domains. The Role will therefore form the departure point and the centrepiece of the discussions below. At *Time 2: New* after the transition, one or more of the Domains may be both New and/or different. Generally speaking. the more Domains affected, the more intense the transition is for the leader concerned for that particular transition. However, the intensity of the transition is also a function of how radically a specific Domain(s) changes – its novelty – because of the transition, all other things being equal (to be discussed further below). The more frequent the LTs over time, the higher the ongoing demands and impact on the affected leader, regardless of the LT experience build-up over time.

The transition, given by the arrow between *Time 1: Current* and *Time 2: New*, are made up of four elements: (i) triggers to the transition: what sets it in motion; (ii) the conditions affecting the transition process once it has been activated; (iii) the transition process itself represented by the arrow; and (iv) transition outcomes.

The next four sections deal with these four elements making up the transition between *Time 1: Current* and *Time 2: New* relative to the five interdependent Domains, in the order listed above: from trigger to outcomes.

Possible Triggers to a Leadership Transition

An LT is essentially about crossing any number of the *boundaries* of the five Domains shown in Table 4.1: moving within, up, down, across, and from-into. The more boundaries crossed, the more intense the LT.[9] Table 4.1 provides an overview of the possible major triggers to LTs, and by implication movements across boundaries.[10]

Table 4.1: An overview of possible major LT triggers

			Trigger		
	Person	**Role**	**Relationships**	**Organisation**	**Context**
Moving within	Person recrafting his/her current role	New superior leader(ship) – immediate or more removed – redefining Role of Person	• Person redefining relationships with regard to the Role, including a new stakeholder(s) • Changed relationships because of a new superior	**Intra-organisation:** Redefined Role because of an organisational redesign/restructure and/or a merger/ acquisition	
Moving up				**Intra-organisation:** Vertical move to a higher Level of Work – Promotion within same Function/ Area or within another Function/ Area within the same organisation	

Trigger					
	Person	**Role**	**Relationships**	**Organisation**	**Context**
Moving down				**Intra-organisation:** Demotion within the same Function/Area or to another Function/Area within the same organisation	
Moving across				**Intra-organisation:** Horizontal move: Rotation for development purposes within same Function or into another Area within the same organisation	**Intra-organisation:** • Same Role, but in a new Operating Arena • Different Role in new Operating Arena
Moving from-into				**Inter-organisation:** Move to another organisation into the same or different Role within the same/different Function within the same Operating Arena and/or same Sector	**Inter-organisation:** Move to another Role in another Organisation within a different Operating Arena and/or same/different Sector

At any given point in time a multitude of these LT triggers may be active in an organisation. The more LTs that are underway at a given point in time, the more vulnerable and unstable the organisation. This is one of the reasons an organisation is so highly vulnerable during a full-blown merger: the whole leadership community is in transition. It is thus critically important that an organisation carefully considers the number of LTs active at any given point in time in the organisation. This point will be returned to later under critical success factors.

To illustrate some of the challenges accompanying LTs, "Moving Up" will be used. One of the best-known, integrated conceptualisations of LTs as "Moving up" is the Leadership Pipeline,[11] depicted in Figure 4.2. The Leadership Pipeline is also reflective of the requisite complexity, a Levels of Work (LOW) approach to organisational work.[12]

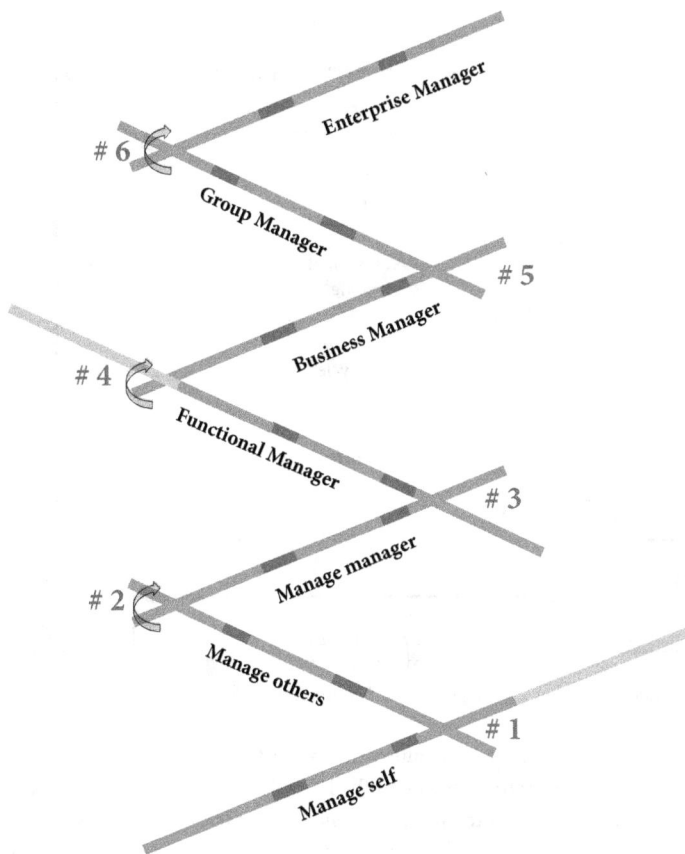

Figure 4.2: The Leadership Pipeline

Each of the inflection points (#1, #2, and so on) in Figure 4.2 represents a "Moving Up" LT with an increase in the requisite LOW. Being able to operate at the requisite LOW poses certain risks, called "leadership traps" (not discussed here because of space constraints), which need to be mitigated through a formal LT plan.[ii]

The LT has been set in motion, it has been triggered, and the move is imminent. What conditions may affect the process of moving?

Conditions Affecting the Activated Transition Process

Figure 4.3 depicts the major conditions (given in the blocks around the inner two semicircles [half-circles]) affecting the activated transition process (the inner two semicircles) in terms of its nature, dynamics, and evolution. These conditions must be viewed in a systemic and integrated fashion: conditions affect one another. The LT conditions therefore form an interdependent whole which have to be considered systemically (although discussed individually below) in their impact on the transition process.

---

ii The leadership traps are compression, vacuum, depression and inflation (see Nel and Beudeker, 2009).

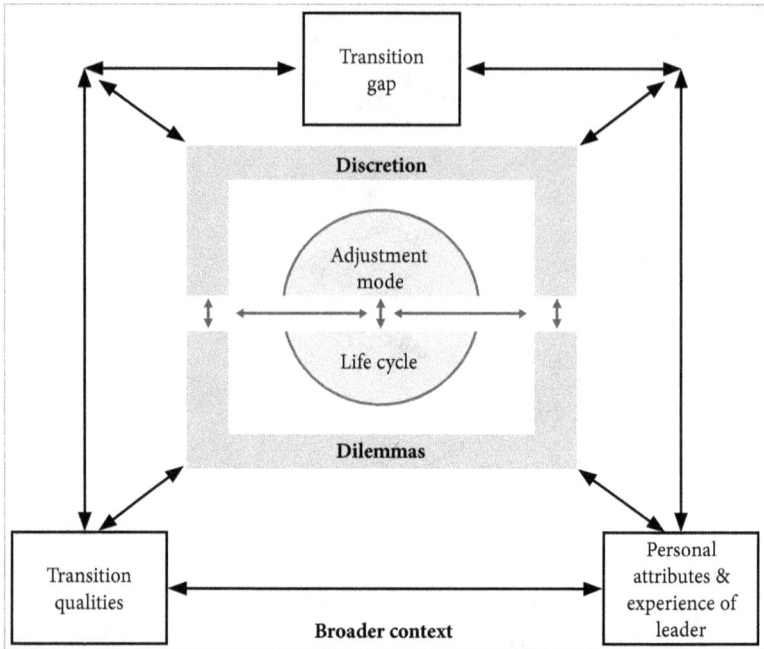

Figure 4.3: The major conditions affecting the transition process

According to Figure 4.3, the Broader Context (in contrast to the Immediate Context) forms the macro backdrop against (or setting in which) the LT will unfold. The Transition Gap, Transition Qualities, and Leadership Attributes and Experience set the basic parameters applied overall to the transition process. Discretion and Dilemmas (to be discussed in this section) demarcate the control over and "shape" of the transition decision space. Adjustment Mode and Life Cycle refer to the unfolding dynamics of the transition process itself as impacted on by the aforementioned conditions. They will be discussed in the next section, which deals with the transition process.

Broader context

The Broader Context refers to the macro setting in which the LT process is embedded and unfolds. This setting is similar to that faced by the leader under "everyday, normal" conditions in the current – but content-wise now has to be made specific to the specific LT triggered with respect to the New. In other words, what features of the Broader Context will inform and shape the LT set in motion?

In the final instance, in considering the Broader Context, an LT boils down to considering the impact the LT will have on the Leader-Context fit now, during, and after the LT.[13]

Transition gap

The Transition Gap pertains to the scope of the transition to be addressed in terms of the difference between the Current and New. The Gap is three-dimensional in nature, in the form of a "Transition Gap Cube"":

1. **The *Domains activated*:** A handy way of determining the activated Domains is to do a cross-impact matrix to detect where the differences are by comparing the Current versus New states of Domains: 'Same' or 'Different', with how many of each. The higher the frequency of 'Differents' found in the cross-impact analysis, the bigger the Transition Gap between the Present: Current and Future: New, and hence the more intense the LT. The higher the 'Sames', the smaller the Transition Gap, and the less intense the LT.

2. ***Novelty*:** The nature of the difference between the Current and New as pertaining to uncovering the nature and degree of the differences regarding content, process, and complexity of the change;[14] and

3. **The *Facets affected*:** An LT is more intense if deeper Facets have to change per Domain, and if multiple Facets have to change across Domains, as illustrated in Table 4.2 below.[15]

Table 4.2: Major Domain Facets that can be affected by an LT

Depth	Role	Person	Relationships	Organisation	Context
Deep	Requisite LOW	Identity	Range of stakeholders	Requisite contextual complexity of Operating Arena	National cultural orientations
	Core Purpose	Frame of reference/ worldview	Diversity of stakeholders	Interpretative Scheme(s)	National customs and habits
	Key Performance Areas	Values and norms	Informal networks	Strategic intent	Desirable leadership attributes
	Critical Outcomes	Attitudes	Formal networks	Ideology	
	Mode of Working	Thinking, Feeling, Judging, Doing		Culture and climate	
	Accountability/ Responsibility	Abilities		Leadership	
	Authority	Experience and Expertise		Organisational Design	
	Technology used	Conduct		Work rhythm	
	Resources required			Resources	
Shallow	Autonomy/ Authorisation level			Performance requirements	

Transition qualities

The dominant features of an intended LT which affect its intensity as a process are listed graphically in Figure 4.4.[16]

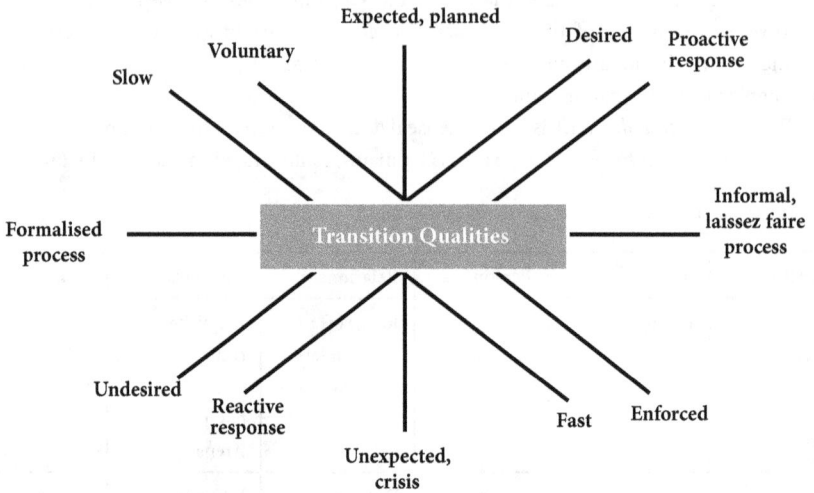

Figure 4.4: Transition qualities

In terms of Figure 4.4, the more an LT takes on a greater number of the qualities given in the lower half of the figure (the qualities from "Undesired" through to "Informal, *laissez faire* process"), the more significantly intense it becomes. Inversely, an LT is significantly less intense if it is imbued by the qualities in the upper half of the figure: from being a "Formalised process" through to "Proactive response".

Personal attributes and experience of a leader

The leader as a person has to make the transition. It appears that a number of Personal Attributes and Experiences enhance the chances that the leader will successfully navigate a transition. In other words, the leader has "resilience" in the transition. These attributes and experiences are listed in no particular order in Box 49.1 (below). The contention is that the stronger these attributes, and the more the leader's LT experience, the better he/she will be able to weather the transition. It has also been observed that as the attributes and experiences increase in criticality, the more intense the LT, and the more frequent the LTs.[17]

Box 49.1: Attributes and experience of a transition wise leader

• Risk tolerance
• Tolerance for ambiguity
• An internal locus of control
• Humble confidence
• Self-insight with an astute awareness of personal strengths and weaknesses
• Flexibility and adaptability
• Personal coherence
• A willingness to experiment
• An openness to personal change
• Prior transition experience

Discretion

This transition condition sets the degree of autonomy the leader has regarding the shaping of the transition process. Put differently, this is a reference to the extent that the leader can control the transition process and alter its shape and outcomes to his/her liking. Typical dimensions of discretion are the autonomy to shape or not shape the Role's make-up to his/her preferences; the form, pace and duration of the transition; the resources and stakeholders that can be accessed and deployed to enable the transition; and deciding when the transition has been successfully and formally concluded.[18] Essentially, Discretion allows a degree of independence or autonomy as to how the "fitting in" of the leader with the New will proceed. Box 49.2 gives the three intertwined transition-fit processes.

Box 49.2: Transition-fit processes

Transition-fit processes
• *Individuation.* The Person can shape the other transition Domains of Role, Relationships, Organisation and Immediate Context as he/she sees fit and as it suits him/her – he/she has high personal discretion.
• *Socialisation.* The Person has little freedom of choice and has to fit into the other transition Domains of Role, Relationships, Organisation, and Immediate Context – he/she has low personal discretion.
• *Acculturation.* This transition process pertains specifically to the degree of Discretion the Person has regarding his/her transition with regard to the needed cultural changes within the New Immediate Context, which is typically applicable to expatriates. Can the leader continue freely living his/her life in the New Immediate Context according to his/her cultural orientations/preferences, subject to high personal discretion? Or does he/she have to fit into the cultural orientations, habits and customs of his/her New Immediate Context, implying that he/she has to adopt the cultural orientations, habits and customs of his/her New Immediate Context, subject to low personal discretion?

Dilemmas

From the triggering of the transition, and moving through the transition, a leader has to balance a number of tensions in the form of complementary polarities. The polarities therefore represent dilemmas faced by the leader in transition. Essentially, the dilemmas pertain to how the leader wants to engage with the New upon entry. For example, he/she may opt "to shake up things immediately" versus "to maintain the status quo initially"; "to prescribe" versus "to seek answers/ solutions"; "to engage with only one person [the leader's superior or team only" versus "to engage with multiple constituencies (several stakeholders)"; and "adopt an autocratic style" versus "adopt a participative style". Figure 4.5 provides a graphic summary of the major dilemmas faced by a leader in transition towards taking up the New.[19]

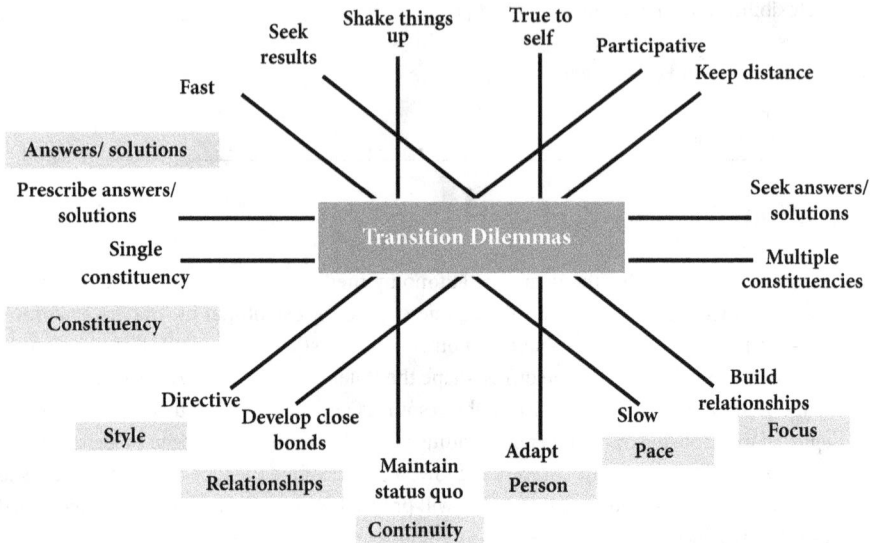

Figure 4.5: *The major dilemmas faced by a leader in transition towards taking up the New*

In summary: the Transition Gap, Transition Qualities, and Leadership Attributes and Experiences set the basic, overall parameters of the transition process. Discretion and Dilemmas demarcate who controls the transition decision space and its "shape". All these conditions relating to transition impose a certain tone, and hence a certain intensity, on the Transition (depicted as an arrow in Figure 4.1). Now that we have dealt with the transition conditions, the transition process is addressed next.

The Transition Process

According to Figure 4.3, the Transition Process is made up of two components, **Adjustment Mode** and **Life Cycle,** the two semicircles in the centre of the figure. **Adjustment mode** refers to the approach (or strategy) the leader will use to adjust to the New. **Life Cycle** pertains to the stages making up an LT. A narrow or a broad approach can be taken to an LT. In the former approach – predominant in the literature – an LT is limited to only the entry into and settling-in of the leader into the New.[20] [iii] This period typically takes six to nine months, all other things being equal.[21] In the broader approach, LT is seen as a **Life Cycle** made up of a number of stages over time with the leader moving into, through, and out of a Role.[22] LT in the narrower sense is just one stage of this Life Cycle: the initial stage of moving into the New.

---

iii In this regard Nicholson (1990) distinguishes the LT phases of Preparation, Encounter, Adjustment, and Stabilisation.

The drawback of the narrow approach is that one falls into the trap of viewing an LT as merely a standalone event – although still a process – of relatively short duration. The need is disregarded to look at the unfolding stages – each with its own distinct nature and dynamics – over the *total* timespan of a leader being in a new Role, which is the broader LT approach. A Life Cycle approach allows the leader and organisation to direct and steer carefully, proactively and effectively the leader's entire occupancy period of a Role, from entry into the Role through to exiting from the Role. A Life Cycle approach will be taken to LTs for the reasons elucidated above.

Adjustment mode

Based on all of the preceding transition conditions being as explicated in the previous section, the leader either chooses – implicitly or implicitly – or is forced to comply with an imposed strategy to adjust and fit into to his/her New Role with its commensurate Domains. The personally chosen or enforced mode is a function of the Discretion condition discussed above. This adjustment has a subjective side – the degree of personal comfort with the New – and an objective side – meeting the performance requirements of the New.[23]

Five adjustment modes can be distinguished, each accompanied by a 'cocktail' of positive and negative feelings:[24]

- *Mode 1: Replication*

  The leader in transition makes the minimal adjustments in him-/herself and the New. It is more of the same. He/she performs much the same as in his/her previous Role, by treating the New as similar to the Old. Positive feelings regarding this mode could be a sense of stability and continuity. Negative feelings may be a sense of being in a rut: more of the same, being trapped, and being helpless.

- *Mode 2: Absorption*

  The leader in transition makes most, if not all, of the adjustments with no or minimal modifications to the New. Most of his/her time is spent absorbing the New through the transition processes of socialisation and/or acculturation. Positive feelings in this case could be the satisfaction of being challenged, having new things to learn, and the extension of his/her skills, knowledge and expertise into unknown areas. Negative feelings may arise out of the letting go of valued skills, expertise and knowledge, and threats to his/her identity, confidence, self-image and self-esteem.

- *Mode 3: Transformation*

  Through the process of individuation, the leader in transition re-creates the New to fit him-/herself, and makes minimal adjustments to him-/herself. Positive feelings in this mode can arise from the opportunity to demonstrate one's ability to be creative and innovative; and the fact that being fully in charge gives one a sense of being in control. Negative feelings would mostly arise in response to others' unhappiness within the New, with the unsettling of the *status quo* being seen as a threat to and a destruction of the valued order and traditions. However, negative feelings may also arise out of the uncertainty of the leader in transition as to whether his/her innovations will work, be accepted, and take root.

- *Mode 4: Co-creation*

  Mutual, simultaneous give-and-take adjustments in the leader in transition and in the New, are made in order to reach a point of "consensus". The processes of individuation, socialisation and acculturation are equally at work. In this case, positive feelings may arise out of personal growth and/or successfully moving through the cycles of thoughtful exploration, discovery, action, reflection, and learning. Negative feelings may be due to the uncertainty arising out of what is untouchable and changeable, and where the boundaries are.

- *Mode 5: Isolation*

  The leader in transition remains unintegrated into and separate from the New. In other words, though physically present in the New, the transition has been unsuccessful. The reasons for an unsuccessful transition are multiple: the leader has been imposed by a Board/ the Executive on the organisation or an organisational unit, typically from externally, resulting in an organisational "revolt"; a serious philosophical and/or style disconnect between the new leader and his/her superior(s); or a hidden critical inability and/or lack of experience in the new leader surfaces, resulting in a detrimental mismatch between the incoming leader and the New. The leader in transition and the New remain separate because there is no real "connectivity". Usually only negative feelings are associated with this adjustment mode: isolation, alienation, rejection, and failure, accompanied by feelings of incompetence, a lack of confidence, and a real threat to one's sense of personal identity and self-worth.

The choice of an adjustment mode – freely chosen or imposed – is typically an explicit or implicit response of the understanding and evaluation of the leader in transition of what it will take for him-/her to settle effectively and efficiently into the New, given the expectations of important constituencies regarding his/her transition. For example, how active is the expectation of "an agenda for action within the first 90 days"?[25]

Life cycle

As has been argued above, a Life Cycle approach as a broader approach to LT is seen as the better one. Viewed as a Life Cycle, an LT consists holistically of distinct stages which a leader in transition goes through during his/her total occupancy of his/her New Role. Moving into – the narrower LT – is seen as only one of the Life Cycle stages, essentially the first stage.

The Life Cycle of LTs has two equally important sides: a subjective, intangible side, and an objective, intangible side. Using the iceberg analogy: the former is below the water, and the latter above. The former is discussed first because it creates the state of mind with which the leader moves into the transition from *Time 1: Current,* on the way to, into, and through *Time 2:* New.

The subjective, intangible LT life cycle

All LTs go through a psychosocial change Life Cycle affecting all parties concerned, namely the personal experiences of the LT – the leader him-/herself – and the stakeholders concerned. This Life Cycle will look different depending on: (i) the intensity of the transition, invoked by the conditions of transition discussed above; and (ii) the feelings arising out of the adjustment mode, freely chosen or imposed, which will set a certain upfront tone (or mood) for the psychosocial change Life Cycle. This Life Cycle predominantly runs its course during the early stages of the objective, tangible LT Life Cycle (to be discussed below). However, if it is not dealt with adequately, the unfinished business of the former cycle will affect the whole of the latter cycle as it unfolds for the new Role.

The psychosocial change Life Cycle affects not only the leader in transition but also applies equally well to a greater or lesser extent to the stakeholders on whom there is an impact caused by the LT, for example, the shock caused among stakeholders when an unexpected leader is appointed to a new (key) Role.

A distinction can be drawn between a less intense and a more intense LT psychosocial change Life Cycle. Each will be discussed in turn.

A less intense LT psychosocial change life cycle

This LT would be one with a few Differences (*vice versa*: many Sames) between the Current and the New; low novelty; being planned, expected, desired, voluntary and proactive; the presence of strong transitional personal attributes and experience; high discretion; and the adoption of a Replication or Transformation adjustment mode. A less intense LT would take on the form of a "mere" transition adjustment process made up of the psychosocial change Life Cycle stages[26] of: *Stage 1: Ending the Current*, by saying good bye, and readying for the New; *Stage 2: Entering the New*, and settling in by getting to know what the detailed New entails; *Stage 3: Ending the New* once it has become the Current.

A highly intense LT psychosocial change life cycle

This LT would be one with many Differences (*vice versa*: few Sames) between the Current and the New; high novelty; being unplanned, unexpected, undesired, enforced, and reactive; poor transitional personal attributes and experience; low discretion; and an Absorption adjustment mode, especially if it is enforced. A more intense LT would take on the form of a change process made up of the Life Cycle stages depicted in Figure 4.6.[27]

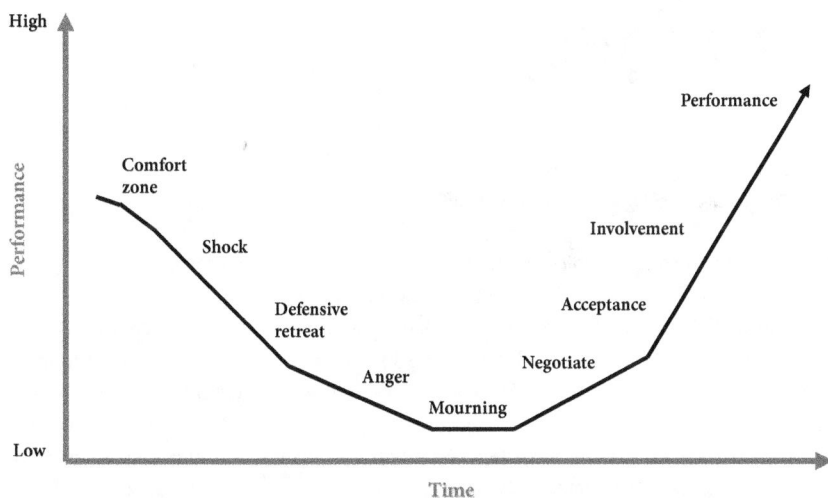

Figure 4.6: Stages of an intense LT psychosocial change Life Cycle

As can be deduced from the Life Cycle stages shown in Figure 4.6, moving from being in a comfort zone through shock until eventual involvement and performance, this LT would be characterised by high levels of resentment, anger, uncertainty, anxiety, isolation, ambiguity, confusion, indecisiveness, and a sense of being totally overwhelmed and incompetent. There would be a significant drop in leader performance – having an impact on team, departmental, and even organisational performance – from which it could take a long period of time to recover. The likelihood is high that the intense LT psychosocial change Life Cycle may continue deep into the objective, tangible LT Life Cycle if the former is not dealt with adequately.

The objective, tangible LT Life Cycle

Objectively viewed, LTs go through a number of formal, tangible transition stages as seen primarily from the perspective of the leader in transition. Figure 4.7 depicts the composition of this Life Cycle.[28][iv]

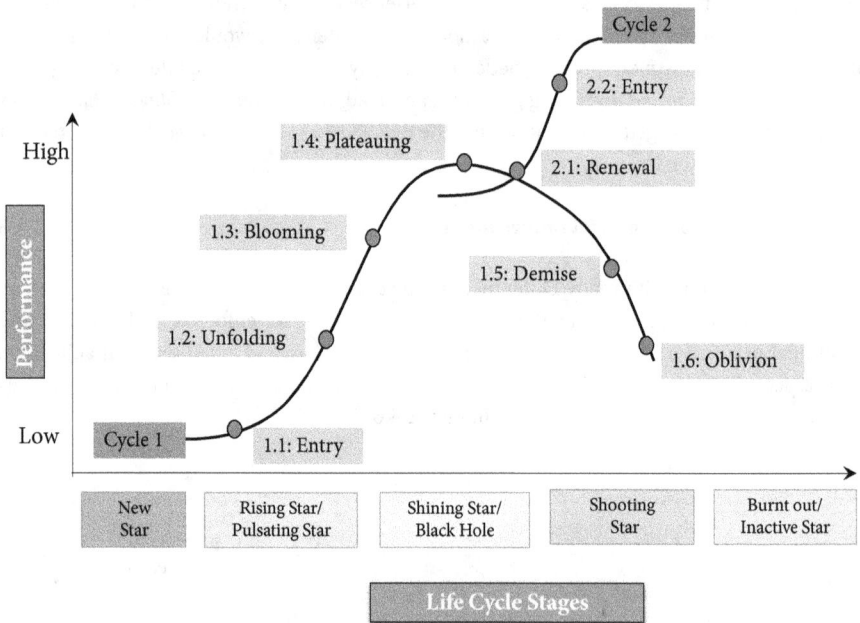

Figure 4.7: The stages making up the objective, tangible LT Life Cycle

According to Figure 4.7, the objective, tangible Leadership Life Cycle consists of six stages, from *Stage 1.1: Entry* to *Stage 1.6: Oblivion*. Two successive Life Cycles are given, Cycle 1 and Cycle 2. Between *Stage 1.4: Plateauing* and *Stage 1.5: Demise*, a leader is at a crucial crossroad: whether to go into *Stage 1.5: Demise* and further onwards to *Life Cycle 1*, the current one; or to move on to *Stage 2.1: Renewal* and then on to *Stage 2.2: Entry*, in this way moving onto a new Life Cycle, *Cycle 2*. Typically, the psychosocial Life Cycle is active, especially in *Stage 1: Entry*, and to a lesser extent, *Stage 2: Blooming*. But if not addressed adequately, its unfinished business may affect all the sequential stages of the objective, tangible LT Life Cycle.

---

iv Ward (2003) proposed a leadership lifecycle model matched to the organisational lifecycle which implies LTs associated and in alignment with the phases of the organisational lifecycle. With regard to my chapter, these phases would form part of the broader context of LTs (see Figure 4.3).

The respective stages are elucidated next. The metaphor of a star will be used to illustrate the "state" of the leader in transition. It is difficult to allocate time-specific durations to a stage, although, as stated above, Stage 1 typically is seen to last six to nine months. A leader may move more slowly or quickly through a stage, or may even be trapped in a stage.

Stage 1.1: Entry – The "New Star"

Having entered the New, the leader is unknown as a *proven* leader within his/her new Role. Generally stakeholders would have a "wait and see" attitude, although some may seek actively to win early favour with the new leader. The leader's *transition need* is to move from being *Unconsciously Unfit* to being *Consciously Unfit* with regard to the demands and requirements of the New in order to make explicit the gap between the Current and the New. Having made his/her team conscious of the gap, the leader can now decide explicitly what actions need to be taken to close the gap.

Some of the critical stage actions making up the leader's transition agenda are given in an approximate priority order:[29] "What must I let go of that made me successful in my previous Role? What is the New that I have to embrace and learn to make me successful in terms of abilities, relationships, information, knowledge, direction, priorities, and ruling culture? Who are the critical stakeholders with whom I have to establish relationships, and build my credibility and legitimacy? How will I go about building relationships with them? How do I ensure mutual and realistic expectations between others and me? What ground rules do I have to establish for our working together? What are the first (symbolic) actions I have to take to make good first impressions?"

Stage 1.2: Unfolding – The "Rising/Pulsating Star"

In this stage the leader is settling in and finding his/her feet regarding the New as he/she increasingly establishes him-/herself. Performance-wise, he/she demonstrates masterful leadership from time to time as he/she is settling in. He/she is starting to make a real difference. His/her *transition need* is to move from being *Consciously Unfit* to *Consciously Fit* regarding the New which has now become the known.

Some of the critical stage actions are building and rolling out a shared direction, agreed-upon priorities and action plan; establishing common values; early successes; increasingly being seen as worthy of trust; growing in credibility and legitimacy in the eyes of stakeholders, and gaining more and more support. The essence of the stage is winning the mandate (or right) to lead; and standing up and out.

Stage 1.3: Blooming – The "Shining Star" or "Black Hole"

The leader has become masterful as a leader in the New, which has now become the known Current. He/she is acting with confidence based on good intelligence and insight, and performing well. He/she has won the support and trust of stakeholders who have awarded him/her the unconditional right to lead. The leader is well and truly on top of the New, doing the right things right. Two types of leaders can be distinguished in this stage in the leadership galaxy: the "Shining Star": the ethical, responsible, performing leader or the "Black Hole": the unethical, toxic, performing leader. During this stage the leader moves in terms of *transition need* from *Consciously Fit* to *Unconsciously Fit*.

Stage 1.4: Plateauing – The "Shooting Star"

The leader's performance in the known current setting is peaking. He/she is in a comfort zone (or rut), being merely in a maintenance mode, performance and relationship wise. It is increasingly more of the same all of the time. The success recipe has been found, and is repeated and defended regardless of its continued relevance. Past successes and the good old days are glorified. He/she has reached his/her "sell by" date. Some stakeholders may find comfort in the predictability, security and continuity of the sameness of the Current. Others may be growing increasingly frustrated as they see that the success recipe is no longer working; only past achievements count; and performance is slipping. A palace revolution may be brewing…

The leader's *transition need* is shifting from being *Unconsciously Fit* to *(Un)consciously Unfit* regarding the Current. If the leader realises that he/she is *Consciously Unfit* – in other words he/she is plateauing – he/she may then deliberately initiate the activation of a new Life Cycle by moving into *Stage 2.1: Renewal*. This is, however, necessary. The leader may be in such a comfort zone that he/she just wants to see his/her time out, typical of a leader close to retirement or at the end of a fixed-term contract, who does not want to rock the boat. If he/she slips into *Unconsciously Unfit*, or does nothing about the realisation of being *Consciously Unfit*, he/she will stay on the same Life Cycle and slide irrevocably into *Stage 1.5: Demise*.

Stage 2.1: Renewal – The "Re-energised (or refuelled) Star"

The *Consciously Unfit* leader who takes action to move him-/herself into a New *Stage 1: Entry* on a new Life Cycle may do so by triggering any of the moves listed in Table 4.1. For example, he/she may redefine/expand his/her current Role, moving into a new Role and/or organisation. He/she has transformed him-/herself into a "Re-energised (or refuelled) Star" in the leadership galaxy, but on a new Life Cycle that demands the next LT. This will invoke a new set of the above stages as described above (*2.1: Entry*, and so on), but on a new Life Cycle. There is therefore also a need for the "last 90 days" exit strategy.[30]

Stage 1.5: Demise – The "Shooting Star"

This leader is increasingly underperforming in the Current. He/she has not initiated a 2.1: Renewal Stage, and is paying the price. It is now publicly admitted and spoken about the leader being Consciously Unfit, and will unfortunately remain so. The leader cannot be saved by him-/herself or others. He/she is becoming increasingly ignored, sidelined, isolated and rejected. His/her views are no longer sought; his/her decisions/actions not taken seriously; and the epicentre of energy is moving away from him/her. He/she is a definite "Shooting Star" in the leadership galaxy.

Stage 1.6: Oblivion – "Burnt out/Inactive Star"

This is the leader who has disappeared totally from the radar screen, and has become forgotten by all, although some may still have fond memories of the person. He/she has gone into *in memoriam*: rest-in-peace stage. However, history is replete with leaders who have gone into ostensible dormancy but have returned with a "vengeance" when the time and place were right to re-emerge as unexpected and unpredictable "Re-energised (or refuelled) Star(s)"; or the period of dormancy has allowed them to re-invent themselves. They are back again as serious contenders.

Another exception are leaders who have gone into dormancy but remain "active" in the minds of people even long after they have gone, and serve as exemplary models because of their lasting, worthy legacy.

In summary: for masterful leadership, a leader must at any given point in time know in which stage of his/her current Life Cycle he/she is, and take the appropriate actions relevant to that stage in order to move him/her along the Life Cycle in order to remain masterful.

Transition Outcomes

The transition process has multiple outcomes across the respective Transition Domains – positive and negative – resulting in an overall LT outcome. Table 4.3 provides an overview of success and failure Domain-specific LT indicators and overall LT outcomes, whether positive or negative.[31]

Table 4.3: Overview of success and failure LT indicators across the LT Domains with overall LT outcomes

DOMAIN	Person	Role	Relationships	Organisation	Context	Overall LT Outcomes
Success LT indicators	Comfortable Confident Authenticity: true self Personal re-invention	On top of Getting things done Future, pro-active work mode	Healthy, constructive interactions Effective team and teaming Trust and goodwill Mandate to lead	Having an impact All round support and acceptance Good reputation	Fitting in	**Positive** Thriving Innovation Moving at ease through Life Cycle Stages Groomed for greater things
Failure LT indicators	Stressed out Overwhelmed Inauthentic: false self Little confidence Personal stuckness	Falling short Present, re-active, crisis fighting work mode Failing	Unhealthy, destructive Ineffective/ no team and teaming Remote and unapproachable Mistrust and ill will No mandate to lead	Isolated Avoided Poor reputation	Misfit	**Negative** Burnout Trapped in a Life Cycle Stage Withdrawal Transfer Resignation Asked to leave

In terms of Table 4.3, what are the possible LT indicator/outcomes scenarios? An LT may be predominantly successful in terms of indicators and positive outcomes, or *vice versa*. In between, many possible permutations across the Domains exist. For example, a leader may be successful in the Person and Role Domains but fail otherwise in the other Domains: this is a leader with a high likelihood of organisational derailment. Or inversely, the leader may be successful in the latter Domains but fail in the former Domains: this is a leader with a high chance of burnout.

In the end, the most successful leader in transition is the one with the best "batting average" across all of the Domains, giving overall positive LT Outcomes. In the end, and over time, real-time systemic, comprehensive monitoring and tracking of the transition outcomes must occur across the total Life Cycle of leaders. Performance management in the organisation provides an ideal platform in this regard.

Critical Leadership Transition Success Factors

The most important LT critical success factors are given in Box 49.3.[32]

Box 49.3: Critical success factors in leadership transitions

Critical Success Factors in Leadership Transitions

- Bring LTs into the *public domain of the organisation* as openly discussed, critical high-risk organisational occurrences that have to be mitigated.
- Adopt the *right mindset* regarding LTs by debunking major LT myths as discussed above in order to deal with the true nature of LTs.
- Craft a *complete conceptual map of LT Landscape* to direct and guide organisational thinking and action regarding LTs.
- In the application of the LT Landscape, however, treat *each LT as unique.*
- See LT as a *Life Cycle process* – a journey – with both a subjective and objective sides, unfolding in stages of longer or shorter durations depending on a specific leader in transition.
- At the individual level, have a proactively conceived, formalised, organisationally supported *transition process and plan* with clear roles to enable and empower the leader in transition and all impacted stakeholders.
- At the organisational level, plan and know the *distribution of the organisation's leadership as a collective* across the respective leadership Life Cycle stages. The ideal collective distribution percentage-wise appears to be: *Entry and Unfolding:* 15–25%; *Blooming:* 60–70%; and *Demise:* 10–15%.
- *Track and monitor* the respective LT journeys by Life Cycle, not only of the leader in transition but also of all implicated stakeholders.

Conclusion

It is hoped that through the in-depth discussion in this chapter of the nature and dynamics of LTs, a strong case has been made to bring LTs into the public domain of the organisation as openly discussed, critical high-risk organisational occurrences occurring on a frequent basis, and which have to be mitigated with foresight and careful planning.

Endnotes

1   Ashforth & Saks, 1995; Cronin, 2013; Gilmore, 1988; Ibarra & Barbulescu, 2010; Nicholson, 1984.

2   Manderscheid, 2008; Manderscheid & Ardichvili, 2008; Nicholson, 1990.

3   Bear, Benson-Armer & McLaughlin, 2000; Manderscheid & Ardichvili, 2008.

4   Elsner & Farrands, 2012; Manderscheid, 2008; Manderscheid & Ardichvili, 2008.

5   Bear, Benson-Armer & McLaughlin, 2000.

6   Elsner & Farrands, 2012; Nicholson, 1990; Petrock, 1990).

7   Denis, Langley & Pineault, 2000; Elsner and Farrands, 2012; Manderscheid, 2008; Nicholson, 1990; Watkins, 2016a.

8   Ashforth & Saks, 1995; Black, 1988; Denis, Langley & Pineault, 2000; Elsner & Farrands, 2012; Lisson, Mee & Gilbert;, 2013; McLeay & Thompson, 2014; Nicholson, 1984; Nicholson, 1990; Petrock, 1990.

9   Ashforth, Kreiner & Fugate, 2000; Elsner & Farrands, 2012; Fisher & Cooper, 1990; Ibarra & Barbulescu , 2010; Nicholson, 1990.

10   Black, 1988; Bear, Benson-Armer & McLaughlin, 2000; Elsner & Farrands, 2012; Fisher & Cooper, 1990; Gilmore, 1988; Ibarra & Barbulescu, 2010; Latack , 1984; Manderscheid & Ardichvili, 2008; Louis, 1980; McLeay & Thompson, 2014; Nicholson, 1984; Nicholson, 1990; Petrock, 1990.

11   Charan, Drotter & Noel, 2001.

12   Jaques, 2006; Jaques & Clement, 1994; Osborn, Hunt & Jauch, 2002; Shephard, Gray, Hunt & McArthur, 2007.

13   Ashforth & Saks, 1995; Nicholson, 1984; Nicholson, 1990.

14   Ashforth & Saks, 1995; Denis, Langley & Pineault, 2000; Ibarra & Barbulescu, 2010; Nicholson, 1984; Nicholson, 1990.

15   Ashforth, Kreiner & Fugate, 2000; Denis, Langley & Pineault, 2000; Black, 1988; Ibarra & Barbulescu, 2010; Latack, 1984; Weiss, 1990)

16   Black, 1988; Nicholson, 1990; Ibarra & Barbulescu, 2010; Dotlich, Noel & Walker, 2004; Van der Merwe & Du Plessis, 2013.

17   Ashforth & Saks, 1995; Elsner & Farrands, 2012; Nicholson, 1984.

18   Nicholson, 1984; Nicholson, 1990.

19   Bear, Benson-Armer & McLaughlin, 2000; Elsner & Farrands, 2012; Petrock, 1990.

20   For example Ashforth & Saks, 1995; Black, 1988; Elsner & Farrands, 2012; Nicholson, 1984; Nicholson, 1990.

21   Elsner & Farrands, 2012; Manderscheid & Ardichvili, 2008; Petrock, 1990.

22   Veldsman, 2002.

23   Black, 1988; Louis, 1980; Latack , 1984; McLeay & Thompson, 2014; Nicholson, 1984.

24   Denis, Langley & Pineault, 2000; McLeay & Thompson, 2014; Nicholson, 1984; Nicholson, 1990.

25   Watkins, 2016a.

26   *cf.* Bridges, 2003.

27   *cf.* Kübler-Ross; Gabarro; Fink, Beak & Taddeco, as cited in Manderscheid & Ardichvili, 2008; Nicholson, 1990; Weiss, 1990.

28   Veldsman, 2002.

29   Bear, Benson-Armer & McLaughlin, 2000; Denis, Langley & Pineault, 2000; Elsner & Farrands, 2012; Gabarro as cited in Manderscheid & Ardichvili, 2008; Gilmore, 1988; Manderscheid, 2008; Petrock, 1990; Veldsman, 2002; Watkins, 2016a, 2016b.

30   Schumpeter, 2015.

31   Denis, Langley & Pineault, 2000; Elsner & Farrands, 2012; Gilmore, 1988; Ibarra & Barbulescu, 2010; Manderscheid & Ardichvili, 2008; Van der Merwe & Du Plessis, 2013.

32   Elsner & Farrands, 2012; Gilmore, 1988; Louis, 1980; Manderscheid, 2008; Manderscheid & Ardichvili, 2008; Petrock, 1990; Nicholson, 1990; Van der Merwe & Du Plessis, 2013; Watkins, 2016a.

References

Ashforth, BE & Saks AM. 1995. 'Work-role transitions: A longitudinal examination of the Nicholson model'. *Journal of Occupational and Organizational Psychology*, 68:157–175.

Ashforth, B.E, Kreiner, GE & Fugate, M. 2000. 'All in a day's work: Boundaries and micro role transition'. *Academy of Management Review*, 25(3):472–491.

Bear, S, Benson-Armer, R & McLaughlin, K. 2000. 'Leadership transitions: An agenda for success'. *Ivey Business Journal*, 8–13, May/June.

Black, JS. 1988. 'Work role transitions: A study of American expatriate managers in Japan'. *Journal of International Business Studies*, 19(2):277–294.

Bridges, W. 2003. *Managing transitions*. New York, NY: Perseus Books.

Charan, R, Drotter, S & Noel, J. 2001. *The leadership pipeline: How to build the leadership-powered company*. San Francisco, CA: Jossey-Bass.

Cronin, S. 2013. 'Reflections on gender issues in work transitions in Chile'. *Work*, 44:89–91, 89.

Denis, J-L, Langley, A & Pineault, M. 2000. 'Becoming a leader in a complex organization'. *Journal of Management Studies*, 37(8):1063–1099.

Dotlich, DL, Noel, J & Walker, N. 2004. *Leadership passages: Personal and professional transitions that make or break a leader*. San Francisco, CA: Jossey-Bass, a Wiley imprint.

Elsner, R & Farrands, B. 2012. *Leadership transitions: How business leaders take charge in new roles*. London, UK: Kogan Page.

Fisher, SF & Cooper, GL. (eds). 1990. *On the move: The psychology of change and transition*. Chichester, UK: John Wiley.

Gilmore, TN. 1988. *Making a leadership change: How organisations and leaders can handle leadership transitions successfully*. San Francisco, CA: Jossey-Bass.

Ibarra, H & Barbulescu, R. 2010. 'Identity as narrative: Prevalence, effectiveness, and consequences of narrative identity work in macro work role transitions'. *Academy of Management Review*, 35(1):135–154.

Jaques, E. 2006. *Requisite organisation: A total system for effective managerial organisation and managerial leadership for the 21st century*. Baltimore, MD: Cason Hall & Co. Publishers.

Jaques E & Clement, SD. 1994. *Executive leadership: A practical guide to managing complexity*. Cambridge, MA: Cason-Hall & Co. Publishers.

Kübler-Ross, E. 1969. *On death and dying: What the dying have to teach doctors, nurses, clergy, and their own families*. New York, NY: Schreiber.

Lisson, S, Mee, l & Gilbert, K. 2013. 'The influence of work-life balance, choice and a meaningful location on work transitions'. *Work*, 44:77–79.

Latack, JC. 1984. 'Career transitions within organizations: An exploratory study of work, nonwork, and coping strategies'. *Organizational Behavior and Human Performance*, 34:296–322.

Louis, MR. 1980. 'Career transitions: Varieties and commonalities'. *Academy of Management Review*, 5:329–340.

Manderscheid, SV. 2008. 'New leader assimilation: mindset An intervention for leaders in transition'. *Advances in Developing Human Resources*, 10(5):686–702.

Manderscheid, SV & Ardichvili, A. 2008. 'A conceptual model for leadership transition'. *Performance Improvement Quarterly*, 20(3–4):113–129.

McLeay, R & Thompson, CF. 2014. 'Inter-sector senior leader transitions: Experience and outcomes'. *International Journal of Public Sector Management*, 27(1):85–93.

Nel, C & Beudeker, N. 2009. *(R)evolution – how to create a high performance organisation*. Cape Town, ZA: Village of Leaders Products.

Nicholson, N. 1984. 'A theory of work role transitions'. *Administrative Science Quarterly*, 29(2):172–191.

Nicholson, N. 1990. 'The transition cycle: Causes, outcomes, processes and forms'. In SF Fisher & GL Cooper (eds). *On the move: The psychology of change and transition*. Chichester, UK: John Wiley. 83–108.

Osborn, RN, Hunt, JG & Jauch, LR. 2002. 'Toward a contextual theory of leadership'. *The Leadership Quarterly*, 13:797–837.

Petrock, F. 1990. 'Planning the leadership transition'. *Journal of Business Strategy*, 11(6):14–16.

Schumpeter, JA. 2015. 'The last 90 days'. *The Economist*, 58, 7 February.

Shephard, K, Gray, JL, Hunt, JG & McArthur, S. 2007. *Organisation design, levels of work and human capability*. Ontario, CAN: Global Design Society,

Van der Merwe, L & Du Plessis, F. 2013. 'Leadership transitions: Talent implications'. *Newsletter of InavitIQ Consulting*, February.

Veldsman, TH. 2002. 'Perspective 3: Navigating galaxies of leadership stars: aligning context, roles and competencies for leadership effectiveness' In TH Veldsman (ed). *Into the people effectiveness arena. Navigating between chaos and order*. Johannesburg, ZA: Knowledge Resources. 72–98.

Watkins, M. 2016a. *The seven biggest traps in the first 90 days… and how to avoid them: What leaders need to know to get off to a great start*. Switzerland, CHE: International Institute for Management Development (IMD).

Watkins, M. 2016b. 'Leading the team you inherit'. *Harvard Business Review*, 60–67, June.

Weiss, R. 1990. 'Losses associated with mobility'. In SF Fisher & GL Cooper (eds). *On the move: The psychology of change and transition*. Chichester, UK: John Wiley. 3–12.

Ward, A. 2003. *The leadership lifecycle. Matching leaders to evolving organisations*. Houndmills, Basingstoke, UK: Palgrave Macmillan.

SECTION 3

LEADERSHIP WELL-BEING

Chapter 5

STRESS, BURNOUT, DERAILMENT AND RESILIENCE IN LEADERSHIP

Jopie de Beer with Renate Scherrer and Ina Rothmann

Case Study

Sam, an operations manager in a corporate environment, had always been a driven individual who had enjoyed the challenges and responsibilities of his job. He had relished interacting with his staff and clients, and had been a popular and respected manager in the organisation. Staff described him as an energetic, enthusiastic, caring, and highly skilled leader who brought out the best in each person while getting the job done. When the global economic decline of 2008 hit the company, positions were not filled, staff numbers were cut to a bare minimum, while the pressure to improve results increased. Sam worked longer hours and took on more responsibilities, time pressures increased, and certain targets were not reached. *"I felt myself running on auto pilot at a very fast pace but staying in the same spot. Eventually I could feel that I was running on empty."* He felt exhausted and inundated, unable to keep up with the constant demands of his position. His performance began to decline, he struggled to focus and concentrate, he had trouble coming to a decision, and then doubted whether it was the right option. He found himself overreacting to unexpected problems and becoming extremely impatient and irritable.

> *"I didn't know who I was any more. I found myself getting irritated with staff, family, and friends, and then switching off from them all together. I constantly thought of ways to avoid interaction with people. To be honest, I did not have the energy to engage in any meaningful conversation with anyone, not even with my wife or children, where before it had been very important to me to take a personal interest in my people and my environment. I doubted my ability to run the operations effectively, and to be a good leader, parent and husband. I felt resentful, cynical and powerless; I could not see a way out ... I knew I was in trouble but I did not know how to fix it ... and the scary thing was that I couldn't have cared less ..."*

Sam's story is an unfortunate but familiar one in the world of work. However, it is also a story that many leaders and managers are reluctant to share or acknowledge. Phrases such as "no pressure, no go, no grow" or "stress is part of the job, that's what managers get paid for!" or "burnout is an excuse for not achieving!" are common. Unfortunately, burnout is a career hazard affecting especially high achievers – high achievers, because they are responsible and passionate about their work; they accept long working hours as the norm; they easily volunteer for more responsibility; and they put pressure on themselves to excel and deliver work of exceptional standard. All of these qualities make them particularly susceptible to stress, burnout and derailment.

Introduction

Leadership failure, particularly during turbulent times, seems to be more common than success.[1] In this regard, understanding the role of stress and burnout in leadership, as well as the possible ways in which leaders derail, can go far in mitigating the risk these factors pose for organisations. Understanding the risk should, however, go hand in hand with methods to build and maintain the resilience of individuals and organisations, given that they are the cornerstone of economic activity in society.

We write this chapter from the perspective that it is impossible to integrate and summarise all the available research and perspectives on stress, burnout, derailment and resilience. However, as per the case study above, it is happening to ordinary people and leaders all around us on a daily basis and at an alarming rate. We need to equip ourselves with as much knowledge as possible in order to recognise it and deal with it. Therefore, we try to provide the reader with a solid analysis of what research has found to be the causes and impact of it, as well as how to prevent it or deal with it effectively. In the case of resilience, we focus on how it can mediate the effects of stress, burnout and derailment.

Figure 5.1 below provides a model overview of where stress, derailment and burnout fit into the experience of the individual in the bigger context of the world of work.

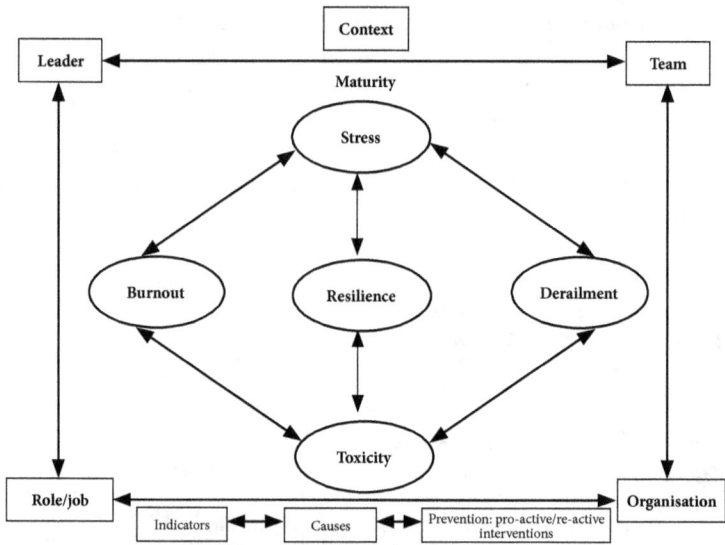

Figure 5.1: Overview of where stress, derailment and burnout fit into individuals' experience in world of work

These aspects never exist in isolation, nor are they impacted on by only one intrinsic factor or external element. Resilience is positioned in the middle, because it is an important coping mechanism or strategy to facilitate successful coping.

The chapter consists of four main areas. There will first be an overview of stress and how it progresses to burnout. Thereafter, an exploration of derailment (as a relatively novel concept) and resilience will follow.

Stress

The reality of stress in the workplace

It is reported that workplace stress in the USA is responsible for 120 000 deaths each year and $190 billion in healthcare costs. In fact, in 2001, almost half of all bankruptcies were related to medical bills, and by 2007 that proportion had grown to 62%.[2]

Doing a meta-analysis of 228 studies on stress in the workplace, it is reported that at least 30% of people experience workplace stress of sufficient severity to affect their health adversely.[3] To add to this figure, work-family conflict increases the odds of self-reported poor physical health by about 90%, and low organisational justice increases the odds of having a physician-diagnosed condition by about 50%. Add to this that job insecurity increases the odds of reporting poor health by about 50%, high job demands raise the odds of having a physician-diagnosed illness by 35% and long work hours increase mortality by almost 20%.

The austerity measures taken when there is an ailing economy further exacerbate the stress.[4] Leaders and employees have heavier workloads and sometimes depreciated incomes. It is reported that work-related stress soared by 40% and absentee rates increased by 25% during the 2008 global recession.

In South Africa, as in other developing countries, the economic strain related to the fall in commodity prices, retrenchments at organisations and the progressive weakening of the SA Rand has a significant impact on leaders who have to navigate this context. It is therefore no surprise that South Africa, following Nigeria, is ranked as the second "most stressed out" nation in the world. El Salvador is ranked third.[5] Given that the direct impact successful CEOs have on organisational performance could be as high as 14% to 29%,[6] failed leadership resulting from stress, burnout or derailment should be regarded in a very serious light.

The nature and causes of stress

Not all stress is bad stress.[7] In small doses, stress can be positive. It keeps you alert and could provide the push you need to finish a task, for instance. Positive stress, called eustress, is an indispensable part of life. With eustress we feel that we have the necessary resources to address the demand and the demand becomes an achievable challenge.

Eustress motivates and focuses energy, is perceived as being within a person's coping abilities, feels exciting, and generates energy and enthusiasm.[8] In contrast, *distress* generates negative energy that causes uneasiness; is perceived as outside a person's coping abilities; that one has no resources to deal with it; feels unpleasant; and generates fear, concern, and anxiety.

It is difficult to categorise stressors into objective lists of those that cause eustress and those that cause distress, because each person is unique and may have different reactions to particular situations. The lists in Table 5.1 may, however, provide a useful indication of different situations causing eustress or distress.

Table 5.1: Personal and work-related triggers for eustress and distress

	Generating Eustress	**Generating Distress**
Personal stressor examples	• Buying a new home or car • Birth of a child • Getting married • Taking educational classes or learning a new hobby • Preparing for a vacation • Helping children with challenging assignments	• Money or legal problems • Death, divorce, abuse, marital strain or moving house • Children or family problems • Injury, illness or waiting for medical results • Unrealistic, perfectionist expectations • Fears and negative thought patterns
Work-related stressor examples	• Promotion • Having the skills and knowledge to execute an assignment • Autonomy to execute tasks and taking responsibility for work outcomes (high job control) • Challenging but manageable work assignments and expectations from others • Providing meaningful inputs in meetings	• Excessive job demands • Job insecurity • Overscheduling • Failing to be assertive • Procrastination and/or failing to plan ahead • Conflicts with teammates and supervisors • Inadequate authority to carry out tasks (low job control) • Lack of skills necessary to do the job • Experiences of dysfunctional behaviour at work e.g. bullying behaviour • Unproductive and time-consuming meetings • Commuting and travel schedules • Work-life interference

Research indicates that certain personality traits can make people more susceptible to stress and burnout:[9]

- Some people are just more sensitive to stress and prone to heightened anxiety levels.[10] This may naturally predispose them to interpret events as dangerous or negative.
- People who are more sensitive have a tendency to become anxious, struggle with self-doubt, and in addition have low levels of conscientiousness, experience a heightened awareness of stress, and have lower levels of resilience.[11] People who suppress their emotions, fear rejection, are perfectionistic and highly driven with a need always to be in control or are by nature more pessimistic, also run the risk of experiencing higher levels of stress and developing burnout.[12]

The body's response to stress

Modern medicine's advances in cellular and molecular biology[13] have made it possible to study what happens in the body when a stressful event occurs. Hypothalamic, pituitary and adrenal hormones are released into the body, creating reactions such as the heart beating faster, sweating, the hair on your skin standing up, and feeling nauseous. At the same time your muscles tense, your breathing becomes faster but your thinking is clear and focused. The body is ready to fight or flee what is perceived to be a danger. All of this happens in milliseconds.[14]

Ideally the body should have time to recuperate after such an event. But if stress is prolonged and becomes habitual, these hormones are continuously secreted and the original benefits turn into symptoms such as headaches, sleeplessness, digestive problems, anger, or depressive moodiness. In addition, when the stress becomes chronic, immune defences become impaired, creating a heightened risk of developing diseases as varied as depression, arthritis, or chronic fatigue syndrome.[15]

It should be noted that it is not just direct experiences of stress, but also memories associated with stress, that can trigger a physical stress response.

If we are chronically exposed to excessive distress day after day after day, the body's need for energy becomes greater than its ability to produce it, and the stress hormone cortisol is released in large quantities. Since cortisol shuts down immune cell responses, we have less resistance to viruses and over time signs of burnout and ill health become progressively more apparent.[16] Extended exposure to stress, especially to a variety of stressors at the same time, adds up to a state of extreme exhaustion that leads to burnout, raising the potential for being diagnosed with a variety of physical diseases.[17]

Burnout

Overview of burnout

Burnout is a destination fed by exposure to excessive and prolonged stress. Physical, emotional and mental exhaustion often lead to feeling overwhelmed, worn-out, and doubting your own ability and contributions at work and in life in general.[18] Figure 5.2 depicts the pathway from stress to burnout and ill-health.

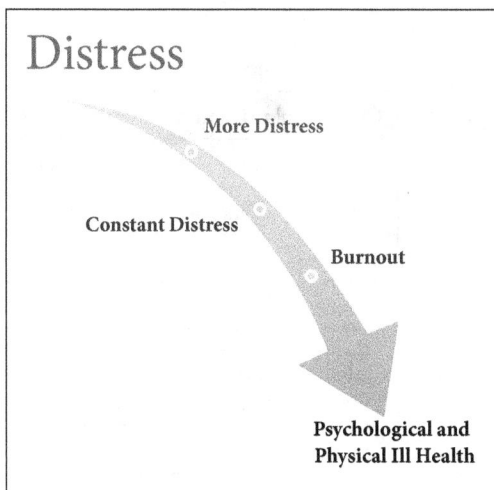

Figure 5.2: Pathway from stress to burnout and ill health

Symptoms of burnout typically include:

- Feeling cynical towards life;
- Having a strong desire to "escape";
- Experiencing a false sense of failure;
- Experiencing negative feelings toward others;
- Displaying emotional distancing, apathy, or numbing;
- Becoming hypercritical;
- Showing inappropriate anger or sadness;
- Enduring a resulting physical illness; or
- Succumbing to depression.

Burnout can also cause long-term changes to the body that make a person vulnerable to illnesses such as colds and flu, heart disease, cholesterol changes, diabetes, depression, and other mental health risks. Moreover, the healthcare expenses of individuals at high risk of burnout are double that of individuals who are not at risk of burnout.[19] Table 5.2 lists the conditions from which individuals are more likely to suffer when they are at high risk of burnout.

Table 5.2: The physical and psychological conditions individuals are more likely to suffer when at high risk of burnout[20]

Area	Condition
Mental health	Anxiety disorders
	Depression
	Sleep disorders
Physical health	Cholesterol risk and cardiovascular conditions
	Headaches and musculoskeletal disorders/pain
	Gastric disorders and stomach pains
	Spastic colon (IBS)
	Diabetes
	Hypertension
Repetitive strain injury	Stiffness in hands and/or wrists
	Eyestrain
	Back, neck and shoulder discomfort

Causes of burnout

Burnout is primarily a work-related distress syndrome. However, any person who feels overworked and under-appreciated is at risk of burnout. The causes of burnout can be found in work-related causes, lifestyle causes, and the personality makeup of the leader.

The job demands-resources theory[21] emphasises that employees excel in their work because they are able to maintain a balance between the energy they have to give (*job demands* expected) and the energy they receive (*job resources* available from the work setting). Burnout in the workplace specifically happens when job demands exceed the availability of job and personal resources to execute successfully the demand,[22] as depicted in Figure 5.3 below. This is typically called the Health Impairment Process, where employees' mental, emotional and physical resources are exhausted, leading to the depletion of energy and resulting in burnout and health problems.

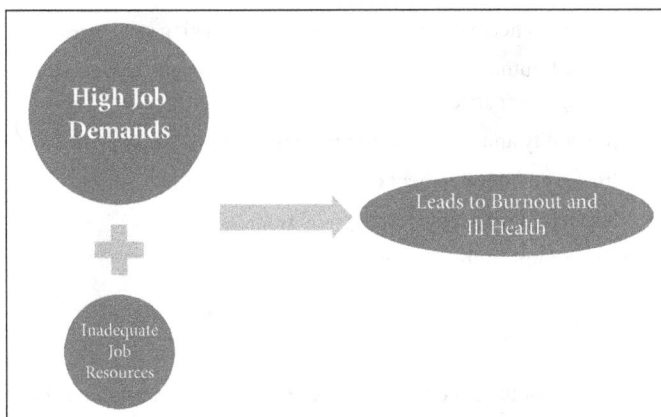

Figure 5.3: The health impairment process

Job demands

The job demand factors which can cause burnout usually form part of the workload, the emotional or cognitive demands placed on an individual, and can be described as follows:

- High-pressure, fast-paced, insecure, chaotic and poorly-planned work context, creating a sense of consistently being in crisis mode.
- Place where management and leadership are perceived as unsupportive, dysfunctional, incompetent, disloyal, overly demanding, or toxic.
- Context where there is a poor job-fit in terms of skills, knowledge, experience and expectations, as well as inadequate physical resources or equipment to execute a high workload.
- System characterised by poor communication, confusion regarding roles and responsibilities, corporate political games and favouritism.
- Work context that disallows autonomy or advancement opportunities – creating a sense of helplessness – so that you have little or no control over how you do your work or the way you execute your work.
- Organisation where there is no or little recognition or rewards for good work, and no opportunities for growth and development.

Job resources

In contrast, the availability of job resources can foster employee engagement (eustress), productivity, initiative and extra-role performance. Several studies have shown that the availability of job resources, particularly in contexts where job demands are high, could have motivational value, drive engagement, and buffer the impact of job demands on stress-reactions.[23]

Job resources include:

- Supportive supervisory relationships
- Good colleague support
- Sound job information, work planning and performance feedback
- Clarity pertaining to role and responsibility
- Good communication
- Clear and effective reporting and decision-making structures
- Level of autonomy and participation in decision-making allowed (management style)
- Availability and quality of physical resources and equipment
- Growth and development opportunities
- Satisfaction with remuneration and rewards
- Career paths in the organisation.

Dealing with burnout

The negative effects of burnout spill over into every area of life, including a person's work, home, health and social life. Burnout spreads from spouse to spouse, from manager to employees, infecting entire teams.[24] Given how contagious stress and burnout are, it is essential for leaders to understand and recognise the effect of their own emotional state on the team or the organisation. Should there be low energy, disengagement and despair from the leader, it will very soon be reflected in the mood and behaviour of the team.[25] Working with a stressed and burnt-out team, trying to find ways for them to become re-energised, engaged and productive again, is not easy.

Recognising burnout

Suffering from chronic stress and then developing burnout is usually an insidious process. Always feeling stressed may become a way of life and continuously lower levels of energy, or physical disease may be accepted or rationalised away.[26]

Given that prolonged distress results in burnout and ill health, it is important to distinguish whether the symptoms experienced indicate distress or burnout. Keep in mind that distress is all about *too much*: experiencing too many demands and pressures that require too much of you. However, one can still imagine that one can get a hold on things and get things under control. In contrast, burnout is about *not enough*: feeling empty, devoid of motivation, beyond caring, and beyond hope of positive change in situations. Distress is about drowning in responsibility. Burnout is about being all dried up. Considering this, people more easily know when they experience distress but often do not notice the gradual development of burnout.

Reversing burnout

There is no quick fix to overturn burnout.[27] Depending on the extent of the burnout, recovery can take years. Treatment must be holistic and multi-faceted. The ultimate goal of the recovery process is to restore energy in order to normalise cortisol levels, to break the bad habits fuelling burnout, and to address the situational factors that caused the burnout in the first place. Once the burnout cycle is broken it is important to continuously build resilience in order to prevent relapse.

Derailment

Overview of derailment

Derailment occurs where managers or leaders are involuntarily plateaued, demoted or fired before the manager reaches his/her anticipated level of achievement, or after reaching that level, unexpectedly failing.[28] These are therefore high-potential candidates, destined for the "fast track", but somehow failing to meet expectations. They are then fired, demoted, or stopped in their leadership path.[29] Because leadership is generally seen as the domain of exceptional people,[30] it attracts a great deal of attention when examples of poor or bad leadership are reported in the media.

Although no official information is available on the incidence of leadership derailment in Africa or the rest of the developing world, it is interesting to note that the global average tenure of CEOs is 7.6 years.[31] Indications are that two out of five new CEOs fail in their first 18 months on the job,[32] and that the 40% of CEOs with the shortest tenure stayed less than two years in the position. Up to 30% of Fortune 500 CEOs lasted less than three years, and the executive failure rate in this group is estimated as being not lower than 30% but possibly as high as 75%.[33]

Based on his own research, Robert Hogan proposes the base rate of incompetent management in the corporate world to be as high as 65–75%[34] and, of this group, between 30–50% will end up being fired or choosing to resign.[35]

It seems that as many as 82% of recently appointed leaders derail because they fail to establish and build relationships in the organisation.[36] In analysing results from climate surveys over many decades, Hogan[37] also states that "*about 75% of the workforce surveyed will say that the worst single aspect of their job, the most stressful aspect of their job, is their immediate supervisor*".

Different types of derailment

Bad management is rampant in the corporate world,[38] and terms such as arrogance, insensitivity and self-centredness are often mentioned by employees and peers about leaders. Although confidence and a high self-regard (for example) are required for effective leadership, it is useful to keep in mind that even strengths used to the extreme can become a way of derailing.[39] Given that most people have derailment potential, it is useful to be able to determine derailment risk.

Grounded in interpersonal and evolutionary theory and the principles of socio-analytic theory, Dr R Hogan developed the Hogan Development Survey that measures derailment in the workplace (dark side of personality). Using the principles of personality structure and personality disorders, Hogan *et al*[40] studied the way in which similar self-defeating expressions of normal personality could appear in the workplace. They posited that behavioural characteristics and personal dispositions are *dysfunctional* if they interfere with an individual's capacity to "get along" (be co-operative, seem compliant, friendly and positive) or "get ahead" (take initiative, seek responsibility, be recognised).[41]

Hogan describes eleven different types of derailment.[42] Table 5.3 provides an overview and short description of each derailer.

Table 5.3: Overview of the Hogan derailers[43]

Derailer	Description
Excitable	Tend to be more volatile and sensitive
Sceptical	Distrustful and ready to retaliate
Cautious	Reluctant to take risks
Reserved	Comes across as aloof and detached
Leisurely	Seem stubborn and independent
Bold	Acting confident, opinionated and entitled
Mischievous	These people are impulsive, non-conforming and manipulative
Colourful	Expressive, dramatic and attention seeking
Imaginative	Experienced as creative and eccentric
Diligent	Characteristics include being meticulous, critical and perfectionistic
Dutiful	Eager to please and reluctant to take individual action

In other literature, Furnham[44] summarises leadership derailment by referring to three classes of derailed leaders:

- **Bad leaders:** Leaders who display despotic, destructive, malignant, or toxic behaviour which implies that the behaviour is evil, amoral and unjust;
- **Sad leaders:** Leaders who may not have the competence, skills or abilities to function as leaders;
- **Mad leaders:** Leaders who may be anti-social, aberrant, destructive, mentally unstable or psychologically maladjusted.

Causes of derailment

Successful leaders are both similar to and different from the normal adult working population. There are indications that leaders are more stable and composed, competitive and ambitious, outgoing and interested in formal learning than others and that this allows them to climb the corporate ladder successfully. Successful leaders can also persuade others and establish co-operation and cohesiveness among different parties to reach goals.[45] Leaders are able both to "get along" with others and "get ahead" in the corporate context.[46]

Personality traits and styles, as deeply etched patterns of thinking and behaviour, may be so embedded and automatic that the leader may be unaware of the nature and the consequences of these traits.[47] Under conditions of persistent adversity, fatigue, stress, boredom, intense emotion, or situations of ambiguity, such styles could show features of moderate or marked severity.[48] The same may happen with the emotions created by greed, hatred, jealousy, insecurity or anger. These traits can intensify to such an extent that they cause stress and impair social and professional functioning.[49]

Normality and pathology of personality therefore exist on a continuum. As an example, the personality traits referred to as Histrionic, Narcissistic and Compulsive may reflect personality traits that could be highly valued in corporate environments and be seen as leadership strengths.

However, "*when over utilised, possibly under stressful situations, these personality traits may excel at minimising problems, denying difficulties and presenting themselves in a favourable light*".[50] The level of usage of these traits may in some cases be adaptive and in others disruptive – particularly also in leadership and a corporate context.

In general, essential leader attributes should include adequate cognitive abilities, personality strength, emotional stability, positive motivation, strong values, interpersonal skills, and job-related expertise and knowledge.[51] Weaknesses in any of these areas may lie dormant for a long time and slowly emerge over time, often triggered by circumstances in the work environment.[52] In good times, such leadership problems could therefore remain hidden, but in difficult times this could become a recipe for disaster.[53]

Via the essential leadership responsibilities of task management, people management and personal management,[54] the reasons for derailment given in the literature can be clustered in three areas with sub-themes, as listed in Table 5.4 below.

Table 5.4: Overview of the possible reasons for derailment

Area	Leaders who derail are likely to…

Task management	• *Have issues with:*
	  o Judgment;[55] Delegation;[56] Execution;[57] Problem solving and divergent thinking;[58] Prioritising;[59] Complexity[60]
	• *Lack:*
	  o Vision;[61] Business experience;[62] Self-insight;[63]
	• *Ignore:*
	  o Market realities;[64] Organisational reality[65]

People management	• *Struggle with:*
	  o Behavioural complexity;[66] Diversity;[67] Holding employees accountable;[68] Managing conflict[69]
	• *Lack*
	  o Interpersonal skills;[70] Listening skills;[71] Communication skills;[72] Integrity[73]
	• *Be:*
	  o Autocratic and dictatorial[74]

Personal management	• *Lack:*
	  o Agility;[75] Energy and passion;[76] Composure;[77] Self-awareness;[78]
	• *Be:*
	  o Self-centred;[79] Dependent;[80] Overly ambitious;[81] Resistant to feedback;[82] Socially insensitive;[83] Arrogant;[84] Emotionally unstable;[85] Overly cautious;[86] Aloof;[87] Mischievous;[88] Perfectionistic;[89] Defensive;[90] Blaming others[91]

Any single factor mentioned above could cause leadership derailment. In contexts where multiple factors are present, the impact and damage to the organisation may be compounded.

The organisation's role in fuelling/sanctioning derailment

Candidates are often employed, and incumbents promoted into leadership positions, as a result of their strong personality characteristics or excellent technical skills only. Organisations may unknowingly employ or promote leaders who potentially have a high risk for derailment if any (or a combination of) the following factors are at play:

- **Selecting:** The hiring processes are inadequate and the wrong people are appointed because of inappropriate criteria, assessing the wrong traits, using poor methods for selection, or not recognising the fact that leadership does not happen in a static environment.[92] It is easy to confuse intellectual ability, loyalty, or technical skill with leadership ability. Agile leaders may be forced into slow-moving bureaucratic organisations, or slow-moving leaders may be appointed into agile organisations. By improving the selection processes,[93] risks associated with selecting the wrong candidate may be mitigated.

- **Organisational controls and processes:** Very few barriers, corporate systems and controls are in place to limit the harm that could be done by "runaway leadership".[94] People are promoted or appointed to leadership positions without previous or appropriate experience, and before they have had time to learn from their own failures and mistakes.[95] Often, people are not held accountable for their performance,[96] and timeous decisions to move non-performers out are delayed.[97] This is exacerbated when there is a failure to understand that leaders primarily learn on the job and that the availability of appropriate coaching and development opportunities are important.[98]

- **Culture:** The leadership team creates a culture where aggression and arrogance or other derailed behaviour is acceptable and the norm.[99] Together with this, there is often no culture of continuous feedback from colleagues, peers and employees.[100]

Dealing with derailment

The use of 360-degree and other assessments

Assessments such as the Hogan Development Survey (HDS) are often utilised to determine proactively the propensity of the leader for derailment. Since derailment quite often goes hand-in-hand with a failure to lead the organisation because of poor interpersonal relationships, poor morale, low levels of trust, or the inability to meet business goals in an ambiguous and changing environment,[101] 360-degree information also provides perspectives on the impact of the leader's reputation.

Leaders do not behave in the same manner towards all subordinates and other organisational members such as peers and supervisors. In this regard it is invaluable to analyse perspectives summarised in 360-degree assessments by specifically looking at the difference between the leader's self-evaluation and the ratings of others to determine derailment risk.[102] Results indicate that the feedback from all raters is important, but that the feedback from peers is particularly important. Risk of derailment increases where the self-rating of the leader and the ratings of peers are clearly discrepant.[103]

The results from a scientific and well-developed 360-degree assessment, as well as a psychometrically valid assessment tool such as the HDS, are invaluable in creating learning and insight for the leader and timeously identifying risks.

Coaching

Derailment in leadership is a significant event with impact on the leader as well as everybody around him/her. Advice to such a leader would include:[104]

- Get beyond denial. Accept the facts and confront the failure.
- See setbacks and successes as positive learning experiences and try again.
- Show honest and authentic remorse.
- Engage with employees and colleagues and admit your mistakes in an analytical and non-judgmental way.
- Help friends and family also deal with your experience.
- Get the event behind you to be able to move on, get in on the action, do something, show yourself you can do it again, build your confidence.
- Recruit others to help you emotionally.
- Find a new mission and passion that creates meaning in your life.

Resilience

Overview of resilience

Resilience is positioned in this chapter as one of the important buffers to deal successfully with stress, burnout and potential derailment. People who seem to be able to withstand the stress and strain of life more easily than others are often referred to as being "resilient". This is a concept derived from the Latin word *resilire,* meaning to leap or jump back in an elastic manner – resuming the former size and shape.[105]

Resilient people are perceived to regard competition, challenge, danger, change, threat or hardship as an opportunity for development and learning.[106] They believe that everything will turn out all right if they work very hard, take control, are positive, and confidently deal with hardship. By effectively and successfully dealing with difficulties in this manner, individuals and organisations seem to be strong and thriving.

Resilient leaders

In a context of cybercrime, financial turbulence, water and food shortages, terrorism and extreme weather changes as well as skills shortages and global competition,[107] organisational resilience is a crucial, but seemingly impossible task. Organisational hardiness is related to the resilience of its employees, teams, and particularly the leaders,[108] since resilient employees tend to be more able to absorb, deal with, and survive stress, change and turbulence.[109]

It is therefore essential to put mechanisms, structures and management practices in place to sustain, guard and build employee resilience, inasmuch as it is possible. Collectively, these resources have to align and be fostered by the formal organisational structure.[110] Particularly important would be elements such as providing essential resources, building confidence, carefully managing the corporate mood, ensuring emotional management, providing interpersonal support, allowing flexibility, and understanding the impact of leadership.[111]

In these processes, the nature and resilience of the leader play a critical role. Transformational leaders tend to show more of an ability and affinity to work with emotional awareness and cope with emotional management by being able to use positive persuasion, group support, encouragement, respect and trust to enhance the efficacy with which individuals and teams function.[112]

Given the interconnectedness of organisations to society, it is true that building resilience actually requires the alignment of efforts at all levels of society, people, organisations, communities, cities, regions and nations.[113] This is a formidable task for leaders at all levels. Therefore, in addition to selecting leaders who are confident, realistic, intellectually bright, and have a strong value system, it is essential that they also have a positive attitude and adequate emotional and interpersonal resources,[114] as well as learning agility. Leaders with this agility have the ability to learn from, and make sense of, experiences whether good or bad, and can model this behaviour to employees. The willingness to learn in this way separates high potential and resilient leaders from others.[115]

Developing resilience

Resilience and personality

There has been debate as to whether resilience can be measured as an individual personality trait or if it should be regarded as a complex mosaic of traits culminating in the ability to withstand hardship. Some would also say that resilient individuals are not necessarily exceptional people who survive against all odds, and that they may just be people who have a combination of the following characteristics: they accept reality, strongly rely on their stable values, believe that life is meaningful, and possess effective coping mechanisms that allow them to survive and improvise flexibly in stressful or unexpected situations.[116]

Others agree that personality characteristics such as being emotionally stable, optimistic and confident of one's ability to deal with adversity; being sociable, outgoing or interpersonally close with others; having social networks and social support; being conscientious and self-disciplined, all culminate in a person with the ability to endure stress successfully and be resilient.[117]

Resilience and cognitive ability

The intellectual ability of people may support their ability to deal with difficult situations more easily, particularly if they are flexible and open in their thinking and are prepared to learn from experience.[118]

Resilience and emotional management

The effective and intelligent management of emotions plays an important role in the leader's resilience. The ability to identify, use, understand and manage their own emotions and recognise those of others can buffer the onset and progression of stress and burnout of the leader.[119] It also enables the leader to manage the interpersonal relationships in the workplace better – a core and essential aspect of sustainable leadership.[120] Wong and Law[121] also found that leaders' skills in emotional management positively impacts on employee behaviour. Being competent and skilled at maintaining effective self-awareness, being problem-solving oriented, having flexibility, showing interpersonal awareness, having empathy, and reflecting positive emotions, attitudes and beliefs, as well as having a sense of purpose and meaning, all add to the leader being more resilient.[122]

Resilience, character strengths and virtues

Particularly important for resilience[123] is the attitude with which a person deals with hardship and difficulty. Does the person manage difficulties in an optimistic and positive manner? Does the leader see the problem as manageable, of short duration and as an interesting experience – or are problems seen as reason for despair and desperation? Does the person have a sense of purpose and meaning in life, and does the person live with a style of abundance? Factors like these can be seen as protective of and enhancing resilience.[124]

Other factors influencing resilience

There are indications that resilience may be shaped by positive or negative life events[125] and that it may increase with age.[126] A most interesting view of resilience comes from developments in the fields of neuroscience, immunology and genetics.[127] Today it is accepted that the plasticity of the brain allows us to retrain the brain. The brain's anatomy, neural networks and cognitive abilities can be improved, often by learning new skills and becoming "cognitively fit". The more cognitively fit one is, the easier one will be able to deal with stress and change.

Experience gained directly or through observation can activate neurons which accelerate learning and the capacity to learn. Ways to expand such neurological learning – that at the same time makes excellent business sense – is to manage by walking around. An intentional decision to learn, listen and discover engages the pre-frontal cortex. Seeking new experiences, identifying patterns, and engaging in new and challenging activities also involve both the left and right hemispheres. This then allows people to be receptive to novelty and innovation at work, supporting them when in a crisis because they are open to seeing opportunity in even the direst situations.[128]

Even activities which may seem to be a waste of time may have beneficial effects. For example, we spend seven billion hours a week playing video games – 300 million minutes a day on Angry Birds alone – but these activities may support problem-solving, strategic thinking, mood, and interpersonal fun, and as such, support resilience.[129]

In a study done in Britain,[130] 75% of employees reported that their biggest stress was related to managing difficult people and dealing with office politics. Other high-stress factors included the volume and pace of work, feeling personally criticised, not feeling competent to do the work, personal turmoil, and balancing work and family responsibilities. When asked where their reserves of dealing with stress came from, 90% said from themselves, 50% said from relationships, and only 10% reported support from their organisation, which means that people mostly rely on themselves to build resilience and manage stress.

Resilience therefore results from a complex interplay of the characteristics, resources, attitude and skills a person has, and uses, when interacting with the demands of the context. It is also accepted that not only is resilience a complex construct, it is also dynamic and continuously developing.[131] Psychological resilience is therefore best conceptualised as a lifelong process where working through it, and learning from easy tasks and difficult challenges, can build an increased ability to understand and cope with pressure.[132] Being able to show resilience in difficult circumstances will also build confidence and satisfaction making it somewhat easier to cope with difficult demands in the future.[133]

Conclusion

In general, effective leaders are expected to be selfless, hardworking, honest and fair, have the ability to empower others, be wise, have good reasoning capacities, be a hero, seek virtue, and be virtuous.[134] In addition, the research done by CCL in 1989[135] indicated that successful leaders, those who do not derail, have the following characteristics:

- More adaptable to change, better able to deal with ambiguity and complexity.
- Able to learn more quickly from a variety of experiences.
- Able to build teams recognised for their diversity.
- Noted for the respect they have for themselves and others. They seek feedback, acknowledge their own strengths and weaknesses and are appreciative of others.

In a journal article, *"Resilience and burnout: A stitch that could save nine"*,[136] Professor DJW Strümpfer reminds us of something he wrote more than two decades ago which still holds true:

> *"It is necessary to stand still and decide what things are really important and basic in one's life, the things one values most, but it also requires a certain power to do so... [it] is necessary to set priorities, not only for a day or a week, but for quite long periods of one's life. In this connection it may be worth asking some ultimate questions, like 'is it worth dying for?' or 'is it worth getting divorced for?' or 'is it worth losing my son[or daughter] for?' Perhaps this may require 'getting away from it all' for several days or even longer, now and then..."*

Resilience does not only provide benefits as a way of dealing with stress and burnout; it also allows leaders and employees to find work-life easier and to flourish in a complex world where ambiguity, insecurity, and exponential change are common.[137] Resilience may in fact shield leaders from aspects of potential derailment and burnout. People professionals in organisations should therefore focus in a purposeful and planned way on assisting leaders to build and grow their personal coping resources.

Endnotes

1. McGrath, 2011; Schrage, 2010.
2. Goh et al., 2015.
3. Goh et al., 2015; Salomon, 2015.
4. Robertson et al., 2015.
5. Green, 2015.
6. Winsborough, 2013.
7. Le Fevre et al., 2003.
8. Colligan & Higgins, 2006.
9. Swider & Zimmerman, 2010.
10. Hutchinson, 2010.
11. Flint-Taylor, 2014
12. Polman et al., 2010.
13. Popova, 2015.
14. NIMH, 2014; Popova, 2015.
15. NIMH, 2014; Popova, 2015.
16. Melamed et al., 1999.
17. Popova, 2015.
18. Schaufeli et al., 1993; Kahill, 1988; Popova, 2015.
19. De Beer et al., 2013.
20. Rothman et al., 2010.
21. Demerouti et al., 2001; De Beer et al., 2012.
22. Rothman et al., 2005.
23. Bakker et al., 2006; Rothman & Joubert, 2007; Villavicencio-Ayub et al., 2015.
24. Beer et al., 2014; Melamed et al., 2006.
25. Bakker et al., 2006.
26. Bakker et al., 2006.
27. Morse et al., 2012.
28. Hogan, 2007.
29. Lombardo & Eichinger, 1989.
30. Inyang, 2013; Lombardo & Eichinger, 1989; Hogan, 2007.
31. Ekelund, 2012.
32. Dotlich & Cairo, 2007.
33. Williams, 2010.
34. Hogan, 2007, Winsborough, 2013.
35. Fernández-Aráoz, 1999.
36. Williams, 2010.
37. Hogan, 2007.
38. Hogan, 2007.
39. Hogan, 2007.
40. Hogan & Hogan, 2009.
41. Hogan & Hogan, 2009.

42. Hogan & Hogan, 2009; Hogan, 2007.
43. Hogan & Hogan, 2009; Hogan, 2007.
44. Inyang, 2013.
45. Winsborough & Sambath, 2013.
46. Winsborough & Sambath, 2013; Hogan, 2007.
47. Millon, 2006.
48. Millon, 2006; Kets De Vries, 2006.
49. Millon, 2006.
50. Millon, 2006.
51. Antoniakis et al., 2004.
52. WEF, 2015.
53. Zenger & Folkman, 2009.
54. Marshall, 2013.
55. Zenger & Folkman, 2009; Hogan, 2007.
56. Charan & Colvin, 1999.
57. Hogan, 2007.
58. Zenger & Folkman, 2009.
59. Hogan, 2007.
60. Lombardo & Eichinger, 1989; Zaccaro et al., 2004; Hogan, 2007.
61. Zenger & Folkman, 2009.
62. Lombardo & Eichinger, 1989.
63. Zenger & Folkman, 2009.
64. Hogan, 2007.
65. Riggio, 2009.
66. Lawrence et al., 2011.
67. Lowder, 2007; Ekelund, 2012.
68. Lombardo & Eichinger, 1989; CCL, 2001.
69. Charan & Colvin, 1999.
70. Zenger & Folkman, 2009.
71. Inyang, 2013.
72. Hogan, 2007.
73. Zenger & Folkman, 2009.
74. Hogan, 2007, Lombardo & Eichinger, 1989.
75. CCL, 2001; De Meuse et al., 2010.
76. Hogan, 2007; Zenger & Folkman, 2009; McKinsey, 2015.
77. Hogan, 2007.
78. De Meuse et al., 2010.
79. Zenger & Folkman, 2009.
80. Lombardo & Eichinger, 1989.
81. Hogan, 2007.
82. Hogan, 2007.
83. Hogan, 2007.
84. Dotlich & Cairo, 2007; Williams 2010.
85. Hogan, 2007; Zenger & Folkman, 2009; Dotlich & Cairo, 2007.
86. Dotlich & Cairo, 2007.
87. Hogan, 2007; Dotlich & Cairo, 2007.
88. Dotlich & Cairo, 2007.
89. Hogan, 2007; Dotlich & Cairo, 2007.
90. De Meuse et al., 2010.
91. Zenger & Folkman, 2009.
92. Hogan, 2007, De Meuse et al., 2010.
93. Kets de Vries, 2006.
94. Kets de Vries, 2006.
95. Hogan, 2007; Lombardo & Eichinger, 1989; McKinsey Quarterly, 2015.
96. Hogan, 2007, McKinsey Quarterly, 2015.
97. Hogan, 2007.
98. Kets De Vries, 2006; De Meuse et al., 2010.
99. Lombardo & Eichinger, 1989.
100. Lombardo & Eichinger, 1989.
101. Kets De Vries, 2006.
102. Braddy et al., 2013.
103. Braddy et al., 2013.
104. Sonnenfeld & Ward, 2007.
105. Strümpfer, 2003; Van der Vegt et al., 2015.
106. Strycharczyk & Elvin, 2014; Clough et al., 2011.
107. WEF, 2015.
108. Robertson et al., 2015.
109. Shin et al., 2012.
110. Van der Vegt et al., 2015.
111. Shin et al., 2012.
112. Luthans & Youssef, 2007.
113. Van der Vegt et al., 2015.
114. De Meuse et al., 2010.
115. De Meuse et al., 2010.
116. Couto, 2002.
117. Van der Vegt et al., 2015.
118. Flint-Taylor, 2014; Van der Vegt et al., 2015.
119. Batool, 2013.
120. Anand & UdayaSuriyan, 2010.
121. Zaccaro et al., 2004.
122. Flint-Taylor, 2014; Reyzábal, 2014; Luthans & Youssef, 2007.
123. Peterson & Seligman, 2004.
124. Peterson & Seligman, 2004; Minulescu, 2015.
125. Sarubin et al., 2015.
126. Flint-Taylor, 2014.
127. Strümpfer, 2006.
128. Gilkey & Kilts, 2007; Strümpfer, 2006.
129. McGonigal, 2012.
130. Ovans, 2015.
131. Minulescu, 2015.
132. Flint-Taylor et al., 2014
133. Flint-Taylor et al., 2014
134. Zaccaro et al., 2004.
135. Lombardo & Eichinger, 1989.
136. Strümpfer, 2003.
137. Robertson et al., 2015.

References

Anand, R & UdayaSuriyan, G. 2010. 'Emotional intelligence and its relationship with leadership practices'. *International Journal of Business and Management*, 5(2):65–76.

Bakker, AB, Demerouti, E & Euwema, M. C. 2005. 'Job resources buffer the impact of job demands on burnout'. *Journal of occupational health psychology*, 10(2):170.

Bakker, AB, van Emmerik, H & Euwema, M. C. 2006. 'Crossover of burnout and engagement in work teams'. *Work and Occupations*, 33(4):464–489.

Bass, BM, Avolio, BJ, Jung, DI & Berson, Y. 2003. 'Predicting unit performance by assessing transformational and transactional leadership'. *Journal of Applied Psychology*, 88(2):207–218.

Batool, B.F. 2013. 'Emotional intelligence and effective leadership'. *Journal of Business Studies Quarterly*, 4(3):84–94.

Beer, LT, Pienaar, J & Rothmann, S. 2014. 'Job burnout, work engagement and self-reported treatment for health conditions in South Africa'. *Stress and Health*, 10 April.

Braddy, PW, Gooty, J, Fleenor, JW & Yammarino, F J. 2014. 'Leader behaviors and career derailment potential: A multi-analytic method examination of rating source and self-other agreement'. *The Leadership Quarterly*, 25:373–390.

Center for Creative Leadership (CLL). 2001. *The bad news: Derailment happens*. Greensboro, NC: Center for Creative Leadership.

Charan, R & Colvin, G. 1999. 'Why CEOs fail'. *Fortune Magazine*, 21 June.

Colligan, TW & Higgins, EM. 2006. 'Workplace stress: Etiology and consequences'. *Journal of Workplace Behavioral Health*, 21(2):89–97.

Couto, D. 2002. 'How resilience works'. *Harvard Business Review*. [Online]. Available: https://hbr.org/2002/05/how-resilience-works. [Accessed 1 June 2016].

De Beer, L, Pienaar, J & Rothmann Jr, S. 2013. 'Linking employee burnout to medical aid provider expenditure'. *South African Medical Journal*, 103(2):89–93.

De Beer, L, Rothmann Jr S & Pienaar, J. 2012. 'A confirmatory investigation of a job demands-resources model using a categorical estimator'. *Psychological reports*, 111(2):528–544.

De Meuse, KP, Dai, G, & Hallenbeck, GS. 2010. 'Learning agility: A construct whose time has come'. *Consulting Psychology Journal: Practice and Research*, 62(2):119–130.

Demerouti, E, Bakker, AB, Nachreiner, F & Schaufeli, WB. 2001. 'The job demands-resources model of burnout'. *Journal of Applied Psychology,* 86(3):499–512.

Dotlich, DL & Cairo, PC. 2007. *Why CEOs Fail: The 11 behaviors that can derail your climb to the top – and how to manage them*. San Francisco, CA: Jossey-Bass.

Ekelund, H. 2012. *Why some CEOs fail and others succeed*. [Online]. Available: http://www.bts.com/news-insight. [Accessed 1 June 2016].

Fernández-Aráoz, C. 1999. 'Hiring without firing'. *Harvard Business Review*, July-August.

Flint-Taylor, J, Davda, A & Cooper, CL. 2014. 'Stable personal attributes and a resilient approach to work and career'. *South African Journal of Industrial Psychology*, 40(1). [Online]. Available: http://www.sajip.co.za/index.php/sajip/article/view/1137. [Accessed 1 June 2016].

Gilkey, R & Kilts, C. 2007. 'Cognitive fitness'. *Harvard Business Review*, November.

Goh, J, Pfeffer, J & Zenios, S.A. 2015. *Workplace stressors and health outcomes: Health policy for the workplace*. [Online]. Available: https://behavioralpolicy.org/article/workplace-stressors-health-outcome. [Accessed 9 September 2015].

Green, A. 2015. *SA is stressed out and suicidal*. [Online]. Available: http://mg.co.za/article/2015-07-01-sa-is-stressed-out--and-suicidal. [Accessed 1 June 2016].

Hogan, R. 2007. *Personality and the fate of organizations*. New Jersey, NJ: Lawrence Erlbaum Associates.

Hogan, R & Hogan, J. 2009. *Hogan development survey manual*. 2nd ed. Tulsa, OK: Hogan Assessment Systems.

Hutchinson, A-MK, Stuart, AD & Pretorius, HG. 2010. 'Biological contributions to well-being: The relationship amongst temperament, character strengths and resilience'. *South African Journal of Industrial Psychology*, 36(2). [Online]. Available: http://www.sajip.co.za/index.php/sajip/article/view/844. [Accessed 1 June 2016].

Inyang, BJ. 2013. 'Exploring the concept of leadership derailment: Defining new research agenda'. *International Journal of Business and Management*, 8(16):78–85.

Kahill, S. 1988. 'Symptoms of professional burnout: A review of the empirical evidence'. *Canadian Psychology/ Psychologie Canadienne*, 29(3):284–297.

Kets de Vries, MFR. 2006. *The leader on the couch – a clinical approach to changing people and organizations.* San Francisco, CA: Jossey-Bass.

Keijsers, GPJ, Schaap, CPDR, Vossen, CJC, Boelaars, V, van Minnen, A & Hoogduin, CAL. 2000. *Burnout Reïntegratietraining, Therapeutenboek [Burnout Reintegration Training, Therapist Book].* Amsterdam: Cure & Care Publishers.

Lawrence, KA, Quinn, RE & Lenk, P. 2011. *Behavioral complexity in leadership: The psychometric properties of a new instrument to measure behavioural repertoire.* Ann Arbort, MI: University of Michigan Business School.

Le Fevre, M, Matheny, J & Kolt, GS. 2003. 'Eustress, distress, and interpretation in occupational stress'. *Journal of Managerial Psychology,* 18(7):726–744.

Lombardo, MM & Eichinger, RW. 1989. *Preventing derailment: What to do before it's too late.* Greensboro, NC: Center for Creative Leadership.

Lowder, T. 2007. *Five dimensions of effective leadership: A meta-analysis of leadership attributes and behaviors.* Minneapolis, MN: Capella University.

Luthans, F & Youssef, CM. 2007. 'Emerging positive organizational behavior'. *Journal of Management,* 33(3):321–349.

Marshall, J. 2013. *Six factors of leadership derailment.* [Online]. Available: http://marshallconsulting.com/wp-content/uploads/2013/08/Six-factors-of-new.pdf. [Accessed 1 June 2016].

McGrath, R. 2011. 'Failing by design'. *Harvard Business Review,* April.

McGonigal, J. 2012. 'Building resilience by wasting time'. *Harvard Business Review, October.*

McKinsey. 2015. 'When to change how you lead'. *McKinsey Quarterly,* June.

Melamed, S, Shirom, A, Toker, S, Berliner, S & Shapira, I. 2006. 'Burnout and risk of cardiovascular disease: Evidence, possible causal paths, and promising research directions'. *Psychological Bulletin,* 132(3):327–353.

Melamed, S, Ugarten, U, Shirom, A, Kahana, L, Lerman, Y & Froom, P. 1999. 'Chronic burnout, somatic arousal and elevated salivary cortisol levels'. *Journal of Psychosomatic Research,* 46(6):591–598.

Millon, T, Millon, C, Davis, R & Grossman, S. 2006. *MCMI-III Manual,* 3rd ed. Minneapolis, MN: Pearson.

Minulescu, M. 2014. 'Is university capable to build resilience in students?' *Procedia – Social and Behavioral Sciences,* 180:1628–1631.

Morse, G, Salyers, MP, Rollins, AL, Monroe-DeVita, M & Pfahler, C. 2012. 'Burnout in mental health services: A review of the problem and its remediation'. *Administration and Policy in Mental Health and Mental Health Services Research,* 39(5):341–352.

National Institute of Mental Health (NIMH). 2014. *Adult stress – Frequently asked questions – How it affects your health and what you can do about it.* [Online]. Available: http://www.nimh.nih.gov/health/publications/stress/index.shtml. [Accessed 1 June 2016].

Ovans, A. 2015. 'What resilience means, and why it matters'. *Harvard Business Review.* [Online]. Available: https://hbr.org/2015/01/what-resilience-means-and-why-it-matters. [Accessed 1 June 2016].

Peterson, C & Seligman, MEP. 2004. *Character strengths and virtues – a handbook and classification.* New York, NY: Oxford University Press.

Polman, R, Borkoles, E & Nicholls, AR. 2010. 'Type D personality, stress, and symptoms of burnout: The influence of avoidance coping and social support'. *British Journal of Health Psychology,* 15(3):681–696.

Popova, M. 2015. *The science of stress and how our emotions affect our susceptibility to burnout and disease.* [Online]. Available: https://www.brainpickings.org/2015/07/20/esther-sternberg-balance-within-stress-emotion/. [Accessed 1 June 2016].

Reyzábal, MV. 2014. 'Literary practice as a way to promote resilience'. *Procedia – Social and Behavioral Sciences, 132*:121–128.

Riggio, RE. 2009. *Organizations from hell: When leadership fails.* [Online]. Available: https://www.psychologytoday.com/blog/cutting-edge-leadership/200906/organizations-hell-when-leadership-fails. [Accessed 2 September 2015].

Robertson, IT, Cooper, CL, Sarkar, M & Curran, T. 2015. 'Resilience training in the workplace from 2003 to 2014: A systematic review'. *Journal of Occupational and Organizational Psychology,* 88(3):533–562.

Rothman, S, Steyn, LJ & Mostert, K. 2005. 'Job stress, sense of coherence and work wellness in an electricity supply organisation'. *South African Journal of Business Management,* 36(1):55–63.

Rothmann, et al. 2010. *Burnout. The three-headed monster consuming employee health and productivity.* Paper presented at 2010 Annual SIOPSA Conference, Johannesburg, South Africa.

Ross, S. 2014. 'Leadership talent, success and derailment'. *Network Magazine.* [Online]. Available: http://www.ntualumni.org.uk/news_and_events/network_magazine/suzanne_ross/. [Accessed 1 June 2016].

Salomon S. 2015. *Study says stress is as bad as second-hand smoke.* [Online]. Available: http://

www.boston.com/jobs/news/2015/08/27/study-says-work-stress-bad-secondhand-smoke/ zwmw9G7AOoP997K71QGy0H/story.html/. [Accessed 9 September 2015].

Sarubin, N, Wolf, M, Greyling, I, Hilbert, S, Naumann, F, Gutt, D, Jobst, A, Sabass, L, Falkai, P, Rujescu, D, Bühner, M & Padberg, F. 2015. 'Neuroticism and extraversion as mediators between positive/negative life events and resilience'. *Personality and Individual Differences*, 82:193–198.

Maslach, C & Schaufeli, W .B. 1993. 'Historical and conceptual development of burnout'. In WB Schaufeli, C Maslach & T Marek. *Professional burnout: Recent developments in theory and research*. Washington, DC: Taylor & Francis.

Schrage, M. 2010. 'The failure of failure. *Harvard Business Review*, 31 March 31.

Sherman, GD, Lerner, JS, Josephs, RA, Renshon, J & Gross, JJ. 2015. 'The interaction of testosterone and cortisol is associated with attained status in male executives'. *Journal of Personality and Social Psychology*, 24 August. [Online]. Available: http://dx.doi.org/10.1037/pspp0000063. [Accessed 1 June 2016].

Shin, J, Taylor, MS & Seo, MG. 2012. 'Resources for change: The relationships of organizational inducements and psychological resilience to employees' attitudes and behaviors toward organizational change'. *Academy of Management Journal*, 55(3):727–748.

Sonnenfeld, JA & Ward, A.J. 2007. 'Firing back – How great leaders rebound after career disasters'. *Harvard Business Review*, January.

Strümpfer, DJW 2003. 'Resilience and burnout: A stitch that could save nine'. *South African Journal of Psychology*, 33(2):69–79.

Strümpfer, DJW. 2006. 'Positive emotions, positive emotionality and their contribution to fortigenic living: A review'. *South African Journal of Psychology*, 36(1):144–167.

Strycharczyk, D & Elvin, C. 2014. *Developing Resilient organisations – how to create an adaptive, high performance and engaged organisation*. London, UK: Kogan Page.

Swider, BW & Zimmerman, RD. 2010. 'Born to burnout: A meta-analytic path model of personality, job burnout, and work outcomes'. *Journal of Vocational Behavior*, 76(3):487–506.

Van der Vegt, G, Essens, P, Wahlström, M & George, G. 2015. 'Managing risk and resilience'. *Academy of Management Journal*, 58(4):971–980.

Villavicencio-Ayub, E, Jurado-Cárdenas, S & Valencia-Cruz, A. 2014. 'Work engagement and occupational burnout: Its relation to organizational socialization and psychological resilience'. *Journal of Behavior, Health & Social Issues*, 6(2):45–55.

Williams, R. 2010. *Why do CEOs fail, and what can we do about it?* [Online]. Available: Retrieved from https://www.psychologytoday.com/blog/wired-success/201007/why-do-ceos-fail-and-what-can-we-do-about-it. [Accessed 1 June 2016].

Winsborough, DL & Sambath, V. 2013. 'Not like us: An investigation into the personalities of New Zealand CEOs'. *Consulting Psychology Journal: Practice and Research*, 65(2):87–107.

World Economic Forum (WEF). 2015. *The Africa competitiveness report 2015*. Geneva, CHE: World Economic Forum.

Zaccaro, SJ, Kemp, C & Bader, P. 2004. 'Leader traits and attributes'. In J Antoniakis, AT Ciancidos & RJ Steinberg. *The nature of leadership*. Thousand Oaks, CA: Sage Publications.

Zenger, J & Folkman, J. 2009. 'Ten fatal flaws that derail leaders'. *Harvard Business Review, June.*

Chapter 6

TOXIC LEADERSHIP AND ORGANISATIONS[i]
Theo H Veldsman

There is a worrying, accelerating increase in toxic leadership in organisations globally (including South Africa). Current international research indicates that between 20% and 60% leaders are toxic.[1] My personal opinion is that on average three to four out of every ten leaders are toxic (= 30% to 40%). This increase can be attributed *inter alia* to the weakening power of commonly accepted ethical values and norms; the fanatical worshipping of unfettered individualism and egocentricity to the detriment of the common good; unrealistic stakeholder expectations (for example, shareholders forcing leadership to take unethical, opportunistic short cuts); the rampant growth in personal self-interest and self-love (that is, narcissism); and more toxic susceptible followers who are allowing toxic leadership to be in place to serve their personal needs and interests, however unethical and immoral.[2]

If this cancer of toxicity continues to grow unabated, it will endanger in no uncertain terms personal and organisational well-being, as well as sustainable organisational performance and success, in the present and going into the future. A pressing need therefore exists for organisations to understand in a holistic and systemic way the nature, dynamics and evolution of toxic leadership and organisations, and how to recognise its manifestations and deal with it expeditiously.

The purpose of this chapter is to provide a systemic, integrated understanding of toxic leadership and organisations in order to enable organisations to counter this growing cancer, preferably proactively. The following themes are addressed: Theme 1: Defining "toxic leadership and organisations"; Theme 2: Toxic leadership, leadership competence and ethical leadership; Theme 3: The make-up of toxic leadership and organisations; Theme 4: The dynamics of toxic leadership and organisations; Theme 5: An integrated, systemic and dynamic map of toxic leadership and organisations; Theme 6: The recognition of toxic leadership and organisations; and Theme 7: Reducing the likelihood of toxic leadership and organisations.

Defining Toxic Leadership and Organisations

The word "toxic" comes from the Greek "toxikon" which means "arrow poison". In a literal sense, the term in its original form therefore means to kill (= poison) in a targeted way (= arrow). *Toxic leadership* refers to ongoing, deliberate, intentional actions ([shooting of] the "arrow") by a leader(ship) to undermine the sense of dignity, self-worth and efficacy of an individual(s) (the "poison"), resulting in destructive, devaluing and demeaning work experiences.[3] [ii] Such destructive actions may be physically, psychosocially and/or spiritually (in other words, meaning/purpose) related.[iii] [iv] Toxic leadership therefore represents the "dark" side of

---

i   This chapter is an extensive adaptation, update and extension of an article by the author, Veldsman (2014).

ii   Apart from "toxic" leadership, other terms used are "destructive" or "bad" leadership.

iii   In some quarters in the literature a distinction is drawn between toxic leadership conduct and toxic leadership outcomes (e.g., Padilla, Hogan & Kaiser, 2007). Different permutations are possible: toxic conduct having positive outcomes; toxic conduct having toxic outcomes; positive leadership having toxic outcomes; and positive conduct resulting in positive outcomes. The bias of my chapter is more towards toxic conduct, regardless of the outcomes, toxic or positive, within the framework of the medium to long term, lasting impact of outcomes which is bound to be predominantly toxic (see also Krasikova , Green & LeBreton, 2013).

iv   Workplace bullying is a similar concept to toxic leadership, but more centred on individual, one-on-one, physical and/or emotional abuse by any one individual (including a leader) on another person(s). Hence workplace bullying is but one form of toxic leadership when the bullying is done by leadership.

leadership.[v] A *Toxic Organisation* is an organisation which by its very nature and dynamics erodes, disables and destroys the physiological, psychosocial and spiritual well-being of its organisational members in deliberate ways, and often even permanently. In other words, it is an organisation being metaphorically a "poison pill" to its members.[4]

In contrast to toxic leadership, *healthy, authentic leadership* is leader(ship) that nurtures and affirms the dignity, worth and efficacy of an individual(s), concurrently creating enabling, empowering and meaningful work experiences. Correspondingly, a *healthy, authentic organisation* is an organisation that cares for and grows the physiological, psychosocial and spiritual well-being of its organisational members, making and leaving its members better persons than when they entered the organisation.

Toxic Leadership, Leadership Competence and Ethical Leadership

But what, then, is the relationship between leadership toxicity, leadership competence/ incompetence, and (un)ethical leadership? Leadership toxicity and competence/incompetence are not directly related. Competent – getting results – and incompetent leadership – failing to achieve – alike may manifest toxic leadership. If a narrower demarcation of leadership competence is used, focusing only on results using *inter alia* technical/professional competence, then a toxic leader in a narrower sense may still be seen as competent because they are still "delivering the goods", especially if a short-term view is taken.

Over the longer term, however, their short-term success is unsustainable, because they are destroying the very people on whom they are dependent and with whom they have to perform. One of the definitive ways of identifying toxic leadership is to monitor and track the medium- to long-term engagement impact of leadership conduct.

It may, however, be argued that if a comprehensive, long-term, view is taken of leadership competence – which would include personal attributes, technical/professional competencies, values and attitudes, and conduct – toxic leaders are incompetent because they are not competent across all of the excellence domains of a well-rounded leader. The premise of this chapter is that the more comprehensive view of leadership competence should be taken. Therefore toxic leadership, regardless of the level of technical/professional competence and results attained, implies incompetence. The above implies that in viewing toxic leadership, due cognisance must be taken of both leadership conduct (= the process) and outcomes.[5]

The question of the relationship between (un)ethical and toxic leadership also arises. It could be argued that unethical leadership can be toxic but not predominantly so. However, toxic leadership equates fully to unethical leadership, if the unethical leadership is targeting people. Ethical and constructive (= non-toxic) leadership are highly related.[6]

The Make-up of Toxic Leadership and the Organisational Landscape

At least five building blocks making up toxic leadership and organisations can be distinguished: toxic preconditions; potentially toxic leadership conduct; toxic leadership archetypes; the toxic organisation; and toxic organisational archetypes. These building blocks are reciprocally

---

v   "Dark" is used in two ways in the literature. Firstly, to denote toxic, destructive or bad leadership (see footnote ii); or, secondly, to indicate hidden personality defects that can derail leaders and manifest themselves when leaders are under pressure or unobserved (cf. Hogan, 2016). The first use of "dark" is applicable here.

interdependent, and form a systemic, dynamic whole. Their overall interdependency will be discussed further in a later section of the chapter. Each building block is discussed next in turn.

Building block 1: Toxic Preconditions

Toxic preconditions refer to the conditions (or triggers) that create, reinforce and sustain favourable conditions for toxicity. At least four preconditions can be distinguished:[7]

- **Precondition 1: The External Context of the organisation.** *These are demands and requirements, real or imagined, within the operating arena of organisation, imposed on the organisation, the "spirit of the times" and/or contextual features.* For example, these may include a general spirit that people are merely cogs in a machine who can be exploited and abused at the organisation's leisure with no comeback or sanctions; real or subjectively perceived contextual uncertainty and instability resulting in an questionable dependency on a saviour leader; severe competition threatening the continued existence of the organisation; an economic downturn; a market collapse; a hostile takeover bid; the possible/ actual public exposure of an organisational irregularity; regulatory compliance pressure.
- **Precondition 2: Stakeholders** (for example, shareholders). *The expectations held and endorsements by parties who believe or have an interest and stake in the organisation.* For example, anything is acceptable in the pressure to satisfy frequently unrealistic shareholder needs, wants and goals, such as ever-increasing (unreasonable) profits and dividends.
- **Precondition 3: Leadership.** *The predispositions, socialisation and psychosocial maturity of the leadership of the organisation.* These include, for example, the attraction and retention by an organisation of leaders who manifest (mild/borderline) forms of psychopathology; have been socialised into unethical values and conduct while growing up; are psychosocially immature relative to the setting in which they have to function; and/or are mismatched to the requisite contextual complexity with which they have to deal, and therefore need to use any means to meet the contextual and performance requirements of their roles in order to survive.
- **Precondition 4: Internal Context of the organisation.** *The acceptability and condonation of toxic conduct in the organisation because of its culture: "This is the way we see, interpret and do things here"; poor governance; and profile of followers.* For example, these may include aggressive, abusive and coercive leadership conduct forming part of the organisation's very DNA, and the accepted way of conducting its daily business; lack of proper governance checks and balances; and toxic amenable followers, whether as passive, subservient conformers or active colluders.[8]

Building block 2: Potentially toxic leadership conduct

Potentially toxic leadership conduct encompasses leadership conduct that potentially contains the seeds of undermining the sense of dignity, self-worth and efficacy of an individual(s) and teams in the work setting. Table 6.1 gives a typology of typical toxic leadership conduct.[9] Any of the types of conduct listed in Table 6.1 may be manifested by leadership from time to time. It is postulated that it is only when this conduct takes on a certain dynamic by becoming a set (or institutionalised) pattern of conduct in the organisation that incidental toxic conduct becomes very present, very real toxic conduct. This topic will be addressed further in a later section.

Table 6.1: A typology of typical, potentially toxic leadership conduct

Type	Examples
Lack of Integrity	Deception; Bending rules to get results; Blaming others for own mistakes; Covering up own mistakes; Opportunism; Ethics and conduct unconnected; Lying
Demeaning/Devaluing	Personal attacks; Ridiculing; Mocking; Belittling; Disrespect; Inconsiderate; Character assassination
Punitive/Coercive	Rule by fear; Rule by insecurity; Favouritism; Selective distribution of rewards/recognition; Unreasonable, unrealistic personal/work demands; Ruthless elimination of all opposition: real or imagined
Manipulative/ Exploitive	Distortion of facts/reality to serve own ends; Backstabbing; Setting up persons against each other; Rumour mongering; Non-disclosure and/or selective release of vital information
Egocentric/Self-serving	Centre of universe; God's gift to mankind; Claimed sole source of credit/success; Self-promotion; Personal need satisfaction takes precedence; Own and organisational interests completely fused; Consummate self-promoter; Arrogance
Divisive/Elitist	Ostracising; In-Out group; Scape-goating; Marginalisation; Collusion
Abrasive/Abusive	Intimidation; Excessive/Misplaced anger; (Physical) acts of aggression; Harassment; Rudeness
Aloof/Distant	Disengaged; Disinterested; (Deliberate) Ignoring of concerns/ ideas/suggestions; Underestimation of the demands posed by challenges/setbacks on persons
Excessive control	Stifling of dissent; Suppressing (or downplaying) of criticism/ concerns; Micro-management; Over-rigid; Suspicious; Lack of trust; Source of all answers; Blind adherence to past success recipes; power hungry
Unpredictability/ Inconsistency	Mixed messages; Knee-jerk, hasty decisions; Quick fixes; (Frequent) directional changes without proper justification; Emotional volatility; Constant mood swings; Indecision; On-going crisis management

Toxic leadership in an organisation manifests itself in the seven habits of eminently unsuccessful leaders:[10]

- They arrogantly see themselves and their organisations as dominating in their context – they see themselves as the centre of the universe around which the universe turns every 24 hours.
- They identify their egos so closely with the organisation that there is no clear boundary between personal and organisational interests – they and the organisation are one, and serve one another.

- They seemingly have all the answers, frequently dazzling people with the speed and decisiveness with which they deal with issues.
- They ensure that everyone is 100% behind them, in the process ruthlessly eliminating any opposition – real or imagined.
- They are the consummate organisational spokespersons and spin doctors, often devoting the largest portion of their time to polishing their own and the organisation's images, which often are seen as the two sides of the same coin.
- They treat difficult obstacles lightly as temporary setbacks that will easily evaporate like mist before the sun because of their amazing brilliance and ability.
- They revert easily to previous success recipes, regardless of their appropriateness or not.

Building block 3: Toxic leadership archetypes

An archetype represents a set, ingrained personal pattern of conduct, characterising a specific leader, in this case toxicity; in other words, leaders with toxic personalities. Toxic conduct in their case has become and is their personality. Using the typology of typical, potentially toxic leadership conduct (see Table 6.2), Toxic Leadership Archetypes can be constructed. Five typical toxic leadership archetypes can be distinguished as proposed by myself and shown in Table 6.2.[vi] Frequently there is a high degree of overlap in toxic conduct between the archetypes. It is the *leitmotif* (= theme of conduct) that gives the conduct a different "colour".

Table 6.2: Toxic leadership archetypes

Toxic Leadership Archetypes	Leitmotif	Description	Predominant Toxic Conduct (see Table 6.1)
Cold Fish	Only the end results count, nothing else	The ends justifies the any means, however immoral. So any decision and action is justifiable in terms of the results desired	Lack of integrity; Demeaning/Devaluing; Punitive/Coercive; Abrasive/Abusive; Excessive control
Snake	The world is mine, and it serves me	The devious manipulation of everyone and situations in order to satisfy personal needs and aspirations, such as greed, status, power	Lack of integrity; Manipulative/ Exploitative; Egocentric/ Self-serving; Divisive/ Elitist; Unpredictability/ Inconsistency
Glory Seeker	Personal glory at all costs	Personal glory and public visibility at any cost, at all times regardless of any real, meaningful, personal contribution	Lack of integrity; Demeaning/Devaluing; Egocentric/Self- serving; Divisive/ Elitist; Unpredictability/ Inconsistency

---

vi For other typologies of toxic leadership archetypes, see for example, Babiak & Hare, 2006; Kellerman, 2004; Shaw, Erickson & Harvey, 2011; Tourish, 2013; Johnson & Fox, 2015.

Toxic Leadership Archetypes	Leitmotif	Description	Predominant Toxic Conduct (see Table 6.1)
Puppet Master (Power Monger)	Absolute control under all circumstances	Absolute, centralised control over everything and anyone, under all circumstances	Lack of integrity; Demeaning/Devaluing; Punitive/Coercive; Manipulative/Exploitative; Excessive control; Aloof/Distant
Monarch	Ruling my personal kingdom	Ruling the organisation as if it is his/her personal kingdom. Everything is unconditionally and unquestionably available for his/her personal use	Lack of integrity; Punitive/Coercive; Manipulative/Exploitative; Egocentric/Self-serving; Aloof/Distant

In order to arrive at a deeper understanding of the proposed Toxic Leadership Archetypes, given in Table 6.2, it is suggested that a set of underlying dimensions, with contrasting poles, can be distinguished for these archetypes onto which the Toxic Leadership Archetypes can be plotted. For example, the dimension of: Focus – Me versus the World; or Need – Glory versus Power. These dimensions represent the constituent elements of the archetypes. These archetypical dimensions with their contrasting poles are given in Figure 6.1.

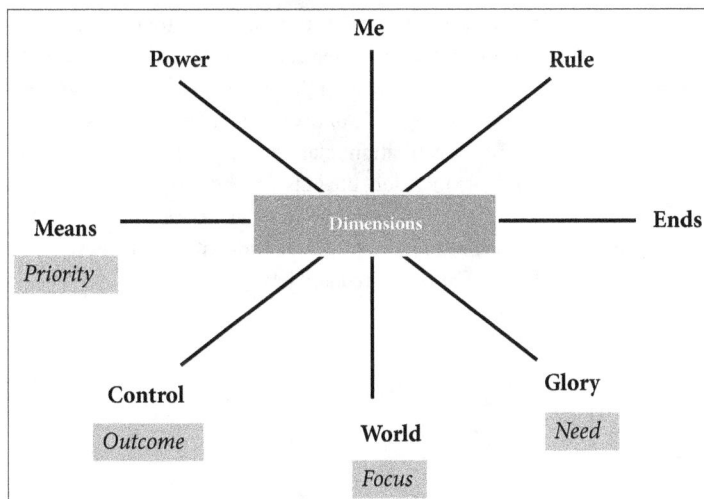

Figure 6.1: Suggested underlying dimensions of the toxic leadership archetypes

Table 6.3 plots the Leadership Toxic Archetypes proposed in Table 6.2 against the poles of the underlying dimensions given in Figure 6.1.

Table 6.3: The toxic leadership archetypes explicated in terms of their underlying dimensions

Dimensions	Cold fish	Snake	Glory seeker	Puppet master	Monarch
	The ends justifies the means	The world serves me	Personal glory at any cost	Absolute control under all circumstances	Ruling my personal kingdom
Focus	World	Me	Me	World	World
Priority	Means	Ends	Ends	Ends	Ends
Outcome	Control	Control	Rule	Control	Rule
Need	Power	Power	Glory	Power	Glory

According to Table 6.3, for example, the constituent elements of the Toxic Leadership Archetype "Snake" are: Me, Ends, Control and Power.

Tables 51.2 and 51.3, in conjunction with Figure 6.1, merely provide the basic skeletons of the Toxic Leadership Archetypes. Full-blown, fleshed-out profiles need to be developed of these archetypes through further research in order to understand in-depth the nature, dynamics and development of the above proposed Toxic Leadership Archetypes fully.

Building block 4: Toxic organisation

The Toxic Organisation is the consequence of institutionalised Toxic Leadership Conduct. Inversely, the Toxic Organisation engenders and reinforces Toxic Leadership Conduct, as well as Toxic Leadership Archetypes, in this way creating the space in which both can germinate and flourish. Consequently, a vicious, recurring cycle of toxicity is created and sustained.

The outcomes of the Toxic Organisation manifest themselves in the interdependent domains of leader, follower, work, organisation, life outside work, and context with the domains of leader and followers sitting centrally, and having so to speak knock-on effects. These domains and their relative positions are given in Figure 6.2. Over time these outcomes may settle into a vicious cycle of toxicity which has to be countered and broken.

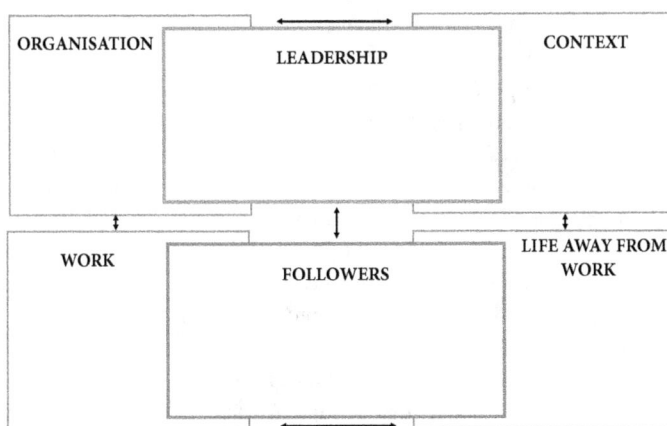

Figure 6.2: Interdependent domains in which toxicity outcomes may be manifested

Table 6.4 provides the outcomes of the Toxic Organisation within the domains of leader, follower, work, organisation, life outside work, and context.[11]

Table 6.4: Typical outcomes of the toxic organisation

LEADERSHIP	FOLLOWERS
• Leadership alienation, mistrust and resistance	• Negative emotional moods and mood swings: anger, despair, despondency, frustration, pessimism, aggression • Destructive and counterproductive conduct • Unethical, deviant conduct: theft, fraud, sabotage, corruption • Poor physical and psychological well-being and health • Withdrawal conduct: high absenteeism and turnover
ORGANISATION	**WORK**
• Organisational power struggles, turf wars and negative organisational politics • Negative organisational climate • Low morale • Organisational dis-identification and low organisational commitment	• Employee physical and emotional disengagement and withdrawal, for example, satisficing performance (= doing the minimum required); lack of contribution • Feelings of disempowerment • Unproductive and meaningless work • Low work satisfaction
CONTEXT	**LIFE OUTSIDE WORK**
(Community, stakeholders, society) • Frequent legal action against organisation • Organisation triggered disasters • Public mistrust • Poor organisation reputation and image • Little stakeholder social capital and goodwill • Negative messaging in social media	• General life dissatisfaction and poor general quality of life • Negative impact on family life

Building block 5: Toxic organisational archetypes

Analogous to the Toxic Leadership Archetypes, it can be argued that Toxic Organisational Archetypes can become institutionalised into organisations; in other words, organisations with-so-to-speak Toxic "Personalities". A Toxic Organisational Archetype is one where toxic conduct has taken on an institutionalised and legitimised pattern of seeing, interpreting and doing things in an organisation. Such a pattern frequently is encoded and formalised into organisational policies, design, structures, systems, and culture; or functions "under the water" as to the way in which the organisation truly functions. Frequently, the above-discussed Toxic Leadership Archetypes are projected onto and engineered into the very DNA of the organisation. An organisation infected by Toxic Organisational Archetype is a terminally ill organisation with chronic toxic symptoms, analogous to the "sick building syndrome".

At least six basic types of Toxic Organisational Archetypes can be distinguished – given in Table 6.5 – and identified in terms of the description of an archetype being the answer to an insurmountable challenge the organisation perceives and believes it is facing; a thematic description of the archetype; and the typical toxic leadership archetypes that can potentially populate and flourish in this toxic organisation.[12] Recursively, these organisations may commence attracting, selecting, and developing leadership that fits these Toxic Organisational Archetypes, in this way strengthening the vicious toxic cycle. An example would be the Paranoid Organisation seeking out Cold Fish Leaders. Such organisations may also seek out members who are willing and compliant to submit to and be abused by toxic leadership and organisations, in other words, subservient, toxic followers. The typical organisational policies, design, structures, systems and culture expressive of these Toxic Organisational Archetypes are not covered here.

Table 6.5: Toxic organisational archetypes

TOXIC ORGANISATIONAL ARCHETYPES	RESPONDING TO	THEMATIC DESCRIPTION	TYPICAL TOXIC LEADERSHIP ARCHETYPES
Paranoid organisation	Anxiety of unknown	An organisation infused by mistrust and suspicion that sees and responds to everything and everyone, both internally and externally, as a threat and danger to its continued safety and security	Cold Fish
Compulsive organisation	Unpredictability and ambiguity	An organisation that is over-planned and over-programmed down to the finest detail in order to minimise, but preferably to eliminate, any surprises, uncertainty and vagueness	Puppet Master
Hyperactive organisation	Accelerating, radical change	An organisation that is directionless, unfocused and impulsive, like an adolescent, acting for the sake for acting in response to changing events, in the belief that any action is better than no action at all	Glory Seeker

TOXIC ORGANISATIONAL ARCHETYPES	RESPONDING TO	THEMATIC DESCRIPTION	TYPICAL TOXIC LEADERSHIP ARCHETYPES
Deflated (or Depressed) organisation	Incapacitating fear of known	An organisation pervaded by a sense of impotence, helplessness and despair because it is infected by inactivity, passivity and a lack of energy	Glory Seeker in form of Saviour/Messiah or Disaster Monger
Delusional organisation	Overpowering complexity, interdependency and variety	An organisation which, through its insulation from and distortion of reality, has created a make-believe world in order avoid the real (or true) reality that is too overwhelmingly intricate to face up to and deal with	Monarch
Conscienceless organisation	Opportunistic exploitation of grey areas between competing/vague value systems	An organisation that has lost the ability to distinguish between right and wrong, good and bad, both internally and externally, because of self-centricity, lack of integrity, opportunism and immorality	Snake

To summarise: it has been proposed that the make-up of the Toxic Leadership and Organisation consists of five building blocks: Toxic Preconditions; Potentially Toxic Leadership Conduct; Toxic Leadership Archetypes; Toxic Organisations; and Toxic Organisational Archetypes.

The Dynamics of Toxic Leadership

The proposed building blocks of the Toxic Leadership Landscape provide only a static picture of Toxic Leadership. All of the potentially toxic styles of leadership conduct (given in Figure 6.1) are displayed at some time or other by all leaders with their consequential toxic individual and organisational manifestations.

It is argued that potentially toxic leadership conduct only becomes truly toxic if and when the **Toxicity Leadership Conduct Index (TLCI)** in an organisation is high. A high TLCI implies that the potentially toxic conduct as depicted in Table 6.1 has become a set pattern of conduct in the organisation: a shared way of seeing, interpreting and doing things on an ongoing basis.

TLCI is the outcome of the *multiplication* of four conduct variables: **TLCI = Intensity x Frequency x Range x Duration of Toxic Leadership Conduct.** According to the formula: (i) the *higher* the *intensity* and (ii) the *frequency* of the leadership conduct; (iii) the wider the *range* of the leadership conduct (that is, how many of these types of conduct are manifested); and (iv) the longer the *duration* of the leadership conduct, the higher the actual toxicity of leadership conduct becomes.

If all of the conduct variables are high, one is dealing with full-blown toxic leadership which would create and sustain a toxic organisation, and in turn would reinforce toxic leadership. As toxic leadership conduct increasingly becomes institutionalised, and takes on the form of manifesting itself in the selection and cloning of toxic leadership archetypes as ideal types, and also toxic followers as a consequence, a full-blown toxic organisation would emerge, expressed in the above-discussed organisational toxic archetypes. These evolving dynamics would further push up the TLCI, resulting in an entrenched, vicious, toxicity cycle in the organisation, which would lead to the implosion and ultimate demise of the organisation (see Table 6.4 dealing with toxic outcomes).

An Integrated, Systemic and Dynamic Map of Toxic Leadership and the Organisational Landscape

Figure 6.3 depicts an integrated, systemic and dynamic map of the toxic leadership and organisation, integrating the above discussion.

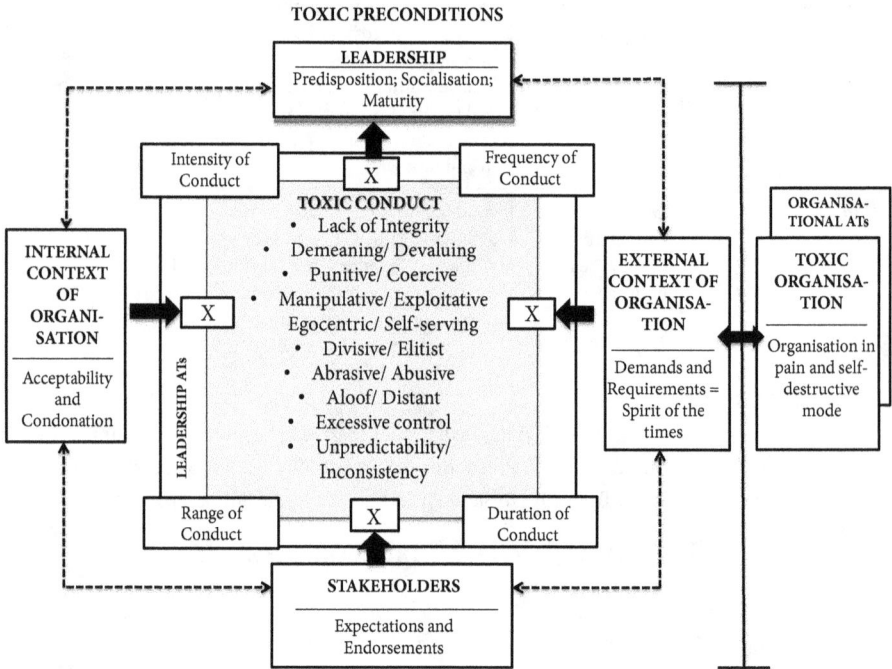

Figure 6.3: An integrated, systemic and dynamic map of the toxic leadership and organisation
Note: ATs = Archetypes; the two-way arrows in the figure denote reciprocal interaction

According to Figure 6.3, the likelihood of toxic leadership and organisation becoming a reality is the consequence of:

- A high prevalence of the four **toxic preconditions**, individually and severally, creating the context in which leadership and organisational toxicity can germinate, flourish and be sanctioned;
- A high **toxicity leadership conduct index**, represented by the multiplicative function (given by the Xs in the figure) of the four conduct variables (for example, intensity, duration), covering the potential toxic leadership conduct given in the centre of the map (for example, lack of integrity, demeaning/devaluing);
- A high presence of *toxic **leadership archetypes*** (for example, monarch) in the organisation for whom the potentially toxic leadership conduct is their natural way of doing things, hence pushing up the TLCI;
- Resulting in a severe, ongoing levels of *organisational pain as manifested in toxic outcomes* (for example, leader mistrust);

- Which is heightened further by the reinforcing manifestation of a **toxic organisational archetype(s)** (for example, a hyperactive organisation); and finally,
- Given the presence of an organisational toxic archetype, the further **spreading of the Toxic Leadership Conduct and Archetypes** already prevalent in the organisation like a virus, with the rapidly heightening chance of eventual organisational implosion.

The description above hence describes the coming about, evolution and trajectory of toxic leadership and organisations.

Identifying Toxic Leadership and Organisations

Toxic leadership and organisations can be identified by at least the following indicators again w.r.t. the interacting domains of leader, follower, work, organisation, life outside work, and context as given in Table 6.6.[13] As the incidence and level of toxicity in the organisation increase, more of these indicators will be manifested, like a virus spreading through and affecting a body.

Table 6.6: Indicators of toxic leadership and organisations

LEADERSHIP	FOLLOWERS
• *All-knowing, all-wise, all-powerful,* claiming *absolute power and authority* resulting in asymmetrical power relations in organisation • Primarily driving *personal agendas for self-benefit and self-glory,* leveraged from the power of their positions, in the process down playing stakeholder needs and interests • The virtual exclusive use of *'me' or the 'royal we'* language • Attributing – and communicating correspondingly – all *successes and achievements* to own personal efforts. Shifting all *failures and under-achievements* to others and circumstances; or, covering up or rationalising them away • Excessive *self-promotion* • An *entitlement attitude* • *Unpredictability, moodiness*	• Creation of an unbridgeable *Us-Them divide* by leadership where followers have to cope on their own with little assistance from leadership apart from leadership relentlessly demanding ever-increasing achievement and ignoring followers' welfare • Followers reduced to being merely *numbers* and judged only for their *usefulness* only • Leadership always *playing the person* and not the ball • No *critique tolerated or disagreement allowed* with only one right opinion: that of leadership • No upward *feedback* to leadership sought/allowed • *Compliance* is rewarded. Mavericks or dissidents penalised, side-lined or 'eliminated' • Followers feel *demeaned, worthless, incompetent* in their interactions with leadership • Leadership surrounds-themselves with *weak, non-critical, benefit-seeking followers*: passive, 'yes'-persons
ORGANISATION	WORK
• Emergence of a *leadership cult and deification of leadership* • *Unethical toxic conduct* allowed, glorified, left unpunished down played and/or normalised • Centralised *control of intelligence and information* with • Deliberate *inability/unwillingness to share* • Absence of leadership during *crises* with the disclaiming of any accountability: others are to be blamed	• Claiming *personal credit* for followers' achievements, or hijacking their achievement for personal gain • High follower *disengagement*. Resistance to going the "extra mile" • Inability of leadership to form *cohesive and stable team* around him/herself

CONTEXT	LIFE OUTSIDE WORK
(Community, stakeholders, society) • Poor *organisational image and reputation* • Lack of *public transparency* • Intense *spin doctoring*	• Choice of *outside life* above being at work • Speaking intensely and continuously negatively of *organisation and its leadership* • Little or no *loyalty* to organisation and its leadership

Reducing the Likelihood of Toxic Leadership and Organisations

The likelihood of toxic leadership and organisations can be significantly reduced through at least the following actions within the interdependent domains of leader, follower, work, organisation, life outside work, and context, as given in Table 6.7.[14] Or, if toxicity is present, these actions can be used to detoxify the organisation. For the highest impact, a comprehensive strategy and contingency plan have to be crafted, covering all of the domains. A single action will in a single domain have little if any effect. It may even have a negative backlash.

Table 6.7: Possible actions to reduce likelihood of toxic leadership and organisations

LEADERSHIP	FOLLOWERS
• An *intensive leadership selection* process during which interviewees have to indicate their decisions/actions regarding situations in which they are forced to make choices between their personal, others' and the organisation's interests, as well as ethical choices • Inclusion of compliance with the leadership charter (see below) as a *key performance area* in leadership's performance contract with regular assessment, also by peers and followers	• Strong, courageous *followers* • *Ethical enablement*

ORGANISATION	WORK
• Set up an organisational *leadership charter* clearly outlining acceptable and unacceptable leadership conduct against which followers and co-leaders can appeal • Build strong and widespread *capacity* for ethical courage, judgement, ability and decision making in organisation • Institutionalise *ethical leadership, culture and climate* in the organisation, and assess on a regular basis • Implement sound *governance* with robust checks and balances • Publicise *leadership role models* worthy of emulating • Public recognition of *constructive and ethical conduct*	• Ongoing surveys of followers' *levels of work engagement* • Real work *enablement and empowerment*: delegate power and authority to where action has to be taken • Establish *information and intelligence* rich work setting

CONTEXT	LIFE OUTSIDE WORK
(Community, stakeholders, society)	• Equip followers to be consummate *marketers of organisation*: what it is, stands for, is doing and achieving
• Bring diverse *stakeholder voices and scrutiny* into organisation	
• Build *public transparency* for leadership and organisational decisions and actions	
• Regular assessment of level of *social capital* with critical stakeholders	
• Craft and roll out *social media* strategy	

Conclusion

The contention of this chapter is that there is evidence for the growing cancer of toxic leadership and organisations, endangering in no uncertain terms the well-being of organisational members, compromising future, sustainable organisational performance and success, as well as threatening the very continued existence of organisations. A dire need therefore exists for organisations to recognise this growing cancer; to understand it in an informed, holistic and systemic way; and to deal with it systemically, expeditiously, and preferably proactively by mitigating the likelihood of toxic leadership and organisations germinating.

Endnotes

1   Aasland, Skogstad, Notelaers, Nielsen & le Einarsen, 2010; Gaddis & Foster, 2015; Hogan, 2016; Johnson & Fox, 2015, p 7, 13; Schyns & Schilling, 2013; Tourish, 2013.

2   Appelbaum, & Roy-Girard, 2007; Goldman, 2006; Johnson & Fox, 2015; Kets de Vries, 2012; Krasikova, Green & LeBreton, 2013; Padilla, Hogan & Kaiser, 2007; Tourish, 2013; Thoroughgood, Padilla, Hunter & Tate, 2012; Schyns & Schilling, 2013; Walton, 2008.

3   Appelbaum, & Roy-Girard, 2007; Aasland, Skogstad, Notelaers, Nielsen & le Einarsen, 2010; Goldman, 2006; Harris, 2016; Johnson & Fox, 2015; Krasikova, Green & LeBreton, 2013; Maheshwari & Mehta, 2013; Reed, 2004; Shaw, Erickson & Harvey, 2011; Schyns & Schilling, 2013; Tourish, 2013; Walton, 2008.

4   Padilla, Hogan & Kaiser, 2007; Thoroughgood, Padilla, Hunter & Tate, 2012; Walton, 2008.

5   Babiak & Hare, 2006; Hogan, 2016; Krasikova 2013; Padilla, Hogan & Kaiser, 2007; Reed, 2004.

6   Johnson & Fox, 2015; Padilla, Hogan & Kaiser, 2007.

7   Appelbaum & Roy-Girard, 2007; Goldman, 2006; Johnson & Fox, 2015; Kets de Vries, 2012; Krasikova, Green & LeBreton, 2013; Padilla, Hogan & Kaiser, 2007; Tourish, 2013; Thoroughgood, Padilla, Hunter & Tate, 2012; Schyns & Schilling, 2013; Walton, 2008.

8   *cf.* Thoroughgood, Padilla, Hunter & Tate, 2012.

9   *cf.* Aasland, Skogstad, Notelaers, Nielsen & le Einarsen, 2010; Babiak & Hare, 2006; Gaddis & Foster, 2015; Goldman, 2006; Harris, 2016; Johnson & Fox, 2015; Kets de Vries, 2012; Krasikova , Green & LeBreton, 2013; Maheshwari & Mehta, 2013; Ouimet, 2010; Padilla, Hogan & Kaiser, 2007; Thoroughgood, Padilla, Hunter & Tate, 2012; Schmidt, 2008; Schyns & Schilling, 2013.

10 Finkelstein, 2003.

11 Appelbaum, & Roy-Girard, 2007; Babiak & Hare,2006; Goldman,2006; Johnson & Fox, 2015; Maheshwari & Mehta, 2013; Ouimet, 2010; Padilla, Hogan & Kaiser, 2007; Shaw, Erickson & Harvey, 2011; Schyns & Schilling. 2013; Walton, 2008.

12 For example, Kets de Vries & Miller, 1984.

13 *cf.* Tourish, 2013; Johnson & Fox, 2015; Kets de Vries, 2012; Krasikova , Green & LeBreton, 2013.

14 Babiak & Hare, 2006; Johnson & Fox, 2015; Kets de Vries, 2012; Krasikova, Green & LeBreton, 2013; Reed, 2004.

References

Aasland, MS, Skogstad, A, Notelaers, G, Nielsen, B & le Einarsen, S. 2010. 'The prevalence of destructive leadership behaviour'. *British Journal of Management*, 21:438–452.

Appelbaum, SH & Roy-Girard, D. 2007. 'Toxins in the workplace: Effect on organizations and employees'. *Corporate Governance: The International Journal of Business in Society*, 7(1):17-28.

Babiak, P & Hare, RD. 2006. *Snakes in suits. When psychopaths go to work.* New York, NY: HarperCollins

Finkelstein, S. 2003. *Why smart executives fail.* New York, NY: Portfolio.

Gaddis, BH & Foster, JL. 2015. 'Meta-analysis of dark side personality characteristics and critical work behaviours among leaders across the globe: Findings and implications for leadership development and executive coaching'. *Applied Psychology: An International Review,* 64(1):25–54.

Goldman. A. 2006. 'High toxicity leadership'. *Journal of Managerial Psychology*, 21(8):733–746.

Hogan, R. 2016. 'Reflections on the dark side'. *Talent Quarterly*, iv, 1–4.

Harris, P. 2016. 'Crazy, stupid, mean'. *Talent Quarterly*, iv, 13–19.

Johnson, CE & Fox. G. 2015. *Meeting the ethical challenges of leadership.* Los Angeles, CA: Sage.

Kellerman, B. 2004. *Bad leadership: What it is, how it happens, why it matters.* Boston, MA: Harvard Business School Press.

Kets de Vries, MFR. 2012. *The psychopath in the C Suite: Redefining the SOB.* Faculty and Research Paper 22012/119/EFE, Fontainebleau, Insead.

Kets de Vries, MFR & Miller, D. 1984. *The neurotic organization: Diagnosing and changing counterproductive styles of management.* San Francisco, CA: Jossey-Bass.

Krasikova, D, Green, SG & LeBreton, JM. 2013. 'Destructive leadership: A theoretical review, integration and future research agenda'. *Journal of Management*, 39:1308–1338.

Maheshwari, GC & Mehta, S. 2013. 'Consequence of toxic leadership on employee job satisfaction and organizational commitment'. *The Journal of Contemporary Management Research*, 8(2):1–23.

Ouimet, G. 2010. 'Dynamics of narcissistic leadership in organisations'. *Journal of Managerial Psychology*, 25(7):713–726.

Padilla, A, Hogan, R. & Kaiser, RB. 2007. 'The toxic triangle: destructive leaders, susceptible followers and conducive environments'. *The Leadership Quarterly*, 18:176–194.

Reed, GE. 2004. 'Toxic leadership'. *Military Review*, 67–71, July–August.

Shaw, JB, Erickson, A & Harvey, M. 2011. 'A method for measuring destructive leadership and identifying types of destructive leaders in organizations'. *The Leadership Quarterly*, 22:575–590.

Schmidt, AA. 2008. 'Development and validation of the toxic leadership scale'. Unpublished Masters thesis, University of Maryland College Park.

Schyns, B & Schilling, J. 2013. 'How bad are the effects of bad leaders? A meta-analysis of destructive leadership and its outcomes'. *The Leadership Quarterly*, 24:138–158.

Thoroughgood, CN, Padilla, A, Hunter, ST & Tate, BW. 2012. 'The susceptible circle: A taxonomy of followers associated with destructive leadership'. *The Leadership Quarterly*, 23:897–917.

Tourish, D. 2013. *The dark side of transformational leadership. A critical perspective.* London, UK: Routledge.

Veldsman, TH. 2014. 'The growing cancer in organisations: Toxicity'. *Human Capital Review*, March 2014.

Walton, M. 2008) 8. 'In consideration of a toxic workplace: A suitable place for treatment'. In A Kinder, R Hughes & CL Cooper (eds). *Employee well-being support.* New York, NY: John Wiley. 9–24.

Chapter 7

A LEADERSHIP LAMENT

Johann Coetzee

When approached to contribute a chapter to this book, I requested the editors to exclude me from the list of invited authors. As I continue to work with leaders in executive encounters (not coaching), I discover compelling and convincing evidence that the spirit and culture within an organisation is not determined by leaders, their leading, or their general leadership effect, but by personality and character. This realisation has guided me toward discovering the nature and effect of the *corporate soul*, being the guiding set of commandments which regulate conscience and conduct. I continue to search for answers as to why corporate crooks flourish, bad people rise to the top, and the majority of employees slavishly endure abuse.

In this chapter I am unashamedly subjective, deliberately confrontational, and evidentially open about where I lacked the courage to say it all before.

In this chapter about leadership issues at the front line, I elect not to report on, describe or espouse scientific perspectives on leadership research and publications. This has been recorded exhaustively by pioneer researchers, and in impressive autobiographies of noted leaders. I decided rather to invite executives whom I have had the privilege of counselling, coaching and treating in therapy over the past 35 years to co-author this chapter, focusing on the auto-ethnographical evidence shared during such sessions. It is what I have been told, taught and witnessed at the critical leader interface that I have attempted to integrate into a synopsis, obviously also tinged with a dimension of subjectivity and cynicism. I take licence to "tell it the way it is" (even if this calls for compromising literary finesse).

In order to authenticate the author somewhat, it is pertinent to record that I have counselled and coached in excess of 28 000 executives throughout my protracted career. I have worked on the inside with most of the top 100 companies in South Africa, facilitating leadership and executive development programmes, organising renewal interventions, and discussing corporate ethics, as well as undertaking forensic investigations. The compelling information and evidence which emerged from these engagements has been distilled into this chapter.

Leadership and Organisational Pathology

There is a significant difference between becoming a leader, leading, and leadership. Many apparently suitable candidates become leaders. But there is no evidence of their leadership, or any effective leading. They become incumbents by appointment and aspiration, and have even studied the subject of leadership comprehensively. They emerge from business schools with MBA qualifications and return there to attend executive development programmes (EDPs). Yet many remain the reprehensible personalities and characters they essentially are.

Yes, leading, leadership and leader are more about character than charisma, more about intrinsic virtue than values capable of being listed and recited, and much more than the semantics that (sheepishly) depict codes of conduct, credos, visions and missions.

I was surprised when my Masters students challenged me as I was regurgitating the attributes of the ideal leader and the contemporary theories of, and publications on, leadership. They asked me: "Why do individuals who are the total opposite of the ideal leader specification make it to the top, and then cause total organisational havoc?" The debate that followed resulted in a snap assessment about leader acceptability and respectable behaviour manifested by their leaders. Eighty percent reported that the dichotomy between the ideal definition and description of an authentic leader, and the contrary version they were at the time enduring, refuted the credence of my attempt to teach them. In fact, to continue to transpose the ideal theoretical model would discredit any such attempt and cause a significant disconnect between teacher and student. Using the luxury of inversion, I enquired why eighty percent of the class tolerated such a *leaderless* situation. The reply: "It pays the bills and the children's school fees!"

Yes, corporate conformism is the way in which those who are actually disconnected from the organisational ethic and (so-called) leadership often pander to individuals they actually despise. In this dishonest demonstration of (pseudo) continued loyalty and support, they falsely signal apparent support and approval. The compounded lie now becomes the leadership model, while seniority, status and stature of such leadership continue to flourish, and are even more generously rewarded.

The ideal leader and leadership

To define the ideal leader and leadership is easy and even over-stated. The skill of stringing an array of superlative leadership characteristics together has been perfected by all the noted and respected global researchers and authors. The predominance of normative dimensions as typical and preferred descriptors are as impressive as they are potentially disqualifying and disappointing. Truth, Trust, Integrity, Honesty, Consistency, *blah-blah-blah*. These (and more) spiritual semantics often actually become the leader disqualifiers. It is like passing the written exam on the subject but flunking the practical.

Knowing about leadership, being appointed into the lofty position, and enjoying all the incumbent benefits and *power*, do not comprise the essential set of criteria. Moreover, I believe that modern, intelligent and essentially self-directed people have become sceptical about conventional leadership theories and such leaders. Modern people are no more led. They will join, co-operate and collaborate with convincing direction and logic, presented by individuals who are authentic in purpose, endeavour, and inspiring effect by virtue of credibility. And they will participate spontaneously only where common courtesy and basic human decency are evident.

The corporate cabaret

The Corporate Cabaret is not actually entertainment. It is tragic and pathological. Yet the organisational stage is so often invaded by clowns and stooges who entertain some other coerced fools, but irritate most. The escalating phenomenon of BULLYING within schools has arrested the minds of the media and the concerned hearts of parents and teachers. Sadly, and strangely, the corporate bullies do not receive similar attention or ridicule as a result of the power interplay which renders the recipients thereof not only vulnerable to, but also tolerant of, such abuse. The power and authority of providing employment and sustaining such a prized property in an economy where unemployment is rife at all levels makes people suffer the abuse and the bullying. Resistance and retaliation typically trigger that (false) power, inevitably resulting in separation.

The stories shared by executives, particularly in exit counselling and therapy, are actually too ghastly to process against the background of innocent people becoming the victims of tyrants who survive and flourish within such (sick) organisations. When considering the descriptors of the soulless organisation, they actually also serve as the indicators of heartless bullies who thrive in their obliterating onslaught on vulnerable people, yet continue to derive their warped gratification from such reprehensible power display. The fact that such abuse is mostly tolerated by vulnerable people also conceals such pathological conduct. Moreover, such power-predisposed personalities thrive on the demise of the victims, as they gloat in false victory. These characters are not leaders at all. They are dictators suffering from a strange dimension of inferiority, who exploit the institutional stratification to exert themselves while unaware of their actual weakness. Sadly, they mostly survive, are even promoted, and receive more handsome rewards.

The mutual protectionism within the inner circle is the despicable incubator in which such bullies' successes are bred and nurtured. These debutants pander to the behavioural models of their principals, and in turn become the champions of their blemished protégés. Unfair budget objectives, cruel austerity impositions, unilateral decisions of a personal nature (such as refusing and cancelling leave), and personal and performance ratings of such subjectivity that they damage image as well as future career prospects, are but a few examples. The corrupt system allows this conduct to exist and to continue, while those who fear the dire consequences of remonstration suffer in silence while the bullies reign.

There is no such thing as organisation behaviour. An organisation as an entity does not generate conduct – people behave. Such dominant individual and collective behaviour constitutes the *behaviour* of the organisation. Likewise, you cannot enrich a marriage. Individuals (partners) have to become more attractive in behaviour, and less worthy of rejection in relational conduct in order to establish the basis for repair and adjusted future conduct. The consequence is an improved relationship.

Organisations as terrible places

Organisations are terrible because well-intentioned people assemble there with good motives, and then become blemished by the inescapable toxicity organisations succeed in generating. Having spent the past forty years working as an Industrial and Organisational Psychologist, I worked very hard to effect real transformation and change, but achieved little. Most organisations practise the actual reverse of what they state as their sense of purpose, moral corporate call, and virtuous motive and intent. People who unconditionally sing the praises of organisations are few and far between. Executives criticise the commitment and contribution of *the people*. The very same people despise executives removed from operational realities, yet earning (receiving) fifty times the wages of those people. This corporate crevasse constitutes the gap between the *haves* and the *have-nots* that serves as the agenda for incessant gossip.

I stopped coaching executives five years ago. True executives *are coached*, particularly through constructive *self*-development and positive *self*-esteem. Mature executive encounters replaced stereotypical meetings during which the sensitive and unspeakable become topics, and complex issues constructive debate. These unconditional encounters inform my perspectives now. It is fascinating to discover that the very custodians of organisational values simultaneously experience and announce disenchantment with the very same institution which they philosophically promote, yet morally endure.

The objective here is not to trash organisations, nor question their fundamental intent. After all, if it were not for organisations as employers, then job and wealth creation just would not happen. The issue disclosed here, and the question asked, is: why do the noble and universally respected motive and intent become so vulnerable when corrupting forces are allowed, or even inadvertently ignored? If employees have to continue to flaunt corporate commitment, because if not also masqueraded, it can be career limiting, then such sick organisational cultures will continue to generate frightened slaves. Moreover, if the truth is feared because of the dire consequence of challenging the lie, then leadership is inauthentic and such an organisation becomes a feudal space.

Leadership virtues and attributes

Given my lifelong exposure to, and coaching and counselling of executives, I reflected on the most outstanding personalities in four categories of leadership virtue and attributes. In doing so, I not only allowed subjectivity, but also incorporated information received from peers and other colleagues obtained via a specifically developed leader effectiveness inventory. I have restricted the results to the seven most prominent characteristics, but in no specific order. The one notable paradox which emerged from the table is the phenomenon that leaders who are universally despised are also very often successful and even followed, owing to the fear of evoking their wrath and subsequently being victimised. Table 7.1 provides an overview of leadership virtue and attributes.

Table 7.1: Four categories of outstanding personalities of leadership virtue and attributes

Genuine	Effective	Revered	Despised
Humane	Uniting	Followed	Feared
Personable	Inspirational	Remembered	Egotistical
Approachable	Successful	Emulated	Suspect
Humble	Visionary	Respected	Mysterious
Consistent	Strategic	Consulted	Insensitive
Dependable	Wise	Authentic	Tolerated
Honest	Disciplined	Generous	Successful

Bad leaders are actually and fundamentally bad people. It is the rotten human factor within a leader that makes him/her shout, swear, oppress and ridicule others. They allow anger and temper to rule and dominate within their perceived power domain. They successfully relegate everyone into subservience. Eventually, when out of favour with their condoning peers and principals, they turn on them as well.

Classic examples are found in politics and leaders of countries. Some of the worst human beings have made it into the highest office and then succeed to entice and unite party political support and *crony* endorsement. It is actually unfathomable to note how such reprehensible (so-called) statesmen rally support and coerce intelligent people to sanction such conduct as if it represents preferred leadership. More examples are apparent in churches, governments, corporate enterprises, welfare institutions, sports agencies, and cultural organisations. Many names spring to mind! How do such buffoons and crooks rise to leadership positions in the first place? How do they muster support and favour until they are eventually exposed for who they really and truly are, and then collapse while their historical support spectacularly disappears? The media is full of these examples daily. We need to become far more critical in the adjudication of candidatures and remain morally vigilant as incumbency progresses. Some of the strongest and most astute *leaders* have feet of clay, and hearts and minds of mortar.

Revealing the Corporate Soul

The soul is that mystical sanctum where the deepest beliefs, thoughts, conscience and judgement are shaped and stored. It is a place and condition where values are defined and released and where character emerges. The soul is the essence of one's being. It is as private as it is precious. Even the absence of soulfulness still constitutes the condition of every unique soul. An organisation cannot actually possess soul, as it cannot behave. An organisation does not have a conscience or a character, and there is therefore actually no such thing as organisation behaviour.

People behave! It is such unique conduct, decision-making, judgement and recorded values and virtues that ultimately constitute the corporate soul. But influential people, and their sapiential power and influence, cause others to conform and endorse so-called top-down philosophies and guidelines. Even worse, when ownership, seniority and power (status and stature) corroborate, then the situation assumes omnipotence of devastating proportions. The corporate soul is the product of personalities. It is ever-evolving and always subject and subordinate to the style and preference of those in high office. If the CEO propagates transcendental meditation as conducive to lucid decision-making, then slavish cohorts buy the book and quote from it. If his/her successor believes it to be nonsense, and builds a corporate gymnasium instead, then the slavish conformists buy track suits and CEO-like exercise apparel. Likewise, if parents prefer pink as a dominant colour in their home, country music as a favourite genre, and pasta as their food of choice, then the family has this inculcated into them. It becomes the soul of the home. If children must keep quiet during dinner and Sunday afternoons, because daddy is resting, then the tyrant rules and the rest pander. While in such an inescapable culture, it is mostly endured, but later is typically despised and definitely not emulated, or replicated. It is a dark soul to be forgotten.

Reputation as feature of the corporate soul

Reputation is an interesting feature of the corporate soul. Why would the majority of consumers prefer to buy a product from a particular organisation, regardless of price? What is it that sparks such irrational loyalty and enduring trust? Is it vested in the organisational name, logo, results, prominence, market share, or tradition? Or is it a particular prominent personality or collection of people (Exco or board) who cultivate patronage? Whatever the answer is, it is the essence of the corporate soul in perception and action. These intrinsic dimensions of the soul are as silent as they are *loud*. Without being announced or flaunted, they become known, and have an impact on the hearts and minds of the recipients thereof. Prominent authentic people are the propagators of such moral virtue.

One is inclined to think, and even accept, that everything associated with the soul is good, pure and even *holy*. However, often purported good souls are received and judged to be rotten because of the toxicity of such a soul. Sadly, there is abundant evidence of so-called good companies found to be engaged in untoward conduct, completely in conflict with the stated corporate commandments. Again, it is not the organisation which behaves badly, but people in authoritative positions who sanction wayward decisions. Collusion is but a single example of such soulless conduct. The culprit is not the woeful establishment, but those in command and their peculiar behaviours. The Corporate Soul is blemished because individuals are soulless and become custodians of the lie. Shareholders typically do not mind executives who are rude, cruel, dishonest, and unprofessional, as long as they influence handsome dividends. So, too, many recipients of good yields prefer not to question the methods used to arrive at that point. Not surprisingly, during a debate on ethics, when a definition of this ingredient of the corporate soul was being debated, two eventual definitions emerged:

- Ethics is a matter of opinion.
- Ethics is a matter of affordability.

Defining the corporate soul

Not a matter of the absolute truth at work, because in a world of realities and pragmatism, other forces prevail, and must be factored into a workable definition. So, compromise is the issue here, and not the irrepressible soul.

While on an excursion to an African country to negotiate a lucrative potential transaction, the *moral terms* of transaction were established and enforced, resulting in the CEO walking away from the deal, not being prepared to pay the bribe. Half of the team agreed with and supported the CEO, while the other half disagreed and questioned his unilateral decision-making. Yet they all co-authored the moral charter of the company.

Now define the Corporate Soul!

When I was employed within the corporates during the first ten years of my career, I too saluted the corporate gods who were so clever, successful and honest. Later, as a consultant to organisations all over the world, I was mostly engaged in psychological work in organisations, endeavouring to help make workplaces a happier space. I mostly failed, because strange people were in charge, driven by motives and aspirations actually in contrast with the values and codes of conduct they espoused and seemingly believed in.

Since commencing a practice of executive encounter, I meet with executives who willingly and candidly share the real information regarding the inner circle, the corner office, and themselves. Startling stuff! The stuff that constitutes the real corporate soul and the authors of and actors in it. Table 7.2 presents some stock topics and exclamations.

Table 7.2: Executive emotions in encounters

• *Should we do the deal?*	• *I actually hate the bright life.*
• *He has to go, but I cannot fire him.*	• *What is balance and priority really?*
• *I made a mistake here.*	• *I'm not growing – I'm just busy being*
• *I've had enough, but can't afford to leave.*	*successful.*
• *I'm starting to show stress and frustration.*	• *I'm engaged in a marginal thing. How do I get out of it?*
• *It's dangerous here.*	• *I'm battling with some painful regrets I need to get rid of.*
• *I'm tired of the cover-ups.*	• *I can see the political onslaught. They're coming for me.*
• *We say ethics and values and act pragmatism.*	• *How do I outwit the toxic sub-culture?*
• *How do I stop the messing around within the Exco?*	• *I suffer from guilt when not at the office.*
• *I don't have a supportive home life. My relationships are collapsing.*	• *My relationship with the Chairman is false and dangerous. How do I repair this?*
• *I present a façade that all is okay.*	• *My attractiveness is diminishing. How do I maintain dynamism and impact?*
• *My children have everything, but not a family. We're actually morally poor.*	• *It's lonely at the top.*
• *I want to work in the way in which I believe, and to believe in the way I work.*	• *I actually like this thing that is so tough and often so dangerous.*
• *I want to love, and be loved, more.*	
• *I miss romance.*	

It is time to reveal the real souls by virtue of volunteered and researched information in a quest to stop the bluffing and the lies. One cannot accept an organisation's *bona fides* when they receive acclaim for job creation, societal engagement and investment, and lifelong tenure for employees, and then retrench 3 000 employees while hiking executive compensation by 20% and investing billions in offshore projects. Such a corporate soul is sick to its core, yet survives and even continues to flourish.

The difference between executive incumbency and real effort

The obscene amounts of money and benefits leaders receive (not necessarily earn or deserve) have triggered concern about real worth, contribution and relative merit. In South Africa, with its peculiar history of separation, this practice cannot continue. While being rewarded at these insane levels, I started asking questions about some of the leaders, more specifically about the difference between executive incumbency and real effort. There is a marked difference between being in office and being effectively at work! So I compiled a checklist with which I invited a number of (brave) executives to conduct a self-assessment, using criteria other than grand job descriptions and personal profiles. I merely asked the confrontational question: "On what basis should I pay you so much?"

The gaps which emerged continue to be my concern and cynicism about many appointed leaders who actually *mis*lead yet continue to flourish. It is remarkable how people-at-the-top continue to find justification for exorbitant self-reward, even when the masses suffer financially. Forfeiting a portion of the millions received as bonuses is mere tactical tokenism which will neither impress nor quieten the worker. Real moral leadership is called for here as the groundswell of disenchantment compounds. Moreover, it is advocated herewith that executives be comprehensively appraised before the remuneration is authorised by using this *pro forma*, and answering the question: "Why should you be paid so much?" Table 7.3 provides a summary of criteria for executive appraisal, their definitions with some space for personal comments.

Table 7.3: Criteria for executive appraisal

CRITERION	DEFINITIONS	COMMENTS
Performance	• Return on effort • KPI outcomes • Agreed performance charter • Specific operational/functional contributions	
Potential	• Future employable talent and capacity • Substance diversity • Latent developmental attributes • Growth capacity • "Worth"	
Position	• Status, stature and substance as incumbent • Positional effect and impact • Integration of resources • Complexity of job • Interface dynamic	
Posture	• Finesse, elegance and demeanour • Professionalism • Standing and Impact	

CRITERION	DEFINITIONS	COMMENTS
Properties (*inter alia*)	• Analytical and deductive skills • Leadership and managerial maturity • Independence and courage • Innovative flair/creativity • Situational effect/impact • Sensitivity/EQ/people skills • Energy and enthusiasm • Vision and guidance • Communication skill • Delivery/contribution/productivity • Office efficiency	
Personal	• Work Life Integration • Stimulated self-growth • Relational maintenance • Self-management	

As part of an *informal* process of executive assessment, I have occasionally subjected leaders rated as exceptional to this (private) template, and found many to be sorely wanting. Essentially the question remains: How much did you actually contribute, and how much damage have you done?

The Corporate Soul at Work

The centre of the soul can be described as the fifth chamber of the heart – that sacred zone where right and wrong are adjudicated, and morality and true meaning defined. It is also that mystical domain where conscience is at work, judging and guiding motive and intent, as well as ethical consistency. The soul is the activator of conscience when decisions and conduct tend to deviate from the considered truth, favouring opportunism, notably at the expense of innocent individuals.

Like the colour of water, the soul is virtually impossible to define, but at best tentatively described by virtue of its normative functionality. One's soul is an emergent filter, serving as that purifying instrument, separating waste from the essence of goodness and wholesome conduct. Such blemishing residue is convincing evidence of the residing presence of soullessness – this cavity is filled with and consumed by untoward preferential conduct, guided by situational pragmatism, and is not considered an abiding moral and spiritual persuasion.

Uncovering the soul of an organisation

The soul of an organisation is best depicted by the collective conscience of everyone involved and most directly influenced by its leadership. The corporate soul is powerfully revealed by the active moral mechanism which detects and disallows every deviation from the stated truth, and the tendency toward the favoured lie. A soulful organisation defines, implements and maintains values and ethics as *Corporate Commandments*, regulating the consistent practice of the corporate religion. All performance and conduct in such a persuaded organisation is fundamentally regulated by operational and behavioural beliefs, and not nebulous and frivolous semantics. At its best, a soulful organisation assumes a natural inclination towards what is normatively proper. This is achieved by virtue of the character of those who direct the organisation, and who incorporate such virtue in strategic intent. Trading in personal principles, values and moral persuasion is often inspired by a material transaction, influenced by warped ego and the quest for unearned wealth.

Likewise, soullessness is dealing in immoral market conditions where the prevailing currency is corruption, collusion and connivance. It is the engagement in such generous yields which also breeds the irresistible quest for more thereof. The first step in this process of moral collapse is the rationalisation of the compromise on principles and moral personal persuasion. The bigger the return on such subcultural involvement, the more likely the gravitation towards such transactions and the banking of the yield. The obvious properties of such a process become most evident retrospectively. The inevitability of its eventual terminal nature, and its damning effect on the culprit, is retrospectively so evident, and the explanation for such conduct is both intellectually and morally inexplicable. The absence of consistent soulful reconnaissance will create the gap for untoward conduct to permeate the system, the minds of individuals, and particularly the body of leadership, together with the inclinational influence of certain personalities.

While it is difficult to define exactly what the soul is, there is consensus among executives, who are normatively inclined, that it is that mysterious domain where conscience, credence and character reside, and which then guides thinking, decisions and actions. But the soul does not design or define itself, since it assumes the features of the philosophies, thoughts, decisions and actions of individuals. An organisation with a pure soul is one also consistently mindful of the toxicity within. It acknowledges and admits that the nature of leadership can create such toxicity, which renders an environment both poisonous and venomous. An organisational culture where people fear people is a classic example demonstrating that where power rules, seniority dominates, and selective exclusivity disallows inclusive participation. What compounds this toxicity is the paradox between the stated value and virtue of openness and transparency, while mystery and speculation constitute the actual experience of the broad masses.

Soulful and soulless organisations

In a thesis on the subject, executives were invited to provide their version of both a soulful and a soulless organisation, and the unique factors that depict such status. A condensed extract from these findings clearly illustrates that the normative aspects define both the soulful and soulless organisation. The origin and cause thereof are to be found within the personalities and conduct of dominant individuals within that culture. Table 7.4 provides an illustration of a soulful organisation.

Table 7.4: Illustration of a soulful organisation

• Resolved personal normative protocol.
• Clearly defined executive philosophy, style and application.
• Organisation (business) ethics defined and announced.
• Resolute defence of personal beliefs and integration thereof into executive role.
• Fearless non-compromising, considered, normative stance.
• Not succumbing to collective peer pressures, nor pandering to conformist intimations of principals.
• Being personal custodian (and champion) of the stated corporate intent, purpose and commitment (offerings).
• Challenging all iniquities and *neutralising* the perpetrators thereof.
• Engaged in constant normative vigilance, by respecting human weakness, and fallibility proneness.

- Maintaining, and promoting intimate relationship with (forensic) auditors.
- Demonstratively eradicating all instances of criminal and/or unethical conduct/practice.
- Assuming a *constructive suspicious* stance anent transactional temptations, relationships and affiliations, most likely to stimulate wayward/delinquent behaviour.
- A genuine people-centric disposition and discernible manner, noted for its caring humanity.
- Recognising and professing the sanctity of work and labour, and the grateful upholding of its virtues.
- Fair and equitable (self) remuneration.
- Effective conflict resolution and restoration of goodwill.
- Status aversion: humble infiltrative stance.
- Employment of the best people. No nepotism.

Nelson Mandela was not a great leader – he was a remarkable human being whose philosophies about life and living inspired all and placated even those most angry. He was universally revered because of his contrarian soul and not his quest to lead. He wanted to influence both an angry and a guilty people – and succeeded. What he believed so deeply, he revealed so sincerely. His leadership impact and legacy are his personality and morality and not his title or office. So why do other leaders not emulate this exceptional and successful model, and why not propagate the enduring virtue of this man? After all, it worked, and against all odds. The answer is simply to be found in motives and needs other than those of *real* leaders, noted for their exemplary human(e) substance and universal impact. And this tragedy does not relate to politics and government only.

Leading Organisational Renewal: Remove Irritations

As mentioned repeatedly, there is no such thing as organisation behaviour, and one cannot actually renew an organisation. The thinking and feeling of prominent individuals need to adjust, and in the context of the moral leadership purported, embrace those lasting character strengths and virtues, driven by humanity and not only by the pursuit of wealth.

I have been taught by leaders on both sides of this continuum that to espouse the characteristics and moral constituent ingredients of organisation renewal, in pursuit of the ideal institution, is as futile as it evokes cynicism. Consequently, I decided some years ago to engage in a *Corporate Irritation Audit* so as to detect what those overt, but even more so, covert irritants are that prevail; who the irritators are; and what the impact is, but also the desirable remedial intervention. It is remarkable how people, duly facilitated, will honestly announce and subsequently purge this corporate *sewage* which turns the organisation into a toxic space and contaminates the health of everyone. More significantly, it is sad to detect why people would tolerate such poison and surprisingly, also ultimately those who are the instigators and causal cluster of such irritations. The list of dominant irritations included in Table 7.5 (below) is evidence that the irritations do not create and embed themselves. They are the consequence of the conduct of people, notably the leadership of any enterprise. People create havoc. Havoc does not create itself.

Ultimately, when engaged in honest and even embarrassing executive encounter, open and honest leaders admit that the greatest irritation experienced at personal and professional level, is to be found not only in the participation in the production of such irritants, but also becoming progressively used to, and tolerant thereof. Truly courageous leaders will ask the people what those irritations are, with the guarantee that there will be no negative recourse or ridicule, but only a commensurate commitment that it will be removed and eliminated from returning. Most organisation renewal interventions commissioned by corporate leadership contain a dimension of cruelty. When the anticipated reformist pain is anticipated to be severe, then external agents are typically employed to do the surgery and butchery. Austerity, reduction in size, complement and capex are the main areas of attention, as *renewal* is being engineered and affordability improved. Not surprisingly, exorbitant executive compensation remains untouched. Removing the real irritations that create corporate lethargy and cynicism is the constructive version of visionary leadership.

Through numerous renewal interventions, the following clusters have emerged as protocol of irritations that corrupt the corporate soul and frustrate everyone. Table 7.5 provides a protocol of organisational irritations.

Table 7.5: Protocol of irritations

Sustainability
• This Irritation Audit is to be viewed and implemented as a serious definitive intervention.   • Disciplined consistent review of effect: Part of collective corporate performance appraisal.   • Integrate into every individual job description.   • Replicate the exercise into the entire organisation.   • Assume a mentality of irritability so as to disallow sneaky stuff!   • Intensive/thorough monthly review of progress and effect regarding irritation management.

Communication and Reporting
• Question the significance, necessity and contribution of ALL reports.   • Establish absolute necessities and their influence on decision-making.   • Nice-to-haves to be eliminated.   • Consider some standardisation, such as templates and pro forma documents.   • Less magnitude and more message in all reports – both written and verbal.   • Do not run the business twice by over-reporting.

Discipline
• Assume a productive NO culture. Refuse irrelevance and unproductive, even invasive, dictates.   • Liberate a conducive YES culture.   • Develop a culture of no excuses.   • Internal integrity must be 100%. No talking-out!   • Absolute mutual support and reciprocal helpfulness.   • Whistle-blowing : Use this medium appropriately.   • Manage the identified irritation away – both individually and collectively.   • Each Executive to assume responsibility for every aspect in Irritation Audit.

Corporate Spirit
• Constantly rekindle the (lost) spirit. Define the corporate soul.   • Is corporate citizenship dwindling, as well as the sense of belonging and morale?   • Local embracing leadership to prevail.   • Engage with the people – Executives to mobilise themselves toward people's space, physically.

Corporate Spirit (continued)
• Insist on work-life balance.   • Manage and lead with more variety and surprise and not only replication and predictability.   • Constantly measure the local temperature.
Pride: Identify the disallowers

• Assume proper Corporate Executive status and stature. Work on:
     o   Presence
     o   Authentic stature
     o   Finesse
     o   Professional polish.

Time and Capacity
• Create capacity by disallowing time wastage.   • Find more free time.   • E-mail discipline. Discipline ALL communication in respect of absolute necessity.   • Meeting prioritisation: Need, Content, Preparation and Duration.   • IT and IM must create time efficacy and not be invasive.   • Disconnect all irrelevancies.
Professionalism
• Link this item with PRIDE.   • Stimulate growth in others and accelerate development of talent.   • Delegate more: Get rid of what you should not be doing.   • Get your own house in order first.   • Continued stimulated, self-growth as leader.   • Assume autonomy and executive standing and give same to others selectively.
Sensitivities
• Decide and agree to tell it as it is.   • No holy cows.   • Review relationships and personalities at the top.   • Do not fear yourselves.

When I finally realised that conventional organisation renewal interventions are actually counterproductive, and values clarification sessions are the source of cynicism, I decided to research the real, authentic leadership disqualifiers by interviewing the people who (have to) suffer the lie. It was remarkable how these people rallied to the occasion to say it the way it actually is. Twenty-two disqualifiers (shown in Table 7.6) emerged which actually depicted the recognisable features of a collapsed corporate soul and questionable leadership.

Table 7.6: Twenty-two disqualifiers of a collapsed organisational soul

1. Propensity for power and dominance	14. Blame and shame of others for own misconduct
2. Situational omnipotence – Assuming import	15. Narcissistic nature – pre-occupation with the self
3. Controlling predisposition – Superiority	16. Leadership exclusivity – not inclusively embracing
4. Suspicion creation – Secrecy	17. Centricity – own comforts and luxuries. Feudal culture
5. Audience/attention addiction	18. Incumbency not leadership
6. Rulership – not leadership	19. Position and title representing worth – not real substance
7. People as subjects – not colleagues	20. Territorial Imperative. Isolation
8. Thriving on meetings – Chairmanship	21. From good to great (= god) – goodness is missing
9. Confusing seniority with efficacy	22. Subtle personal wealth creation
10. Disallowing competition – Challenged/threatened	
11. Unilateral decision-making. Autocracy	
12. Disguising incompetence. Tactical invisibility and untouchability	
13. Growth in (pseudo) stature – little authentic substance	

The Applied Truth at Work

Yes, this is a better and more realistic definition of Ethics. There is no question about the relevance and universal acceptance of ethics as an abiding leadership virtue and character strength. Yet situational *realities* mostly guide the application and maintenance thereof. Unethically inclined leaders refer to such inclination as behavioural (= financial) pragmatism. To lecture on ethics is as easy as it is futile. Everyone agrees with the subject and its moral content and intent. Answering the uncomfortable questions (= normative leader encounter), is the real issue, the responses to which actually depict and define the real, ethical, upstanding leader. Having answered these questions, the discomfort of inescapability also becomes an integral part of the ethical conditionality. Passing a theoretical exam on the subject is not at issue here, but the exemplary influencing of the organisational morality by revealing your own. Not many leaders possess this courage. Table 7.7 provides a list of possible enthical encounters.

Table 7.7: Ethical encounters

- Are you prepared to declare and defend your personal ethics as directed by your beliefs?
- Would you display the courage to go against the group if the consensus challenged your values/beliefs?
- Would you tell the client everything?
- Would you become part of secrecy if it were expected of you despite your convictions?
- If the employer expected you to neglect your marriage/family in favour of work, how would you react?
- Would you "speak up" if the organisation were "lying"?
- Would you address a colleague if he/she were overstepping the agreed values?
- Do you help market the social conscience of the company if you know the fundamental motive has a different motive and intent?

- What about affiliations against your convictions, but which are expected of you in the interest of good external relationships/contracts?
- The power of the silent: Aggressive challenge or silent conformity? Where do you stand?
- What are your views/practice on bribing?
- Personal commandment with regard to consistent ethical behaviour: does it exist?
- Is the truth career limiting or career enhancing where you work?

In an attempt to reach consensus about a pragmatic definition of ethics, I have put the tantalising questions in Table 7.7 to numerous executive teams, MBA and EDP students and delegates over the years. The vigorous debates continue to oscillate between pragmatism and *avoidism* in order not to reach a single conclusive and emphatic definition. By analysis of the discussions and derivations of the tentative conclusions, the emotional debates suggest that ethics is essentially a matter of affordability, as well as a matter of opinion. Yet in each and every organisation where I have worked within this normative construct, the published corporate values and code of conduct contain emphatic statements on honesty, truth, trust, openness, co-operation, support, and ETHICS.

An organisation can never be or become ethical. The integrity and ethical consistency of individuals naturally evolve into such public perception and noted respect when evident. In the absence of such individual ethical predominance, the image and reputation of such an organisation assumes a negative impact. It is also remarkable to note how the critical and powerful adjudicators of ethical conduct employ euphemisms while judging the decision-making of executives. In one instance in an African country, the CEO of a large mining organisation was not prepared to entertain the bribe to be awarded the tender, and consequently walked away. Two of the largest shareholders within that organisation subsequently called me in order to discuss the collapse of the negotiations, referring to the CEO as being too dogmatic and disengaged in a world of commercial realities.

Much has been written about the CORPORATE RELIGION, and more lately, about the corporate soul. Without entering all of the philosophies and theories on these two pertinent subjects, I merely ask executives during executive encounter sessions this one inescapable question: "Do you work the way you believe, and do you believe the way you work?" It is interesting how most respondents argue the merits of selective compromise and even the benefits of postponing the truth. So, who is the ethical leader, and what would make him/her respected and supported by all audiences? If it were true that normal behaviour is defined as that behaviour which dominates in a particular time and space, then it could be concluded that, if everyone manipulates the truth for the desired outcome, then such conduct is the norm and normal. If, however, the corporate values, debated and defined by the executive stipulate truth, trust and honesty as virtues and character strengths, then why would the very authors of such a testament of moral intent hesitate to define ethics as the absolute applied truth at work, and disapprove any dimension of compromise thereof, regardless of the situation? The answer is that it remains the human factor within the leader that exposes weakness and vulnerability. It is as much evident as disturbing that POWER, GREED and EGO constitute the human frailty, regardless of the presence of other remarkable attributes such as resilience, fortitude and courage.

Human weakness is at issue here. Some of the most devout believers collapse their faith under temptation. Being the authors and publishers of corporate commandments (= ethics) is merely a literary exercise, mostly impressively formulated. The definitive encounter for all leaders is to answer the ethical encounter truthfully and re-visit the applied version thereof.

Leaders I Remember and Admire – And Why

Among the most remarkable leaders I have encountered throughout my life, the majority were not deliberately behaving like, or presenting themselves as, important individuals holding noticeable office or title. They were *just persons* whose humanity and humility were dominant. When subsequently learning about their status, stature, qualifications, achievements and universal appeal, I was startled by their authentic, unassuming nature, and even avoidance of recognition and acclaim. They naturally exuded dynamism and impact. They commanded attention and respect by virtue of very unique characteristics, and not popular embellishments. Remarkably, many of these men and women grew up and schooled in the platteland (= rural area), where urban sophistication, exposure, and even opportunities did not exist. But they possessed a solid family extraction and principles and a heritage which grounded careers and shaped personalities. In most instances, their semi-literate parents formed their values base, and focused aspirations and achievement motive. They were *decent* people and did not consciously deviate from what were inculcated as enduring values and sustainable conduct.

The eight outstanding leaders I remember best and admire most are revered for the attributes and characteristics shown in Table 7.8.

Table 7.8: Characteristics of outstanding leaders

• Vision and anticipation	• Penetrative influencing
• Unorthodox thinking	• People centric: interested in others
• Compelling wisdom	• Successful in endeavours, honest in failure
• Entrepreneurial flair	• Not pre-occupied with wealth – focused not on what they have, but **who** they are
• Impeccable manners	
• Gentle souls	• Assertive without aggression
• Intuition	• Humble but never timid
• Uncompromising principles	• Being available

By contrast, for the executive competencies profile I currently use when assessing leaders and managers, see Table 7.9 which contains many of the above dimensions by implication, but mostly specific performance-defined attributes. Organisations still preferably insist on this protocol.

Table 7.9: Executive competency profile

Analytical Ability
• Deductive reasoning
• Mental alertness
• Logic and common sense
• Cognitive skills and creative thinking
Business Mindedness
• Understanding the business ethic (complexity and singularity), acumen and merchant mentality
• Astuteness in business perspective and the commercial arrangement of dynamic factors.
• Understanding the big picture

Communication skills
<ul><li>Communications sophistication commensurate with level</li><li>Formulating skills</li><li>Creating comprehension</li><li>Arrangement of relevant information</li><li>Communicative style. Vocabulary indicative of culture, exposure and professional maturation</li></ul>

Emotional intelligence
<ul><li>Appropriate sensitivity, empathy and interface skills</li></ul>

Enthusiasm
<ul><li>Mental and physical energy</li><li>Inspired achievement motive</li><li>Appropriate passion and drive</li><li>Realistic goal orientation</li></ul>

Independence
<ul><li>Decisiveness, situational courage and personal/professional resourcefulness</li><li>Stress tolerance and self-control</li><li>Stability of performance (non-erratic) skills in encounter, confrontation and debate</li></ul>

Innovation
<ul><li>Originality of thought, unconventionalism and non-stereotypical style</li><li>Innovative substance and impact</li><li>Creative thinking</li></ul>

Inquiring stance
<ul><li>Constructive curiosity – dynamic inquisitiveness, penetrative questioning</li><li>*General knowledge*</li></ul>

Leadership
<ul><li>Inspirational effect. Stimulating followership. Initiating direction</li><li>Eliciting followership</li><li>*Charisma*</li></ul>

Situational competence
<ul><li>Personal and professional presentation</li><li>Anticipatory alertness</li><li>Appropriate behaviour and responses</li><li>Receptiveness and general social conduct</li></ul>

Visioning inclination
<ul><li>Prognosticative orientation, transformational dynamic and adaptability</li><li>Exploratory and anticipative stance</li><li>Pro-activity and speculative anticipation</li><li>Intuitive inclination</li></ul>

A pragmatic critic challenged my preferred profile of the eight noted leaders by referring to the protocol as ideological, philosophical, and *syrupy*. He also added that leaders of such virtue typically come last. My retort: "But they are competing in an entirely different race!" Field Marshall Montgomery was rarely seen in tunic, or at HQ. He wore battledress and spent his time with troops in the trenches. During the first anniversary of the tragic Marikana incident, the CEO was notably absent on stage during the memorial service. When trying to find her to take her lofty seat, she declined, because she was busy distributing water to the thirsty congregants.

Real leadership substance shows naturally. Flaunted stature and status disappears – naturally! If I have to make money at the expense of people, I prefer poverty. If my CV has to announce my worth, then I prefer being *worthless*. If the grand challenge is to progress from good to great, then I prefer the pursuit of goodness.

It would seem that I am suggesting that nice guys always come *last*, and that leaders noted for compassion, sensitivity and a genuine caring disposition don't last. Of course this is not universally true, although such personalities are potentially vulnerable and even terminal, as is so often proved.

If the soul is that sacred domain where good and bad, right and wrong, fair and unfair, and gentle and callous are adjudicated and regulated, then why would essentially soulful individuals tend to become soulless leaders when at work? Why does the pursuit of profit and *making budget* release tyrannical and demon-like behaviour? In numerous counselling and therapy sessions with ex-executives who have been *invited* to early retirement, they declare that naivety, consistent display of humanity, and fair leadership practice cost them their careers, and even their lifelong status. They retrospectively admit that there is actually no such theory or practice as tough on task and soft on people! They also, retroactively, admit that the virtues of resilience, fortitude and assertiveness are actually only euphemisms for uncompromising toughness, unforgiving management, and virtually no concern for the person in the guise of the employee.

Effectively re-humanising the workplace calls for an appropriate application of leadership style and inspirational effect. If you swear at people for whatever reason, then you are not a leader – you are a savage! If you instil fear into people, notably those who are forced to endure such abuse, then you are a tyrant. If you exploit your false immunity because of perceived seniority, then you are actually a weakling, hiding behind corporate drapings. If you do not convert all your education, training and development in management and leadership, and the applied behavioural science into fair labour practice, then you have not grown at all – you have only become more senior.

My Leadership Apprehensions: An Imbalanced Scorecard

In order not to regurgitate contemporary theories and philosophies about leadership, I decided I should demonstrate the candour and courage by stating here what I have witnessed as facilitator and organisation psychologist and not as student, see Table 7.10 below. At my age, stage and phase, I do so fearlessly now! I also invited other leaders who have become tired of the lie and the masquerade, to join the throng of leaders also tired of pandering to the *nonsense*, and now intolerant of the buffoons who should never have qualified for such office in the first place. It is also with painful hindsight that I similarly revisit my own leadership façade which irritated many and helped so few.

Table 7.10: Leadership apprehensions

- The culture and climate in any organisation is fundamentally determined by the personality of the CEO.
- Stated values and codes of conduct are the stimulants for cynicism and a checklist to isolate current wayward executive conduct.
- Everybody gossips about everyone else, yet endorses the virtues of openness, support, collaboration and synergy.
- All executive committees are busy with something untoward, despite the commitment to transparency and integrity.
- Most appointed leaders have never been truly nurtured, guided and ushered into such position, just as most lecturers have never been taught to teach – they just have PhDs.
- A great place to work is not a physical address – it is the impact and effect of people with common courtesy and devoid of status and power pre-occupation.
- Of all the leader attributes still being researched, debated and recorded, *humility* has always been the most important and will remain so.
- Sustainable success is very difficult to attain, notably admired leadership. Success is actually lethal.
- Scrap all stated codes of conduct, values treaties, visions and missions. Ask and answer the question: What are we actually doing here?
- The truth is career limiting – notably in organisations where a sub-culture of crooks and tyrants are ruling.
- You can never achieve any semblance of a collective corporate spirit if executives continue to receive and accept obscene amounts of money.
- Within any democracy, the majority will rule. In South Africa at enterprise level, leaders still rule as if seniority, wealth and power will prevail.
- Yes, No. 13: Despite their reprehensible selves, some of the worst human beings still lead large enterprises and even enjoy support and following. The paradox obliterates every leadership theory.

Leaders and Self-management

Leader education, training and development consists mostly and typically of skills and attributes according to the demands of the position charter, key performance areas, shareholder expectations, and growth imperatives. Business schools do this well. Leaders are highly regarded for their prowess, acumen, delivered results and performance successes. Yet they are often in a personal pathological state of self-abuse and imbalance. Sick people cannot lead others well!

Work-life integration constitutes an enormous challenge to all leaders. As seniority increases, so does the corporate call, and consequently self-neglect. It is during the first semester of the typical four decades at work that the greatest damage is done, and marital and family relationships are most vulnerable. Leadership talent and capacity are identified. So, too, are employees accelerated, promoted and rewarded, and sadly, candidates become addicted to it. While wellness and wellbeing are promoted and purported as part of the core values of any responsible organisation, the disciplined enforcement thereof is woefully absent.

It is true that the typical successful and highly talented leader will have worked roughly ten years' overtime for free after three decades at work (by the age of 50). The advent and availability of modern connectivity is compounding this dilemma as a result of the portability of the office and its interchangeability regardless of address. While the laptop and iPad have become incredible instruments facilitating efficiency and productivity, they are likewise so invasive that this militates strongly against the achievement of any semblance of wellbeing.

The likelihood of becoming addicted to recognition and corporate applause is not only evident, but severe. For those in pursuit of seniority and wealth creation, the obscene rewards for top executives will remain a highly desirable pursuit if not obsession, and will corrupt and even collapse the very moral foundation on which such career aspirations should be built.

Selective compromise, the ability to say NO to career inconsequentials, and the willingness to LIVE the preferred quality of life model, constitute the agenda for authentic wellbeing. While this subject has become prominent on the syllabi of both MBA and EDP programmes, only 20% of delegates report that they actually engage in some form of rehabilitative interventions. Even more sadly, of the 20% converts, 40% will relapse, and of that 40%, 80% will get worse and never return to *normality*.

True moral leadership, in the context of wellbeing, will disallow any invasive factor that distorts the mechanism and ingredients for such leadership and organisational wellness. To illustrate, while facilitating a weekend session on the subject for the Board of Directors and spouses, with remarkable impact and even emotional effect, the CEO concluded the session by apologising to his colleagues for organising the session over the weekend, since "it is actually family time, private property, and therefore a violation". He declared then that it would never happen again at any level. He expanded his persuasion into an announced set of corporate commandments which also insisted that nobody should be at work before 07:30 in the morning and absolutely not later than 17:30. He concluded that people should want to go home, and want to return in the morning, and should be likewise received at both ends of the day.

In an attempt to discover the factors that militate against wellness, well-being and balance the profile shown in Table 7.11 emerged.

Table 7.11: Factors against wellness, well-being and balance

• Excessive ambition • Materialism: greed, wealth • Career acceleration: too much, too fast, too soon • Competitiveness: win syndrome • Normative collapse: neglect of values • Institutional disintegration: marriage, family • Addictions: success, applause • Friendship neglect • Ego: image, status, stature, power preconditions	• Self-neglect: priorities collapse • Fears: failure, losing • Tolerance of nonsense • Fun deprivation • Sensorial poverty: only doing, not feeling • Mechanistic living: too prescriptive • Make-believe: "It will get better". False future focus. • Slavish commitment to the corporate call • Invasiveness: universal availability • Future uncertainty – provision • Addiction to condition

By contrast, the one factor that would leverage the conversion from self-neglect to a balanced integrated life and lifestyle emerged from adversity, notably loss. It is as sad as it is remarkable that tragedy and trauma mostly bring astute individuals to their senses, but typically just in time to be too late. A second factor which also ignites realistic career gratification and lasting fulfilment is the achievement of the condition – ENOUGH. When successful leaders detect and define what is enough money, enough status, and even enough career, they also discover the virtue and mechanism of realistic compromise, and in this process, without collapsing competence nor skills. Such converts merely continue their career and lives by working hard differently.

Some Tips for Un-leading – More Influencing

This compendium of ideas and suggestions in Table 7.12 emerge from personal persuasion and the compelling evidence of brave and authentic leaders' conduct I have had the privilege of witnessing.

Table 7.12: Tips for authentic leadership

Surprise your people with the unexpected
• Meet and treat them in their space.   • Make critical incident notes and share observations about their personal circumstances.   • Think and demonstrate unconventionalism.
Get rid of all features of physical opulence
• Never outsmart your people.   • Disallow the top-floor syndrome.   • Never eat more expensively than your own colleagues.   • Preferential parking, *en suite*-toilets and grand crockery only create distance.
Declare war against meetings
• Be careful about *renting* an audience.   • Try meeting on your feet. If you sit, you waffle.   • Disallow all "matters arising".
Invite all people into your space
• Randomly invite colleagues (from all levels) to lunch.   • Host people in informal meeting and discourse.   • Reveal your sincere social manner.
Respect personal time and space
• Disallow gatherings over weekends.   • Insist on wellbeing and work-life balance.   • Legislate for all leave to be taken.
Consistency
• All people prefer order and joy to chaos and pain – just give them the appropriate version.   • Never compromise discipline and respect.   • Reveal your own weaknesses and ask for help.
Differentiate and individualise
• You are not all things to all people.   • Know your people very well – then give each individual the nourishment that will make them flourish.   • Find the common denominators within your team and then service that appetite.

Find and reveal your unique style
• Conventions are predictable – think alternatives and surprising stimulants.
• Authenticate yourself not with designation, but with proximity and availability.
• *Do* the values: Honesty, Openness, Support, Enjoyment and Growth.
• Demonstrate your genuine interest in people. Make sure you know them thoroughly – and their families.

Celebrate
• Generously celebrate contribution effort, success and achievements – budget for fun.
• Recognise energy and commitment, even when not making budget.
• Be aware of what demoralises people and avoid it. Ask them what it is.

Trust
• You have to trust people, but remain ready and be prepared to be disappointed.
• Relocate those who abuse trust, immediately.
• Demonstrate your intolerance of the lie publicly.
• Trust your own human vulnerability.

Dependence
• Empower the right people with an unconditional mandate.
• Practice devolution of autonomy and authority selectively.
• Underpin yourself with the smartest people available – and make it affordable.

Move
• When you're at your smartest, it lasts a maximum of five years – move on timeously.

Image
• Remove VIP from your mind and your treatment.
• Disallow all forms of pandering toward you.
• Mingle with all people – always.

In Conclusion: The Smouldering Leadership Front Line

Much of what has been written in this chapter points to the progressive de-humanisation of the workplace and the sensorial poverty of leaders. The quest for success, distorted achievement motive, and the addiction to power, greed and ego seem to have become inescapable traps on the leadership ladder. Giants are toppled by enticements, icons fall victim to lures, and gentle souls become tyrants without realising it, or wanting to. The case and call for authentic leader transformation is at the front line and smouldering.

The groundswell of disapproving and disenchanted employees is compounding. While questionable leaders in all spheres think they are leading their people, they are actually not. At issue is not the leader, leadership, or leading, but personality and agreeable conduct. When stripped of status, title and sapiential show, there is not much substance left, other than façade. The corporate soul is rendered fractious by such pseudo-leaders. And those who appoint and tolerate them are as culpable as the weaklings themselves.

While it may seem as if this chapter has singularly isolated the questionable leader as a universal phenomenon, ignoring the exemplary leaders who do exist and survive, the message is deliberately cautioning. So many of the *good-to-great* global leaders survive and are idolised because of the size of the dividend they generate for shareholders and not because of their humanity. The cruel bully still seems to outlive the nice guy.

Talking about courage, try answering these ten concluding encounters as you continue on your leadership executive journey:

- Are you sure you have genuine support from the people you believe you are leading?
- Which behaviours you release do you also actually disapprove of?
- Are you living the stated values in all circumstances? Are all people welcome to adjudicate your conduct?
- How much unproductive clutter and "stuff" do you generate?
- Can you convert adversity into opportunity with ingenuity?
- Do you possess the skill and art to blend disciplined management and inspirational leading?
- Can you be, and are you, absolutely open and honest in all things?
- Do you work the way you believe, and believe the way you work?
- Is your leading impact pleasing to all stakeholders and congruent with your conscience?
- Are you enjoying the leadership role you are in?

Chapter 8

LEADERSHIP MATURITY

Danie du Toit with Theo Veldsman and Deon van Zyl

Many of the visible indicators of poor leadership performance and excellence appear to be attributable to deeper, inner leadership dynamics. It is argued in many quarters that future leadership challenges and the growing leadership crisis will demand more than just the enhancement and/or addition of new leadership competencies and behaviours. Future leadership fit for the radically changing and more demanding world of work will require a far greater insight into the inner, deeper dynamics of leaders, relative to themselves and others. Such an understanding is not at present readily available, though with some exceptions as represented in the work of Kets de Vries.[1] Without this understanding, leadership could be influenced and/or manipulated in adverse and destructive ways, given that people most often base their decisions and behaviour on unconscious belief patterns embedded in deep leadership dynamics.[2][3]

Better insight into the deep inner dynamics of leaders, in particular the concept of leadership psychosocial maturity, could assist in countering the seemingly growing crisis regarding leadership. Furthermore, Carl Jung's concept of individuation may prove to be a valuable way of understanding leaders' journeys towards psychosocial maturity.

The leader who has progressed along the journey of individuation will excel because of a higher degree of psychosocial maturity. A higher level of individuation results in a lowered likelihood of the manifestation of signs of failed leadership, for example, underperformance, mistrust, derailment, and burnout.

In this chapter, leadership maturity is discussed from a Jungian perspective. Jung's concept of "individuation" will be described, and a three-stage model will be applied to the development of leadership maturity. Leadership attributes and behaviours associated with each of the stages will be described. The chapter ends with concluding remarks regarding the application of individuation to leadership maturity.

Jung's Conception of "Individuation"

Jung's original conception of individuation refers to a lifelong development process by which an individual is formed and differentiated in becoming a psychologically unique, separate, whole being.[4][5] Put differently, individuation is a person's journey towards self-realisation and the drive to become him-/herself as an indivisible unity. This progressive integration enables the individual's growth towards greater wholeness and inner harmony.[6] This means that the individual becomes what he/she always was and is meant to be, and grows to his/her full potential.[7][8]

Individuation thus embraces the development of the consciousness from an original state of unconsciousness, leading to an extended and enriched psychological life. During the process of individuation, the unconscious becomes more integrated into the conscious. It necessitates the integration of the dialogue and self-regulating feedback systems between the conscious and the unconscious minds.[9]

What differentiates individuation from other related constructs is its multidimensionality and comprehensiveness, compared to related concepts which are frequently unidimensional and narrowly focused. In contrast, individuation embraces the positive and the negative, the consciousness and the unconsciousness (with the addition of the collective unconsciousness), tension and harmony, the team and the individual, integration and differentiation, and life-long growth.

The individuation process is not a linear developmental process, but can be viewed as a continuous circular process. Though chronological age also plays a role in individuation, growth through a developmental stage is not a once-off occurrence, but a life-long growth process, where the end of one cycle marks the beginning of the next. In the words of TS Eliot, exploration (in other words, growth) is an ongoing process:

> "...[t]o arrive where we started
> And know the place for the first time".

Given these overall features of individuation, it is contended that the concept is most appropriate in enabling a deep and comprehensive understanding of the psychosocial maturity of leaders within the changing world that leaders face, and in which they have to be effective.

Stages of Individuation

The chapter will be based mainly on the three-stage model of Stein, who refined Jung's original theory on the process of individuation. The three stages are:

Stage 1: *Nurturing stage.* During this stage, the fledging leader learns about self-acceptance and building self-confidence.

Stage 2: *Adaptation stage.* During this stage, the challenges of the world are taken on.

Stage 3: *Integration stage.* The leader attains a more holistic, integrated view, is able to forecast environmental changes, and proactively utilises opportunities.

The Three Stages of Individuation

Erich Neumann, in 1955,[10] expanded Jung's original concept of individuation by explicating stage-wise the realisation of the innate potential of an individual in order for him/her to become the person he/she is meant to be. The stages must be understood metaphorically and symbolically, not literally. They overlap, and are interdependent. Personal growth towards maturity is not an absolutely definable process, though the stages and the transitions between them are differentiable. These stages are discussed next.

Stage 1: Nurturing

During the first stage of individuation, a person needs to be nurtured and taken care of. This stage typically starts before birth and continues beyond childhood, and prepares the person for adulthood. The mother, or caring and supporting mothering, is critical during this stage in order for the child to establish self-acceptance. As a child grows up, he/she continuously becomes more independent, self-reliant, and self-sufficient. This stage serves the psychological purpose of supporting and protecting the child's ego. However, the true individuality of a person will emerge only after the person has left the security of the caring and comforting home.[11]

Stage 2: Adaptation

In the second, paternal, stage, the father figure assists the ego to grow away from the nurturing containment of the mother providing security.[12] The person learns the rigour of adapting to the world at large, and facing and living with the consequence of his/her personal actions. The realistic world is experienced, and the ego develops a more realistic self-identity and worldview.[13] If sufficient nurturing did not take place during the first individuation stage, the person could be overwhelmed by anxiety, and shy away from the challenges faced during this stage.

During this stage, the person needs to learn how to deal with and master the world of achievement, work, competition, and interpersonal competence. Typically, this stage of taking on challenges and achieving goals is heavily emphasised and rewarded by organisations. Many leaders, even at executive level, never progress beyond this individuation stage of dealing with external challenges, performance, and achievement.

Stage 3: Integration

One of Jung's biggest contributions towards the psychology of personal growth is the emphasis on the third stage. This stage makes Jung's contribution unique among other psycho-analytical approaches. Jung[14] believed that, during this stage, the search for meaning and purpose becomes important. The task during this stage is not to become a responsible citizen, be independent, or to achieve career success – these tasks of adaptation and achievement need to have occurred already during the previous stage.

During the integrating stage, the person embarks on an internally focused journey of finding his/her own unique individuality, and casting away the trappings of external conformity. The social reality does not disappear, but adjustment to society is given less personal time and energy. The focus is not on survival, but on meaning. The person also strives to integrate opposing elements within his/her own psyche in order to gain full access to his/her total psyche. During this stage, the person becomes centred, whole, and connected to transcendent, higher-order realities.

The main focus during the first two stages is to separate the ego from its surroundings, while the main focus during the third stage is the integration of the entire person.[15] This third stage is highly relevant in understanding the highest level of leadership psychosocial maturity. The third stage enables the leader to identify with meaning and purpose beyond him-/herself, in order find a calling through which to serve a greater good and be differentiated from the external world (inter alia, his/her team), while simultaneously remaining connected and exerting influence.

Attributes of Each Stage of Individuation

Ten attributes, which accompany each of the three stages, have been identified.[16] These attributes explain the stages and attempt to make them accessible and understandable. The attributes are then operationalised into leadership behaviours. These leadership behaviours will be described to make it possible to gain insight into a leader's stage of individuation by observing his/her behaviour.

Stage 1: Containing/Nurturing

The containment/nurturing stage can be seen as culminating in the leader's emergence as a fully-fledged leader. The successful leader in the organisational world is expected to have grown beyond this primary development stage of individuation. However, important developmental tasks need to have taken place during this stage.

During this stage, the person needs to experience acceptance, be afforded the opportunity to take risks in a safe environment, try out and experiment with different roles and behaviour styles (including leadership roles), and experiment with the different facets of relationships (such as power, caring, and team dynamics). If these tasks are not completed successfully, and without growing confidence, the person will not be able to grow confidently into the leadership role with all of its associated risks and challenges, but will be fixated on safe, immature activities. The building of healthy relationships, self-esteem, and self-confidence are the minimum outcomes of successful individuation in this stage.

Unfortunately, there are many leaders who have not even achieved the first stage of individuation. They can be recognised by their frantic search for constant reassurance from others because of a lack of self-confidence and security. Often, addiction or substance abuse is an indication of unmet nurturing needs. Repeated patterns of self-devaluation and self-sabotage can also indicate their unmet needs of security, self-confidence, self-awareness, and risk-taking. Unindividuated leaders see the world with wounded vision. Their defences make genuine self-awareness impossible. Consequently, they can never really embark on a journey of growth towards further individuation. They seek out the warm security of the known and validation by others.

Individuated Leadership Attribute: Pre-leadership

During this stage, the fledgling leader prepares to take on the challenges of the external world head on. Leadership approaches, styles, skills, and behaviour are practised in a safe environment. He/she starts experimenting with the ways and means of really taking up the leadership role.

Table 8.1 summarises the individuated and unindividuated leaders' attributes as well as the leadership theme of this attribute and its behavioural manifestations.

Table 8.1: Pre-leadership of individuated and unindividuated leaders

ATTRIBUTE: PRE-LEADERSHIP		
Theme: Builds security as base for further development		
Attribute: Pre-leadership	**Leadership theme of stage**	**Key leadership behaviour manifestations**
Individuated		
Nurturing needs met. High self-esteem. High self-confidence.	Prepares to become leader by exploring, testing boundaries and building insight. Explores relating to others. Tests waters as prospective leader.	Challenges and questions status quo. Keen to take on leadership roles. Gets noticed because of impact in teams.
Unindividuated		
Strong nurturing needs. Low self-esteem. Low self-confidence.	Accepts external sources' views or models of leadership uncritically and applies compliantly.	Applies leadership style mechanistically with little concern for requirements of the situation. Avoids leadership roles.

Individuated Leadership Attribute 1: Self-awareness and insight

Self-awareness is a key concept at this stage of the individuation process. Individuation is predominantly about increased self-awareness. The unaware person is in the grip of and ruled by his/her instinctual and archetypal reactions.

Self-awareness also is seen as the keystone for developing emotional intelligence.[17] Self-monitoring of one's personal dysfunctional behaviour is the first step towards change. A lack of self-regulation could lead to a discrepancy between what leaders say and what they do, the much-needed congruence between "talking" and "walking". This degree of congruence directly affects a leader's perceived integrity. Incongruence is rooted in leaders' unawareness of their own drives and mood states. Leaders need to develop a sensitivity of how they affect people in achieving their goals. Without self-awareness and access to one's inner wisdom, it is difficult to take action with authentic conviction, or to give objective, impartial guidance.[18] A contained, nurtured leader is therefore not only aware of his/her inner thoughts, but also actively listens to and respects the opinions of team members.

In his study of the lives of some great leaders, Collins detected signs that Washington, Lincoln, Roosevelt, Nixon, Carter, and Clinton were in the grip of a mother-complex: they all lived out aspects of their mothers' unlived, projected lives.[19] The "shadow" is the first layer of the unconscious. The shadow contains unintegrated aspects of the individual personality, which the person does not yet own, and does not accept as part of him-/herself.[20] To survive, an organism has to recognise what is not self. Aspects of the personality that are experienced as "not me" are repressed into the shadow. The unconscious content of the shadow is of an emotional nature, and therefore charged with energy. The energy must be discharged in one way or another.

The unindividuated person ascribes unacknowledged parts of him-/herself to others. He/she then discharges the blame onto others. They are blamed for aspects the leader has not yet acknowledged in him-/herself. This overreaction to and judging of others is called *projection*. Shadow projections usually involve a person of the same gender,[21] and the person is usually unaware of performing these projections. The leader finds excellent reasons why his/her reactions and behaviour are justified. It is usually very clear to others that the leader is irrational.

If a leader is caught up in the grip of his/her own shadow, the consequences can be disastrous. Whether the object of the leader's projection is a follower, the leader's leader, or a client, the leader is bound to destroy trust and be viewed as immature. Leaders often tend to focus on positive aspects to build morale and mobilise followers towards a positive vision of the future. They emphasise great deeds and winning, because they wish to activate, mobilise, and move their followers. In doing so, they increase the danger of ignoring their shadow side. The more the shadow is ignored and suppressed, the more it grows in strength. Because a leader is in a position of power, followers are usually careful in dealing with the leader. His/her "blind spots" and irrational behaviour are therefore not referred to; this reinforces the leader's rationalisations by giving him/her a "blank cheque", allowing the shadow to flourish and expand unchallenged.

If the reality of a projection is denied, the person increasingly identifies with it.[22] The leader is likely to take diminishing notice of the responses from his/her environment. Many organisational leaders derail because they are in the grip of their shadow side.[23] Projection always serves the same purpose: it allows one to pass on blame and not take personal responsibility and accountability.

To acknowledge and integrate the shadow means genuine growth in terms of taking a real step towards becoming a whole, integrated person. More individuated leaders acknowledge both the light and the dark sides of their lives. They accept the good and the bad sides. They know that the one side can exist only because of the other. Because the shadow contains mostly personal, unconscious content, Jung[24] believed that it can be made conscious without too much difficulty. He stated that a person with some self-criticism can see through his/her own shadow.

A more individuated leader thus becomes more than his/her persona or socially acceptable way of presenting him-/herself. These leaders are able to tolerate followers seeing behind their social masks. They need not conceal their true nature behind such a mask. They admit to it, and do not allow their dark sides to rule their lives. This public vulnerability and transparency by the leaders allow followers to experience them as authentic in their openness. These leaders do not lose any power by being their true selves; they in fact, paradoxically, gain power.

If the leader's ego becomes inflated to the point where he/she sees him-/herself as a super-strong hero, beyond good and evil, and capable of doing and justifying anything according to reality as he/she perceives and shaping it to his/her ends,[25] his/her downfall is usually imminent.[26] In contrast, more individuated leaders are aware of their shadow sides, and they do not deny, repress, or project them. Their awareness of their shadows gives them humility and humbleness. They know that they are fallible and human, with human faults, and not superheroes. In this way, they gain the power to deal honestly and openly with their weaknesses.

Table 8.2 summarises the individuated and unindividuated leader's attributes as well as the leadership theme of this attribute and its behavioural manifestations.

Table 8.2: Self-awareness and insight of individuated and unindividuated leaders

ATTRIBUTE 1: SELF-AWARENESS AND INSIGHT		
Theme: Faces the shadow		
Attribute 1: Self-awareness and insight	**Leadership theme of stage**	**Key leadership behaviour manifestations**
Individuated		
Self-aware of own inner world. Aware of own core complexes. Accepts uniqueness of others.	Aware of own impact on others and own reaction to actions of others. Forms genuine and deep relationships.	Open to give and receive feedback. Builds trust of followers with congruence between what he/she feels, thinks, says and does. Respects and appreciates diversity and uniqueness of others. Makes own vulnerabilities transparent.
Unindividuated		
In grip of unconscious, instinctual reactions. Has many blind spots. Tends to judge people who hold different views from him-/herself.	Tough and keeps a safe distance from followers to ensure that they believe the façade.	Does not welcome unfavourable feedback. Sees self as super-strong, beyond good and evil, and therefore does and justifies anything according to reality as he/she sees it. Destroys trust of followers by being incongruent: not meaning what he/she says and actions not in line with what was said.

Stage 2: Adaptation

The individuation challenges during this stage are about facing the real world as it is, and adapting to and performing in such a world. The person has to learn to take care of him-/herself. The person leaves the safe, nurturing containment offered by the mother (or mothering). The ego experiences the anxiety invoked by the challenges of the world. If this anxiety is introduced in moderate amounts, the person learns to master the challenges with growing confidence. He/she needs to learn about fitness, achievement, and competition.

The growth process can be described as a "hero's journey" that starts with facing true reality, and becoming independent and self-sufficient. The hero crosses the safety threshold of "home", leaving the comfort of the known zone for an unknown, insecure world. The ego needs to identify with a hero figure in order to muster the energy to "slay the dragon" (that is, to face the challenges of life) and "free the princess" (that is, to liberate his/her own soul).[27] In other words, symbolically expressed, the journey entails moving from the nurturing stage of individuation to the adaptation stage.

Individuated Leadership Attribute 2: Balancing engagement and disengagement from self and others

To implement and manage change is one of the major responsibilities of a leader, as reflected in the above descriptions and definitions of leadership. Despite the attention change management is receiving, and the efforts made to ensure that change intervention processes run smoothly, very few organisational change processes, whether it is a major take-over, a new computer system, or just moving offices, can be described as really successful.

A possible Jungian attribution of the problems encountered during most change interventions is to low levels of individuation. When a new orientation or adaptation is needed, as happens during change, a constellated archetype is usually activated. There is only a limited number of such constellations. Hence the same typical patterns of resistance will occur over and over again. These archetypal patterns function at a primitive, instinctual level, and are therefore not reachable by logical arguments or reasons. An example would be the often immature reactions of employees when an organisation announces retrenchments. The insecurity of employees could activate an archetype, such as that of the orphan. Employees in the grip of the orphan archetype then behave, not like mature human beings, but like children abandoned by their mother. Because these patterns function at an unconscious level, people caught in such patterns will rationalise their resistance to change. The more individuated a person is, the less the tendency to regress to unconscious, instinctive patterns. The person will deal with the reality as presented to him/her and will be in the moment.

Individuation takes place as a two-fold movement: temporary identification with the unconscious images in order to make them conscious, followed by dis-identification with them, and reflecting on them as an individual. In this way, a person obtains psychological distance from the collective archetypal images, and does not get caught up in unconscious patterns. The same patterns that make change processes difficult cause leaders to derail. The unindividuated leader is attached to reactive, archetypal patterns such as micro-management, being overly concrete, conflict avoidance, and the tyrannising and victimisation of subordinates.[28] Leaders must constantly renew themselves and let go of the past, which includes letting go of outdated patterns of instinctual reaction. The individuated leader is more capable of detaching from patterns that have become outdated. He/she is more capable of change, of fitting his/her responses to a situation/context, and of inviting and receiving honest feedback.

Showing empathy is impossible for the leader who has not arrived at an adequate level of individuation. Empathy in action means that a leader is able to have insight into another person's internal state, then exit, and move to a point of distancing, in order to assist the other person to move on. The capacity to engage and disengage appropriately is a clear indicator of individuation, and a critical requirement for effective leadership.

There needs to be "authentic intimacy" between the leader and the team. The leader needs autonomy to ensure that he/she does not become absorbed by "groupthink" and is able to exercise discipline and change direction. Autonomy is not the same as isolation – the more individuated leader establishes interdependence. The leader is part of the team; he/she is able to engage, but is also able to disengage in order to remain objective in the face of brutal truths, such as his/her team's performance. If the leader is psychologically merged with the team, it becomes very difficult for him/her to give direction, to give honest feedback, and to know when to change direction.

During this phase of individuation, the leader learns that it is not enough to stand out and step away from the collective. He/she must learn to engage and disengage as is needed by others, in situations, as well as by parts of him-/herself. To disengage is not a once-off, brave step away from the collective, but is a constant process of engaging and disengaging.

Table 8.3 summarises the individuated and unindividuated leaders' attributes as well as the leadership theme and its behavioural manifestations.

Table 8.3: Balancing engagement and disengagement from self and others in individuated and unindividuated leaders

ATTRIBUTE 2: BALANCING ENGAGEMENT AND DISENGAGEMENT FROM SELF AND OTHERS		
Theme: Open to change, breaks archetypal patterns		
Attribute 2: Balancing engagement and disengagement from self and others	**Leadership theme of stage**	**Key leadership behaviour manifestations**
Individuated		
Lets go of past. Remains objective. Distances self from others at times and reflects on events.	Relationship and network building while maintaining own sense of purpose.	Exercises healthy discipline while maintaining relationships. Initiates and implements meaningful change. Destroys anything hindering excellence. Builds coherent, performing team.
Unindividuated		
Holds on to the past. Subjective. Unable to take meta-perspective.	Self-centred or overly team driven, or oscillating between the two.	Resists change and avoids conflict. Tyrannises subordinates with micromanagement practices. Gets sucked in by "groupthink".

Individuated Leadership Attribute 3: Embracing and managing ambivalence and paradox

The world is growing not only more and more complex and chaotic, but also increasingly ambivalent. Right and wrong, important and unimportant, are often unclear. During ambivalence, leaders frequently have to choose between the lesser of two evils, with no clear precedent to guide them. Difficult ethical decisions usually have negative consequences, whatever the leader decides. Under these conditions, decisions are also often beyond an ethical code, and beyond a leader's usual expertise and experience. The objective and rational analysis of facts, the weighing up of alternatives, and risk evaluations do not provide clear and comprehensive answers in these ambivalent situations.

Under these circumstances, the leader's intuition and inner wisdom need to guide him/her to a seemingly acceptable answer. If a leader is not in touch with his/her inner wisdom, biases, preconceived ideas, and projections, appropriate decisions in these ambivalent and paradoxical situations are almost impossible. The unindividuated leader seeks out the security of knowing that he/she is on the "good" and "right" side. If anyone suffers because of a decision by the unindividuated leader, he/she finds the justification of a projection: ethical values that differ are rejected and pathologised. Unindividuated leaders need a clear choice between good and bad, important and unimportant. In contrast, the individuated leader tolerates ambiguity and difference. He/she has an appreciation for, and is not threatened by, values and viewpoints that differ radically from his/her own.

Some situations have clear-cut, final solutions. Others cannot be solved by a single decision or solution. The advantages and disadvantages of both sides of a decision create a dilemma that needs to be managed. The unindividuated leader, unable to deal with dilemmas, desires to find final solutions to problems, due to his/her own one-sidedness. An example of such a dilemma is whether to centralise or decentralise decision-making in an organisation. This type of decision calls for the fusion of opposites at a higher level. Dynamic opposites need to be balanced simultaneously, and fused. Both points of view have advantages and disadvantages. This is readily accepted by individuated leaders.

Instead of taking a decision and managing the consequences, unindividuated leaders often reverse a decision to counter the disadvantages. One thus sees organisations forever wasting energy: they go through the continuous pendulum swings of centralising, decentralising, centralising again, and back to decentralising. Unindividuated leaders often see decisions as "either-or" choices, and find it near impossible to see "and" decisions. The more individuated leader is able to handle, confidently and comfortably, the tension created by seemingly conflicting ideas. He/she knows that solutions are often not clear-cut and readily established.

Jung described the masculine side of human beings as the *animus*, and the feminine side as the *anima*.[29] At this stage of the individuation journey, the male hero needs to encounter his/her own anima, or feminine intuitive side. In modern organisations, the animus seems to be encouraged, and is sought at the expense of the anima. Leadership tasks, however, in complex organisations require more than only the energy and goal-directedness of the animus. The self-confident hero now finds that brute force and the indiscriminate application of animus energy to ambivalent and paradoxical situations do not work. He/she needs to balance the forceful animus with the reflective depth of the anima. Far from easy or unheroic, Jung described this stage of individuation as follows: "The only adventure that is still worthwhile for modern man lies in the inner realm of the unconscious psyche."[30]

To manage ambivalence and paradoxes requires a different approach. Considering and caring about the impact of decisions on a broader constituency and environment becomes critical. It is crucial for leaders to balance goal-directedness with humbleness.[31] The leader who is unable to do this cannot progress to a higher level of leadership. The masculine and feminine principles are not given upfront to any person. They manifest through real-life experiences. To get to know one's anima is much more difficult than to get to know the shadow. Knowing the anima is not a return to the maternal nurturing that the wanderer longs for, but necessitates a progression towards integration. At this stage, the hero no longer has a need for, and does not long for, external nurturing and support.

The anima is about relationships. The leader needs to learn to accept people as they are. He/she needs to build authentic relationships, without projections, compensations, or compulsive demands. Knowing one's anima, particularly, impacts on relationships with people of the opposite gender. The more individuated leader does not suffer from the compulsion of anima (or animus) projection.[32] An unindividuated leader is often, at heart, a sexist, and bound to derail because of underplaying the criticality of healthy interpersonal relationships. If genuine and deep relationships are not cultivated, one's orientation towards life remains infantile.[33] The unindividuated leader finds it very hard to trust others, especially those of the opposite gender, because he/she does not trust him-/herself.[34]

The anima contains hidden wisdom about the laws of life. The anima is not only the counterpart of the animus. In its own right, it also carries ambivalence and paradoxes.[35] By knowing his/her anima, a person's ability to deal with external ambivalence and paradoxes increases as he/she becomes more comfortable with the duality of his/her inner self, since he/she has wider access to more inner wisdom. Just as a man needs to encounter his anima, a woman needs to encounter her animus, in order to be a balanced, integrated person. At this stage of the individuation journey, the hero is responding to an inner call, far more than reacting to externally imposed doctrines. The more individuated leader starts to learn that true opposites are never incommensurables. Seemingly opposite sides are interrelated: the one can only exist if the other exists. This relationship between opposites is further explored in the discussion of the unfolding of the next attribute.

Table 8.4 summarises the individuated and unindividuated leaders' attributes as well as the leadership theme of this attribute and its behavioural manifestations.

Table 8.4: Embracing and managing ambivalence and paradox in individuated and unindividuated leaders

ATTRIBUTE 3: EMBRACING AND MANAGING AMBIVALENCE AND PARADOX		
Theme: Faces and balances own anima and animus		
Attribute 3: Embracing and managing ambivalence and paradox	**Leadership theme of stage**	**Key leadership behaviour manifestations**
Individuated		
Balances dynamic opposites simultaneously. Balances forceful anima with reflective depth. Considers conscious and unconscious wisdom in inner dialogue.	Manages and integrates opposites.	Seeks progressive solutions for paradoxes. Keeps to a decision, but manages the problems the decision has created. Listens to apparent "opponents" and respects their views, even if he/she differs with them.

Attribute 3: Embracing and managing ambivalence and paradox	Leadership theme of stage	Key leadership behaviour manifestations
Unindividuated		
Not in touch with inner wisdom. Uncomfortable with ambivalence and paradoxes. Clings to all-knowing persona.	Focuses on single aspects of issues, constantly changing between opposite poles.	Constantly reverses decisions and shifts priorities. Has racist or sexist tendencies or shows low tolerance for people with differing religions. Takes costly decisions which do not resolve the intended paradox.

Individuated Leadership Attribute 4: Balancing self-sufficiency with a team or team orientation

To break from the tribe or team representing the collective a person belongs to requires extraordinary energy and courage. The tribe/team does not encourage or tolerate any member standing out. This tendency discourages and suppresses genuine leadership. Unspoken fear of the negative consequences of creative leadership exists. This fear traps everyone into conformity, complacency, cynicism, and inaction. The team, no matter how sophisticated on the surface, does not want any member to stand out and be counted in order to face and solve the problems of the time. There is also the fear of ineffective and/or unethical leadership being exposed.

The "hero myth" represents the ego's desire to replace dependency upon unconsciousness with conscious self-direction and purpose. The main task of the hero is to attain independence. The hero as a leader has a critical burden: to take his/her team with him/her. The myth of the independent, Lone Ranger-type leader needs to be transformed into interdependence. The leader has the task of mobilising his/her team to pursue a shared vision and being committed to achieve this vision. In so doing, the leader is giving life to something bigger than him-/herself: a lasting, worthy legacy.

Table 8.5 summarises the individuated and unindividuated leaders' attributes as well as the leadership theme of this attribute and its behavioural manifestations.

Table 8.5: *Balancing self-sufficiency with team or team orientation in individuated and unindividuated leaders*

ATTRIBUTE 4: BALANCING SELF-SUFFICIENCY WITH TEAM OR TEAM ORIENTATION		
Theme: Independent, self-sufficient wanderer, forms ego-identity		
Attribute 4: Balance self-sufficiency with team or team orientation	**Leadership theme of stage**	**Key leadership behaviour manifestations**
Individuated		
Independent and self-sufficient. Self-directed and purposeful. At peace with own life history.	Stand up and be counted. Finds own voice relative to others, time and place.	Takes unpopular stance in such a way that others are likely to follow. Ensures that goals are achieved, standards are met, and plans are implemented. Comfortable to engage with others without letting go of own stance; is in touch with the world on his/her own terms.
Unindividuated		
Conforming and others-directed: safety of collective defines comfort zone. Lacks purpose. Uncomfortable with own life history.	Goes with team. Follows only own agenda or gets absorbed in others' agendas. Succumbs to team pressure.	Maintains *status quo*: unable to get buy-in and ownership of collective vision, values and interests. Uncomfortable to take stance which opposes the team. Unable to convince others to follow him/her on a quest.

Individuated Leadership Attribute 5: Maintain composure and mental clarity amidst complexity and chaos

As mentioned above, organisational life is growing increasingly complex. Employees often experience it as chaotic, particularly if they expect and believe linear, cause-and-effect principles to operate. In contrast, instant, real-time decisions, ongoing innovation at all levels, agility, and quick adjustments are needed, and occur continuously in the world today. Even stock markets have caught on to the fact that agile and responsive leadership makes the difference between winning and losing, and between being and staying ahead of the game.

Under these conditions, the danger of overload is most real. Overload comes from many sources: information explosion, task complexity, role ambivalence, matrix reporting structures, and project work in combination with routine tasks requiring detailed attention. Followers look to leaders for clarity and direction. Ambiguity triggers dependency needs and, consequently, higher levels of anxiety. Followers expect leaders to contain their anxiety.

One of the key tasks of the leader is to face up to reality without denying problems and challenges, and then to give direction and bring hope. To simplify is a key task of an effective leader, given these conditions.[36] An inspirational, well-articulated vision is a very practical tool to contain anxiety,[37] and thus to ensure that followers do not feel overwhelmed, but are purposefully enabled. The leader's authentic presence is critical to give followers a sense of control over their context. To have things done faster in organisations necessitates leaders making intelligent, timeous decisions, and then implementing these effectively under conditions of ongoing, radical, and fundamental change.

In a complex world with multiple variables, the individuated leader is able to distil the critical issues from the overwhelming mass of less important ones. Clarity of thinking is critical, but so is the ability to stay calm and focused. The individuated leader is centred and able to take a meta-position, providing him/her with a better position to keep his/her perspective and remain calm. In contrast, the unindividuated leader is characterised by too narrow a focus, infused by low self-confidence and uncertainty. He/she finds it difficult to let less important issues go unattended. Such leaders tend to micromanage. In spite of the ongoing turbulence, the effective leader ensures that a setting is created in which employees can still single-mindedly focus on their work and be fully engaged in their tasks/roles, in order to ensure excellent performance.[38]

Table 8.6 summarises the individuated and unindividuated leaders' attributes as well as the leadership theme of this attribute and its behavioural manifestations.

Table 8.6: Maintaining composure and mental clarity amidst complexity and chaos in individuated and unindividuated leaders

ATTRIBUTE 5: MAINTAINING COMPOSURE AND MENTAL CLARITY AMIDST COMPLEXITY AND CHAOS		
Theme: Able to enter into flow state, accepts that he/she is a "good enough" leader		
Attribute 5: Maintaining composure and mental clarity amidst complexity and chaos	**Leadership theme of stage**	**Key leadership behaviour manifestations**
Individuated		
Comfortable with complexity and ambiguity. Comfortable with imperfection, fluidity and change. Comfortable with lack of structure.	Creates clarity amidst chaos. Embraces fluidity.	Focused on key deliverables. Simplifies complexity for followers to make it manageable. Able to give direction when priorities are unclear and goals vague.
Unindividuated		
Ambiguity triggers dependency needs and anxiety. Perfectionist tendencies. Needs clear structure.	Unable to lead without clear structure and unambiguous goals.	Unable to make decisions without precedents and in uncertain situations when all variables are not known. Gets bogged down in detail. Expects perfection in less critical areas. Disappears in times of crises.

Stage 3: Integration

The third stage of individuation is unique to the Jungian approach. Other psychodynamic approaches are limited to Stage Two: Adaptation.[39] During the integration stage, the search for meaning comes to fruition; the person becomes centred, whole, and connected to both transcendent and immediate realities. During this stage, the often fragmented ego becomes integrated, and is in dialogue with the self as the ultimate destination of individuation. In other words, the leader is able to utilise his/her unconscious wisdom effectively by having a high degree of access to it.

Individuated Leadership Attribute 6: A sense of deeper meaning and destiny

Individuation is a summons to find and free oneself. For the more individuated leader, this freedom implies the relative freedom from collective prescriptions, as well as from instinctual, archetypal urges. For the more individuated leader, freedom and destiny merge to form meaning. He/she creates the future as he/she sees it, rather than reacting to it. The more individuated leader has a deep sense of purpose and a transpersonal awareness. He/she has a well-developed philosophy of life, and is able to articulate it eloquently and with genuine sincerity. The more individuated leader takes the agenda of his/her inner spirituality (or soul) seriously, and lives his/her own myth. These leaders follow their destiny as they see and believe in it.

Individuated leaders shift the nature of commitment. They are not blindly and obediently, in a compliant way, committed.[40] They will do what it takes to achieve their goals, but in a state of flow. They are not narrow-mindedly driven, but achieve their goals and vision at their own pace, and with wisdom, flexibility, and agility. Being in a flow state implies having the patience to actively listen to and respond to one's true calling. These leaders are in a state of surrendering to a higher purpose of their own choice. This state of surrender creates an authentic presence, acknowledged by all. Individuated leaders belong to themselves, and are persons in their own right. This attracts people to them, because of the authenticity being conveyed. Leadership, for individuated leaders, truly becomes a state of being, more than a mere state of doing.

Self-awareness increases one's ability to control and direct one's life. Actualities and potentialities are continually uncovered through living, working, relating to others, and contemplating one's life. Meaning in life is therefore a continuous process of discovering and uncovering, rather than a single insight or event. The collective unconscious contains archetypes of human experiences and patterns, such as birth, death, marriage, the mother, the father, the hero, and the wise old woman. These archetypes link people to other people and to their ancestors. They represent a vital link connecting a person to the past, present, and future.[41] The incorporation of such images into the self is vital for the individuation process on the way to wholeness.

The individuated leader claims his/her personal stake in the wider cosmos. He/she sees him-/herself connected to something transcendental, something bigger than him-/herself. Individuation is about separation from the collective, but in such a way that the leader remains meaningfully connected, also at a symbolic level. The leader creates meaning for his/her followers through the meaning he/she has found. The hero, at this stage, has a strong sense of vocation (or calling). He/she knows exactly where he/she is heading, given his/her calling, and also knows where he/she is leading his/her followers in terms of the "light" he/she has received. At this point, individuation comes close, in some respects, to Indian Vedic psychology, which describes the ultimate form of consciousness as transcendental (or cosmic): a wholeness of pure consciousness, beyond the division of subject and object, being fully aware of one's own unbounded nature and multiple possibilities, as yet unexpressed, accompanied by a deep understanding of the underlying order of things.

Table 8.7 summarises the individuated and unindividuated leaders' attributes as well as the leadership theme of this attribute and its behavioural manifestations.

Table 8.7: Sense of deeper meaning and destiny in individuated and unindividuated leaders

ATTRIBUTE 6: SENSE OF DEEPER MEANING AND DESTINY		
Theme: Incorporates archetypal images and creates collective meaning		
Attribute 6: Sense of deeper meaning and destiny	**Leadership theme of stage**	**Key leadership behaviour manifestations**
Individuated		
Takes responsibility for own happiness and growth. Utilises learnings from the past, lives fully in present, considers impact of present on future. Driven by deep sense of higher purpose and making contribution or difference; rises above own self-interest.	Inspires and actualises a shared vision. Transcends self-interest to greater purpose.	Creates vision and values for followers. Models way to live vision and values for followers by making personal sacrifices. Takes ethical decisions, even at a high cost to self.
Unindividuated		
Views life as snapshot events. Reacts to events without considering broader implications and context. Could be stuck in past, living only for moment or overly concerned about future.	Driven by short-term goals and self-interest.	Leads in reactive manner, does not give clear direction. Unable to model way to live organisational vision and values. Takes unethical decisions for short-term gain.

Individuated Leadership Attribute 7: Balancing self-empowerment and the empowerment of others

Unlike most other approaches to leadership, the Jungian approach places less emphasis on charisma, and much more emphasis on the leader's duty to ensure that those entrusted to him/her are also encouraged to individuate. This means that a major task of the leader is to understand the psychological make-up, emotional responses, and personality characteristics of team members. The effectiveness of a leader's actions is ultimately judged by his/her team and other stakeholders. Aspects such as the performance and growth of the team, the preparedness to deal with change and crisis, team members' satisfaction with the leader, their commitment to team goals, as well as their development and growth, are measures of the leader's effectiveness.

The more individuated leader will thus practise empowerment with the growth of his/her employees in mind. Empowerment will never be an excuse for overloading people. The individuated leader is able to build trusting and genuine relationships with team members. He/she does not demean and destroy relationships when mistakes are made. He/she is able to tolerate imperfections in both him-/herself and others, because, as a leader, he/she is not overly anxious about achievement. He/she accepts mistakes as a natural part of risk taking, experimentation, and learning. The effective leader will ensure that every employee has the opportunity to reach his/her own potential while concurrently working towards organisational goals.

Table 8.8 summarises the individuated and unindividuated leaders' attributes as well as the leadership theme of this attribute and its behavioural manifestations.

Table 8.8: Managing polarity: balancing self-empowering and empowering others in individuated and unindividuated leaders

ATTRIBUTE 7: MANAGING POLARITY: BALANCING SELF-EMPOWERING AND EMPOWERING OTHERS		
Theme: Allow others to individuate		
Attribute 7: Managing polarity: balance self-empowering and empowering others	**Leadership theme of stage**	**Key leadership behaviour manifestations**
Individuated		
Tolerates imperfection. Insight into own strengths and weaknesses. Growth orientation for self and others.	Growing others and self to achieve in a complementary fashion.	Understands psychological make-up, emotional responses, and personality characteristics of team members. Ensures team members are challenged and consequently develop and grow. Ensures knowledge is managed effectively.
Unindividuated		
Overly anxious about achievement. Overly confident. Main concern not own or others' growth.	Narrow task and goal achievement focus. Concern for achieving goals overshadows growth of people.	Overloads subordinates. Under-communicates. Denies mistakes and tends to blame.

Individuated Leadership Attribute 8: Psychological integration and wholeness

At the third individuation stage, the more individuated, centred, and integrated leader is connected to something infinite, to other people, and to an overarching purpose and meaning. He/she also is more intimately connected to the realities of daily life. African tradition emphasises the deeper and more purposeful connection to other people much more than most Western cultures. This connection finds its expression in the African term "*Ubuntu*", best described in the

Zulu expression: "*Umuntu ngumuntu ngabantu*", meaning that a person is a person only because of and through others.

Ubuntu fits in very well with the Jungian concept of a deep and meaningful connectedness to other people while fulfilling one's destiny. An individuated leader is able to understand and relate to the collective without totally immersing him-/herself therein. This probably makes the concept of *individuation* at the third stage more aligned to African philosophies of personal growth than to most western philosophies in this field. Most of the latter philosophies emphasise the individual's right to self-actualisation and to fulfil his/her ego-centric destiny, without giving much attention to the person's responsibility towards and connection to his/her team.

However, no person will ever fully know him-/herself. The end of one's journey of exploration, Stage Three, marks the preparation for the start of a new journey. Beginning is an end; an end is a beginning. The human psyche contains everything necessary to grow, adapt, and heal itself.[42] At this stage of the individuation process, the leader has moved towards wholeness. He/she has grown in awareness of him-/herself, and has uncovered his/her potential. The more individuated leader can form authentic relationships with others, free from projections and compulsive demands. The ego and the more transcendent self are functioning as a whole in relation with others, while preserving their intrinsic qualities. The unification of the whole personality is thus not a once-off event, but a never-ending, life-long journey.

Table 8.9 summarises the individuated and unindividuated leaders' attributes as well as the leadership theme of this attribute and its behavioural manifestations.

Table 8.9: Psychological integration and wholeness in individuated and unindividuated leaders

ATTRIBUTE 8: EXPERIENCING PSYCHOLOGICAL INTEGRATION AND WHOLENESS		
Theme: Experiences unification of personality		
Attribute 8: Experiencing psychological integration and wholeness	**Leadership theme of stage**	**Key leadership behaviour manifestations**
Individuated		
Aware of self and own potentialities. Healthy dialogue between parts of self while parts maintain independence. Deep awareness of total self, known and unknown, good and bad, strength and weakness and accepts self.	Has wisdom and accepts stewardship. Takes action in spite of own preference; integrated, shared leadership.	Is seen as wise by most people. Takes action to ensure wellness of team members. Takes care of everything entrusted to him/her.
Unindividuated		
Feels fragmented and compartmentalised. Overly individualistic or immersed in collective. Remains a stranger to him-/herself.	Fragmented, self-alienated. Caught in earlier stages.	Acts frustrated and fragmented. Not emphasising lifelong growth. Not considering wellness of team members.

Individuated Leadership Attribute 9: Living interrelated and interconnected

Globalisation, in particular, has brought the importance of systemic thinking to the fore. The leader has to maintain some distance from the everyday functioning of the organisation in order to maintain a healthy perspective. He/she cannot afford to become over-involved in the detail – to the extent that he/she loses sight of the "big picture." The big picture is growing in both size and complexity. Globally, systems are also increasingly becoming interconnected and interdependent. A seemingly small change in one country may snowball into global consequences, the so-called "butterfly effect", as was seen during the deep 2008/2009 worldwide recession.

Chaos contains hidden patterns. The person at this level of individuation is not only able to tolerate, but also to live comfortably with, chaos. The more individuated leader makes sense of the chaos, sees the underlying patterns, understands the rules giving rise to these patterns, and is able to visualise possible/probable future patterns. Such sensitivity does not come from studying only market trends and the like in isolation, but also from an inner sensitivity and intuitive insight. The individuated leader takes a systemic view of life, and sees phenomena as interconnected. The philosopher, Bohm, has already said that everything in the universe is related.

The leader who is deeply connected to his/her inner wisdom is more sensitive to the outer world, and can make sense of the seemingly chaotic. He/she can intuitively foresee future events, make the best of opportunities, and take timeous precautions to counter threats. To the unindividuated leader, these seemingly planned "miracles" make the individuated leader seem like the archetypal magician. In reality, a leader at this stage of individuation has progressed beyond the enactment of any archetype. He/she is coming close to being a fully unique human being, living out his/her chosen destiny while remaining connected.

This characterisation of the individuated leaders by Jung resonates highly with the currently propagated chaos/complexity theory of reality. In short, this worldview sees reality as consisting of a holistic set of reciprocally influencing and interdependent variables, which, in collectivity, continuously go through unpredictable states of order and chaos as their interdependencies change. Order is expressed in the form of emerging, self-designing patterns, governed by a few underlying rules. In some quarters, it is argued that leaders need to adopt this world view if they want to be truly effective in the emerging new world order.

The more individuated leader, at this stage, is in a flow state: his/her intuitive connectedness overcomes aloneness and separation. He/she can allow life's creative forces to flow through him/her. In his/her cosmic connectedness, he/she finds his/her highest purpose and meaning. Flow means allowing life to happen, instead of trying to control everything. Even the individuation process itself is, at this stage, not a deliberate decision, but must be allowed to happen, to flow. Jung wrote:

> *"The process of unification is only partially under the control of our will; for the rest it happens involuntarily. With the conscious mind we are able, at most, to get within reach of the unconscious process, and must then wait and see what will happen next."*[9]

The more individuated leader has the trust and patience to go with the flow of life. He/she also enables others to perform at their respective optimal levels and experience a flow state. The hero is now ready to serve something beyond him-/herself.[43]

Table 8.10 summarises the individuated and unindividuated leaders' attributes as well as the leadership theme of this attribute and its behavioural manifestations.

Table 8.10: Living interrelated and interconnected in individuated and unindividuated leaders

ATTRIBUTE 9: LIVING INTERCORRELATED AND INTERCONNECTED		
Theme: Aware of interconnectedness and synchronicity, expects small miracles, enters into true dialogue		
Attribute 9: Living interrelated and interconnected	**Leadership theme of stage**	**Key leadership behaviour manifestations**
Individuated		
Allows life to happen. Connected to transcendent world and practical realities. Ready to serve something beyond him-/herself.	Has a theory of how life works. Big-picture thinker: sees variables as interrelated, in healthy interaction.	Focuses on strategic issues. Could be described as person ready to serve a higher cause or other people. Considers broader implications of decisions for example, impact on community and environment.
Unindividuated		
Tries to control everything. Feels alone and separated. Is self-serving.	Only sees causal links between variables; drowns in detail.	Focuses on operational issues. Could be described as self-serving. Trusts no one and tries to control everything.

By this point, the three stages of individuation, namely nurturing, adaptation, and integration, have been translated into ten stage-related leadership psychosocial maturity attributes and behaviours.

The Development of Leadership Psychosocial Maturity

Individuating individuals

The development of the psychosocial maturity of leaders is a seemingly impossible challenge. Current literature, both in the Piaget and Jungian traditions, maintains that maturity depends on chronological age. Given the dire need for competent leadership as well as the worldwide population becoming younger and younger, there is no option but to take on the challenge of "fast-tracking" the maturation process of individuals with high leadership potential. Though very little robust scientific research has been done on the development of psychosocial maturity, some individuals clearly attain high levels of maturity at early ages. Some recent research has found that the level of individuation is not as dependent on chronological age as it had been made out to be.[44]

The starting point for developing a person's psychosocial maturity is an "inside-out" rather than the usual "outside-in" approach. The "inside-out" approach starts with self-awareness. Change, and personal growth, are not forced but are allowed to happen. Where the "outside-in" approach starts with skills training, this approach considers inner transformation as necessary to take place first before any lasting behavioural change. Techniques to develop psychosocial maturity are therefore based on the premise of "know thyself" first and foremost.

An array of in-depth psychology techniques can be used to guide a leader through the stages and attributes of individuation towards greater maturity. Techniques that can be utilised in this approach include coaching, mentoring, counselling, art therapy, music therapy, equestrian therapy, utilisation of stories in its many forms (for example, in the Ericsonian way, where a story is created to reflect the client's inner world, or myths or fairy tales, which can be used to gain insight into archetypal patterns), dream analysis, film, theatre, and nature encounters. This approach does require intensive interventions. Although training courses can be part of the process, they are seldom enough. Some form of one-on-one sessions is usually needed to assist the leader to reflect on and gain insight into his/her inner world.

Individual coaching or counselling is probably the most effective way to develop a person's maturity. Regularly seeing a coach or psychologist for personal growth is gradually becoming less stigmatised. As more and more senior leaders in organisations openly say: "I am off to see my coach/psychologist," others will realise that it is showing seriousness with one's own personal growth. During sessions, the main aim would be to make the leader aware of unconscious, archetypal patterns of reactions and behaviours. For instance, many leaders are stuck in stage 2: Adaptation.[45] They have experienced neither the nurturing of stage 1, nor the freedom of the Integration stage 3. Coaching/counselling can address specific individual developmental issues. The stages and attributes can be used as a "roadmap" to guide the developmental process. The behaviours associated with the attributes and stages can give an indication of aspects which need attention.

Individuating teams

Teams and organisations, and even whole systems, can individuate. In the same way as an individual, a team of people can collectively be conscious or unconscious, mature or immature. There are well-known examples of teams of people who collectively have had much lower levels of consciousness than any individual member of the team. After corporate scandals, such as Enron and Parmalat, and more recent less well-known ones, individuals who were part of the decision-making process said that they individually knew that what they were doing was wrong, but went with the collective, unconscious decisions of the team.

Teams can individuate in a similar way to individuals. The team's individuation also starts with consciousness. Teams where the norm is open communication, open feedback, members not being over-sensitive to criticism and no "sacred cows" (topics not open for discussion) has a chance to become more conscious and as a result could become more individuated, and therefore more mature. Permission to counter "groupthink", which means any member of the team is allowed to point out a blind spot without any negative consequences for him-/herself, is therefore an important practical step towards psychosocial maturity of a team.

Immature teams often "scapegoat".[46] Scapegoating is an unconscious process whereby team members all agree that a particular team member, or department, is useless and everything that goes wrong is blamed on the scapegoat. The scapegoating process unites team members in a primitive, unconscious way in their condemnation of the scapegoat. The management team of an organisation will, for instance, all agree and openly ridicule the Information Technology or

Human Resources departments. As long as the team scapegoats, it does not face the real issues and remains immature. Individual psychosocial maturity of team members is a prerequisite for team psychosocial maturity. It is individual team members who must be mature enough in the first place to handle direct feedback and criticism.

The leader of the team sets the tone for the norms which govern the levels of maturity expected of team members. The leader therefore plays a major role in the psychosocial maturity of the team. The team as an organism can also develop its level of maturity in very similar ways in which individuals develop their maturity. The team's unconscious issues and stage of individuation can be explored and developed, for instance through team coaching sessions.

Individuating organisations

In order for organisations to become more mature, it will have to be the leaders of the organisations that drive the process. Greenleaf had already confronted leaders with this question more than 30 years ago: *"Are the people entrusted to you growing as persons in their own right, are they becoming healthier, wiser, freer and more autonomous as a result of your leadership?"*[47] As a first step towards a more individuated organisation, leaders should have the personal growth, maturity and psychological wellbeing of their team members as part of their performance contracts. The growth and maturation of team members can be traced by means of measurements such as multirater feedback and an annual wellbeing assessment utilising interviews by wellness experts, who could use indirect measuring techniques such as analysis of drawings, which have been shown to give a fairly accurate "picture" of a person's psychosocial states.[48] [49] Because growth and maturation are largely unconscious (very few people would openly admit that they are immature), self-report questionnaires are probably the least accurate form of assessment, although team members could evaluate and give feedback on steps a leader had taken to ensure personal growth.

Organisations can potentially be places where organisational members can grow, develop, and fulfil their needs and aspirations while contributing towards the organisation's success. Sadly, with the current stagnant world economy, coupled with the pressure on productivity caused by global competition, the way in which organisations engage with their employees reminds one of the factory "sweat shops" of the middle of the previous century. Organisation members' growth, development and well-being are not seen as a priority in many organisations. Imagine how organisations would change if the growth and maturity of organisation members became a strategic imperative, and leaders were measured on more than outputs such as profit, safety records, quality of products, and services. Organisations can then, once again, become the wonderful places for people to work that they have the potential to be. Such an organisation would be conscious, mature and individuated.

Conclusion

In this chapter, Jung's constructs, individuation in particular, were proposed as an approach towards leadership maturity and leadership development. With the increased demands on leaders, leadership maturity is an essential foundation to successful leadership. An "inside-out" approach has a chance of bringing real growth and depth to leadership development. The identified critical leadership attributes and behaviours give a practical starting point to the assessment, development and evaluation of progress for leadership development and wellbeing.

Endnotes

1	Kets de Vries, 2006.	26	Sternberg, 2008.
2	Kets de Vries, 2006.	27	Stein, 2012.
3	Pearson, 1998.	28	Kets de Vries, 2006.
4	Jung, 1948.	29	Jung, 1964.
5	Jung, 1968.	30	Jung, 1964.
6	Jung, 1968.	31	Collins, 2011.
7	Jung, 1948.	32	Jung, 1968.
8	Jung, 1968.	33	Jung, 1964.
9	Jung, 1968.	34	Jung, 1968.
10	Neumann, in Stein, 2012.	35	Jung, 1968.
11	Jung, 1968.	36	Kets de Vries, 2006.
12	Stein, 2012.	37	Kets de Vries, 2006.
13	Jung, 1968.	38	Kets de Vries, 2006.
14	Jung, 1968.	39	Stein, 2012.
15	Jung, 1968.	40	Kets de Vries, 2006.
16	Du Toit, 2011.	41	Jung, 1968.
17	Kets de Vries, 2006.	42	Jung, 1968.
18	Kets de Vries, 2006.	43	Greenleaf & Spears, 2002.
19	Collins, 2011.	44	Du Toit, 2011.
20	Jung, 1968.	45	Du Toit, 2011.
21	Jung, 1968.	46	Colman, 1995.
22	Jung, 1968.	47	Greenleaf & Spears, 2002.
23	Kets de Vries, 2006.	48	Du Toit, 2011.
24	Jung, 1968.	49	Du Toit, Botha & Koen, 2015.
25	Jung, 1968.		

References

Colman, D. 1995. *Up from scapegoating: Awakening consciousness in groups.* New York, NY: Vintage Books.

Collins, JC. 2011. *Good to great: Why some companies make the leap… and others don't.* London, UK: HarperCollins.

Du Toit, DH. 2011. *A Jungian perspective on the psycho-social maturity of leaders.* Doctoral dissertation. Johannesburg, ZA: University of Johannesburg, Department of Industrial Psychology and People Management.

Du Toit, DH, Botha, E & Koen, V. 2015. *The measurement of unconscious constructs.* Paper presented at the Jopie van Rooyen Conference, Skukuza, ZA, May.

Greenleaf, RK & Spears, LC. 2002. *Servant leadership: A journey into the nature of legitimate power and greatness.* 25th Anniversary ed. Mahwah, NJ: Paulist Press.

Jung, CG. 1948. *The integration of the personality.* 5th ed. London, UK: Kegan Paul.

Jung, CG. 1964. *Collected works: Civilization in transition.* Vol. 10. 2nd ed. London, UK: Routledge and Kegan Paul.

Jung, CG. 1968. *Collected works: Researches into the phenomenology of the self.* Vol. 9, Part 2. 2nd ed. London, UK: Routledge and Kegan Paul.

Kets de Vries, MFR. 2006. *The leadership mystique: Leading behavior in the human enterprise.* 2nd ed. London, UK: Prentice Hall.

Pearson, CS. 1998. *The hero within: Six archetypes we live by.* 3rd ed. San Francisco, CA: HarperCollins.

Stein, M. 2012. 'Individuation'. in RK Papadopoulos (ed). *The handbook of Jungian psychology: Theory, practice and applications.* Brighton, UK: Psychology Pressp. 196–214.

Sternberg, RJ. 2008. 'Why leaders fail'. In D Barry & H Hansen (eds). *The Sage handbook of new approaches in management and organization.* London, UK: Sage Publications, Inc. 481–484.

SECTION 4

LEADERSHIP STORIES

Chapter 9

LEADERSHIP STORIES

Introduction

In its very essence, the organisation is a dialogical network of interpersonal interconnections based on conversations, expressed in the form of stories. Stories are naturally-occurring phenomena in organisations through which information, shared experiences, expectations, culture, and identity are passed on. Stories are the very fabric of organisational life. They add a psychological dimension to organisational life through its feeling and experiencing dimension in the form of sense-making, meaning-giving, as well as emotional attachment and involvement which rational, empirical information and lack of knowledge cannot provide.

Storytelling infuses the whole Strategic Leadership Value Chain. It is persuasive leadership-in-action. A story as a form of conversation is capable of representing and transferring complex, multidimensional organisational realities to listeners in a simple and effortless way in order to make sense of, and give meaning and purpose to, organisational reality.

At its most basic level, storytelling as a conversation (or dialogue) refers to what is being said and listened to between people. The word 'dialogue' stems from two Greek roots, "*dia*" and "*logos*", jointly suggesting the sense of "meaning flowing through". Stories help organisational members to make sense of who they are, where they come from and fit in, and what they want to be. They help reduce organisational uncertainty, complexity and ambiguity by quickly and coherently disseminating information; they frame organisational events through their value-laden features; and they promote organisational culture and identification by establishing a context for organisational members.

Using stories is one of the best ways to:

- make abstract concepts meaningful;
- help connect people and ideas;
- inspire imagination and motivate action;
- give "breathing space" in the frenetic and merciless task-driven nature of the organisation;
- allow different perspectives to emerge;
- create sense, coherence, and meaning;
- develop value-centric descriptions of situations, allowing knowledge to be applied and solutions to be found;
- convey organisational values and culture;
- communicate complex messages simply;
- connect people into a shared frame of reference; and
- inspire change.

In the *first instance* leaders are, and have to be, storytellers about themselves: from where they have come; who they are; what they stand for; what they believe in; what they want to achieve and how; and what they want to leave behind as a legacy. The character, competence, connectedness, caring and commitment of leaders are manifested *inter alia* in how well they understand, and are able and willing to share, their personal journeys as leaders: from the past, through the present, into the future. It is a most powerful way in which to connect with others.

In the *second instance*, leaders have to be able to tell the story of the organisation they are currently involved in: the identity and ideology of the organisation; where the organisation has come from; its desired future destination and legacy; the journey travelled to date by the organisation; the journey still to be travelled; and how things are done and not done in the organisation.

This Section provides examples of the first kind of leadership stories: leaders' stories about themselves as leaders.

The accompanying box gives a list of the leaders whose stories follow – with their respective core themes – are included in this Section.

LEADER'S STORY	THEME OF STORY
Thuli Madonsela	*Leadership as the giant leap necessary for an inclusive, prosperous and peaceful future*
Mohammad Karaan	*Intuition, silence, giants and the cattle herder*
Gill Marcus	*What matters is the greater good*
Monhla Hlahla	*Moving effectively through the stages of leadership impact*
Hendrik du Toit	*Good leaders stand or fall by their principles*
GT Ferreira, Laurie Dippenaar & Paul Harris	*Leader excellence asks for a distinct, shared leadership philosophy*

References

Boje, D. 2008. *Storytelling organizations*. Thousand Oaks, CA: Sage.

Boyce, M.E. 1996. 'Organisational story and storytelling: A critical review'. *Journal of Organisational Change Management*, 9(5):5-26.

Christie, P. 2009. *Every leader a story teller – storytelling skills for personal leadership*. Johannesburg, ZA: Knowres.

Denning, S. 2011. *The leader's guide to storytelling*, San Francisco, CA: Jossey-Bass

Gabriel, Y. 2000). *Storytelling in organisations: Facts, fictions and fantasies*. New York, NY: Oxford University Press.

Ibarra, H & Lineback, K. 2005. 'What's your story?' *Harvard Business Review*, 1–7, January.

Veldsman, D & May, M. S. 2012. 'The stories that leaders tell during organisational change: The search for meaning during organisational transformation'. Unpublished Masters thesis, University of South Africa, Pretoria, South Africa.

Leadership as the giant leap necessary for an inclusive, prosperous and peaceful future

Thuli Madonsela

A book on leadership is a timely contribution as South Africa reflects on two decades of transitioning from its dark past in search of catalysts to accelerate progress towards the constitutional promise of a prosperous and peaceful future, where everyone's humanity is affirmed, potential freed and life improved in a strong constitutional democracy anchored in the rule of law.

Why leadership?

Leadership is critical for the future of people, organisations, communities and society. Inspired by a vision of a better future, true leadership conceives, actualises and leaves a sustainable future for all, to the benefit of all. However, leadership is not tied to a single person – the 'messiah' – or a position. It cannot be overemphasised that for groups to achieve the futures they desire, the burden of leadership must be borne by all members with each playing differentiated but complementary leadership roles. No one needs a title to lead. In fact, a person who is not leading without a title cannot lead with a title. Instead she/he will diminish the authority of the title.

Since the test of leadership is followership, anyone can and many do lead unconsciously through the things they do or say that influence and inspire others to do the same or act in a particular way or achieve a desired future. The crucial difference is conscious and purpose-driven leadership, which is at the core of true leadership. True leadership, which is effective leadership, is about consciously influencing others to embrace and resolutely pursue a cause or desired outcome. True leadership requires purpose-driven actions by persons seeking to make a difference through influencing themselves and others to act in congruence with the outcomes they seek.

True leadership is accordingly different from unconscious leadership. The latter often translates into what is often referred to as 'misleading'. An unconscious leader may not even realise they are responsible for others going astray. Accordingly, it is true leadership that is required for impactful peer influence and the success of families, organisations, communities and global quests.

A true leader's leadership is an inside-out conscious exercise that starts with leading oneself to do the right thing or that which must be done to achieve a desired end. He/she is not a whiner but a purpose- and principle-driven problem-solver who identifies or creates opportunities for him/herself and others to achieve desired outcomes when an opportunity presents itself or by creating the opportunity him/herself. The strength of an organisation, community and society is where there is an unstoppable, pervasive desire by everyone to be a leader.

What difference must leadership make?

To my mind, the difference a leader has to make is threefold. Firstly, a leader has to be *purpose-driven*. He/she must be driven by a quest to make difference, fully conscious of their role and responsibility regarding the achievement of the desired future or outcome for the collective he/she serves.

Secondly, a leader needs to be *vision-driven*, which requires a clear sense of the desired future or ideal world that the collective desires to achieve. He or she need not be the originator of that vision but must play a role in helping the collective to develop or embrace the vision of the future end state they want.

Thirdly, leadership is about *service* to one's collective and humanity. For sustained followership, a leader's impact should be improvement in the lives of followers and others. When leadership ceases to be about service, the privilege of being followed is lost. The mantra of leaders should be: 'Do all the good you can do wherever you can, and with all the people you can work with.'

What are the features of leadership who make a lasting, worthy difference?

I believe such leaders have five critical differentiating characteristics: Firstly, they live out uncompromisingly and with *integrity* their values, regardless of the persons, institutions and circumstances involved. They do the right things for the right reasons for the right outcomes, regardless of the level of resistance and critique. Secondly, they are *authentic* as a person in all they do. They are true to themselves, and what they stand for. Thirdly, they are *service focused, selfless and people centric*. They reach out to others from the premise that everyone is trying to do the best they can. And if they knew better, they would do even better. The leader must strive to create win–win situations.

Fourthly, these leaders apply *systemic, big-picture thinking* linked to their *values and principles*. They seek to understand the impact of their daily, transactional actions on the goals and vision they are endeavouring to achieve. These leaders always begin with the end in mind and stay with the end in mind throughout the path they are following towards their vision. Fifthly, such leaders are *resilient by* doggedly sticking to what they have set out to achieve, again regardless of persons and circumstances.

How should leaders go about making a real difference?

My firm belief is that true leaders do things differently. First, in achieving their goals and vision – as informed by their life purpose – these leaders realise that *leadership starts with themselves as persons* in the first instance. One cannot lead others if one cannot lead oneself and those dearest to oneself, like being a true parent to one's children. Second, these leaders *lead from the perspective of being servants*. He/she seeks to find the challenge, issue or problem they were 'born' to solve to the benefit of all, in this way adding value for all. It is not about themselves and their personal interests and benefits. The 'Me' is subservient to the 'Us'.

Third, to make a difference, these leaders infuse everything they do with *passion and dedication* in the way that they want to make the best of whatever area or situation they are entrusted with as a leader, regardless of the resistance and critique. Fourth, such a leader always seeks, as a starting point, to *understand others*, their world views, and circumstances before pushing to be understood as a leader. This requires active listening by the leader, and one-on-one, quiet conversations. In particular, the leader seeks to uncover the unsaid, the undiscussables, what is skirted around, or avoided. She/he realises that she/he may also be hampered by her/his own blind spots. Regardless of what a leader asks her/his followers to do, they will start doing things based on how the leader interacts with them as opposed to what the leader tells them to do.

Fifth, difference-making leaders ensure at all times that their *day-to-day transactional decisions and actions are tied to their overall purpose and vision*. Sixth, these leaders allow *followers to influence* them regarding the vision, the path to the vision, and the pace at which to move towards the vision. Seventh, they *communicate* on an ongoing basis to all concerned parties to keep them informed, and are *personally visible* where it matters. Eighth, though they have 'hard' power which they have the full right to apply, they seek primarily to use their 'soft' power: *engaging people* by appealing to their aspirations, hopes, ideals, needs and dreams.

Ninth, they engender *teaming and team work*: 'We are in this together, and are all needed to realise the vision.' Tenth, they act as inspirational *role models* by setting the example. Eleventh, they are *good followers* which is reflected in assisting fellow leaders to achieve common goals. Twelfth, replicate leadership by building the *next generation of leaders*, especially amongst the upcoming youth, realising that they want to be part of building a new world. With or without leadership's permission, they will play that role.

The future

Many of the ideas I have raised above are explored at great length throughout *Leadership Dynamics and Wellbeing*. It is my wish that this book, in exploring the key topic of leadership, will enable you as a leader, organisations and institutions, leadership teachers and researchers, to go and make that sorely needed difference. I also hope the book will assist our leaders, particularly our young and corporate leaders, to enable our country to make the much-needed and desired giant leap into the inclusive, prosperous and peaceful future we all yearn for so passionately.

Thulisile Madonsela was South Africa's Public Protector. She is also a Human Rights Lawyer and Equality Expert. Madonsela is one of the 11 technical experts who helped the Constitutional Assembly draft the final constitution in 1994 and 1995. Previously, she was a member of a Task Team that prepared constitutional inputs for the Gauteng Province of the African National Congress. She presented the final document at the African National Congress' Gauteng Constitutional Conference in 1995.

Intuition, Silence, Giants and the Cattle Herder

Mohammad Karaan

Article published in Sake Beeld on 1 October 2015.
Translated from Afrikaans. Used with permission

My approach to leadership can be summarised in twenty principles.

1. *Share the future.* An open hand and open systems will better serve you than selfishness and closed systems. To prosper, grow and foster positivity, the benefits of knowledge and wealth must be shared in a conscious manner. Those who are blessed with great vision, carry a greater burden of responsibility.

2. *Find a different path.* Conforming to convention is not how you prosper – the way to do it is to forge a new or different path. Amongst any population group there are a select few who intuitively strive to be different, and leaders are amongst their number.

3. *Intuition first, then logic.* Logic can be misleading. Leaders trust their intuition and their sixth sense, even if it is subjective. Logic is shaped by personal experience and the viewpoints of others. Each being grows from, and is connected to, a bigger truth. Learn to trust this truth.

4. *Channel energy.* Leaders understand that goals are achieved by channelling energy in a certain direction. Inspiration unleashes energy.

5. *Trust swarm intelligence.* The birds and bees do not hold meetings. Lions instinctively know how to hunt. Thanks to swarm intelligence, every animal understands its role. Leaders build organisations in which employees' instincts and innate understanding of their individual critical roles determine the company's language, relations and operations. So that there is no need to be guided by hierarchies or await instructions.

6. *Seeing around corners.* Leaders see the future long before others do, and lead them towards it without necessarily knowing the destination. The future is an uncharted land with unknown challenges, many of which will be revealed in due course. A leader can see around corners.

7. *Actively pursue blessings.* No one can predict the outcome of events with any measure of certainty, and many of our actions are largely dependent on luck. Happiness is a blessing. We create blessings through the goodwill of others. Good leaders surround themselves with people who bless them with their care, protection and nurturing.

8. *Giants and dwarves.* Leaders build their organisations on the shoulders of giants and continuously involve those who are greater than themselves. Growth comes from appointing people who are 'greater than' you are. Conversely, appointing those who are 'lesser than', diminishes you.

9. *All people are the same.* Yes, diversity is a reality which leaders can use to their advantage. But at their core, people are the same regardless of ethnicity. True leaders can lead regardless of the circumstances, even if that means leading groups who are different from them.

10. *Doubt and faith.* Leaders are not hobbled by doubts, but are impelled to act by the strength of their convictions and their unwavering faith in the future. This keeps them on track as their peers run out of steam.

11. *Savour the silence.* Many leaders are loners because they tend to live in a world of their own that is nurtured by a wellspring of silence from within. Silence is synonymous with peace. Contact with a greater Truth allows you to replenish your energy. Leaders know how to savour the silence.

12. *Avoid fools.* Fools not only derail you, their foolishness expends your energy unnecessarily. Leaders avoid fools by keeping the peace and leaving the foolish on their road to nowhere. Yes, leaders are often confronted by angry people, and know that their anger stems from a siege mentality. Man is just a different breed of animal. A threatened animal becomes aggressive. Leaders handle aggression by identifying the root cause and addressing it in a subtle way.

13. *Speak less, listen more.* Leaders know that it is much more important to listen than it is to speak. They also know that sometimes contemplation is more valuable than speaking out. Not everything you know needs to be shared. The right word at the right time is far more effective than an uninterrupted flow of opinions.

14. *Tread lightly on this earth.* True leaders do not threaten, they lure. They tread lightly, knowing that they are but a small part of a much greater and more powerful whole. Their aim is not to take, but to give.

15. *Walk a mile in someone else's shoes.* Many great leaders had difficult childhoods, but knew how to turn this to their advantage. That experience allows them to see life from a different perspective, thanks to the benefits of insight and wisdom.

16. *The further you look into the past, the further you can see into the future.* Today was created yesterday, tomorrow will be created today. The future is uncertain because you are still constructing it today. Leaders are not intimidated by the uncertainty and mystery of the future. They know that because the future is shaped by the past, they need to understand the past. The past is still the best predictor of the future.

17. *Your scars tell a story of who you are.* Many great leaders and prophets grew up in single-parent households. Many successful individuals have reported how their difficult childhoods inspired them to face difficult challenges later in life. Use those tough lessons of your youth to your advantage.

18. *Friends, heroes and travelling companions.* Success is not the preserve of the sage or the slave. It largely depends on the quality of the people with whom you surround yourself. Be discerning and clever in choosing your sidekicks. On the road to success, make sure you choose the right travelling companions when they cross your path.

19. *The truth shall set you free.* The essence of good leadership is to strive for the truth in all things, no matter the risk.

20. *The cattle herder's creed.* Many great leaders learned valuable lessons while working as cattle herders. First, in the morning the cattle herder leads the herd to green pastures, leading the way from the front. Second, once in pasture he keeps a watchful eye on them, praising good behaviour and punishing transgressions. Third, at dusk, when they return to the camp, he walks behind the herd to ensure that there are no stragglers because the cattle already know their end destination.

Prof Mohammad Karaan is an Agricultural Economist and Dean of the Faculty of Agri-sciences at Stellenbosch University. He served on the National Planning Commission, was Chairman of the National Agricultural Marketing Board and worked as an economist at the Development Bank of Southern Africa. He is the Director of Pioneer Foods, as well as several other companies.

What Matters is the Greater Good

Gill Marcus

Interview conducted during March 2013 by Adriaan Groenewald of the Leadership Platform at the time Gill was the Governor of the SA Reserve Bank. Used with permission

Gill never had leadership ambitions. If someone addressed her as a leader she would probably look behind her. She says: "I don't see myself in that role. I never saw myself with an ambition to be a leader. I don't see that now." She simply sees leadership as "an honour bestowed on someone because people want to hear what you have to say, because you reflect, for them what's important".

For Gill it has also been a quest of "what matters to me?" What has been important to her is what kind of society we live in; what kind of values we have; who we are. She believes it is also a challenge of "to be or to have". For her personally 'to be' is more important. To have includes material wealth, your position and all your authority and for her this "has never been a part of what I see as important".

Marcus has never applied for a job in her life. In her teenage years she joined the ANC. From there on life was about what she could do to match her desire to make South Africa a better place. With whatever came her way she did her best and was asked to do more and more. In essence it has been like a symbiotic relationship of adding value by shaping situations and responsibilities, while these very situations shaped her views in return.

Remaining true to her values and purpose was always a given, but on her journey more started to matter. She explains that "when you are exercising your role or responsibility you have to take more into account". This 'more' to her is 'the greater good'. So, as a leader it is not only about what is right for you but what is right for the greater good. Marcus explains: "It (the role) can't be against your values, but it's not about yourself and when you are exercising judgment, it is about the greater good."

According to Marcus this mindset lifts the leader onto another level where, "it is not about how I feel today; this is secondary. I could be feeling totally lousy today but if this is what I have to do then this is what must be done". It seems that it is therefore about understanding yourself, the greater good and then the 'office' or position that is thrust upon you. She says: "The question is to draw the distinction between what is the authority of the office and what is your personal authority, because office has huge authority." Marcus believes the leader's personal conduct can add to the office or detract from it, and "your best combination is when you can combine your personal leadership and authority with the authority of the office, because then you can use that combination to effectively achieve what needs to be done".

Every day is a great adventure for Marcus and she loves waking up to a new day, needing only four hours' sleep. With the world being in its current state it can however be a challenge to sleep well, never mind waking up. She and her team try and understand the current global turmoil, by asking questions like: What are we seeing? How are we seeing it? What are the implications? What is our responsibility to do, "so that we can minimise the impact of an imploding world, because that's what's happening"?

While the Reserve Bank is an independent organisation of roughly 2 200 employees with seven branches across SA, it functions like an integrated stakeholder of society that is part and parcel of it. The independence according to Marcus stretches as far as "exercising our constitutional responsibility without fear or favour". Marcus highlights "we are in many instances the only African country that is a participant in our own right in many of the international forums, like the G20, G24, BIS. We have a voice internationally and try to influence decisions about the world we believe we need to live in". Marcus herself may be unique in that she has been in parliament, government and the private sector, which includes chairing the ABSA Board.

All of the above, and more, enhance confidence in decision making. When Marcus is comfortable that she has sufficient information and views she takes a decision. As a consultative leader she views consultation as a process where, whenever possible, the different parties should be in the same room so that they can bounce their views off one another. In this way it is not only consultation between the leader and individual parties but everyone's views will be aired and influenced one way or the other. This approach improves the chances of arriving at a collective agreement. Of course this necessitates quality, mature individuals that are knowledgeable yet willing to listen and even shift from their original positions, for the greater good.

Marcus expands regarding decision making: "I think there are different levels of decision making. There are decisions about organisational day-to-day issues that must be decided on, and then there is decision making around for example the monetary policy stance." In the case of the latter they do not simply make the decision when they meet as a committee every two months. They build up to that decision every day. So, when the time comes they pull all the preparation together, evaluate and decide. Marcus comments: "I would say it is the quality of the information and the quality of the people around and then the rigour with which you all examine the data and discuss what needs to be done. You want people with strong and thoughtful views, and I believe we have them here."

Marcus comes across as passionate, intelligent, purpose-driven, humble, human, engaging, approachable, fearless, a big picture thinker and authentic. Her weakness may be that she does not necessarily enjoy being a public figure. Then again, this could very well be her strength.

Gill served as Deputy Minister of Finance in the Government of Nelson Mandela from 1996 to 1999. In 1999 she became Deputy Governor of the Reserve Bank. After leaving in 2004, she held the Professorship of Leadership and Gender Studies at the Gordon Institute of Business Science, before going into business. In July 2009 she became Governor of the Reserve Bank. She stepped down at the end of her five-year term in November 2014.

Moving Effectively Through the Stages of Leadership Impact

Monhla Hlahla

Interviewed during 2011 by Adriaan Groenewald of Leadership Platform. Used with permission

In 2005 I met Monhla Hlahla MD Airports Company South Africa (ACSA) for the first time, as the newly crowned Businesswoman of the Year. I can tell you emphatically that the person I interviewed during 2011 and the one I interviewed in 2005 are two entirely different individuals. She carried herself very differently, with more quiet confidence, a certain calmness.

What happened? She allowed herself the time to move through what can be described as the 'four stages of leadership impact' and so gained invaluable experience.

The interview with Hlahla helped me refine this model.

- **Stage one: Understanding and acceptance.** The purpose of this stage is to understand (e.g. the organisation, people, environment, the drivers of organisation) and gain a level of acceptance from all stakeholders which one cannot claim but has to earn over time.
- **Stage two: Credible management/leadership.** The purpose of this stage is to leverage off the understanding and acceptance and lead for maximum impact. However, during this stage the leader may still be mostly focused on the self, e.g. how she leads; how she can become a better leader for the organisation and people.
- **Stage three: Leadership multiplication for legacy.** This is a powerful stage as the leader now mostly starts focusing on others, his/her leadership: how he/she can achieve through them by assisting them to be better leaders and how someone can in fact take over from him/her.
- **Stage four: Successful handover.** This is the exit stage. If the leader has moved through the above three stages, then this stage will mostly be a natural consequence. There will be a successor that is ready to take over, and the leader will feel ready for another challenge in his/her life.

Some leaders get stuck in one of the first three stages and hesitate or even refuse to exit, which could be detrimental to the organisation or country, depending on who the leader is. There are several reasons for this, some being rather obvious, but will not be expanded on here. It takes great maturity to positively and consciously set one's sights on stage four.

Hlahla's views correlate with this 'leadership impact' model as she believes that during her first few years she managed more than what she led. It was during this management period that she acquired more of an understanding of the overall business, and in time attained acceptance. As this happened it became easier for her to lead effectively – positively impacting on individuals, clients, suppliers, and ultimately the organisation.

Her concern is that there are too many leaders who move on to another job before they have had the opportunity to really lead effectively. Perhaps this happens because stage one can be so difficult. So, some leaders may be tempted to give up and move on, especially when a more attractive or lucrative offer comes along. But, just know that if one leaves for the wrong reasons it will be before you have truly added value to the people, the organisation and in fact oneself. There is no short cut to making any meaningful contribution. Hlahla believes very strongly in this principle.

She has now been the leader of ACSA for just on eight years and this is not an easy company to run. To me it seemed she is probably in stage three where she is making a difference with confidence, while focusing on her leadership under her.

Her stage one had serious challenges. The first one was a very difficult Chairman who did not trust her. There were media reports about their unhealthy relationship. Hlahla received lots of advice and counsel from family, friends and colleagues. The pressure to fight the issues through the media beckoned, but she declined and pushed on, even though at times she quietly sat in her office crying. Then she fired her Chief of Security, which of course made headlines on a regular basis. It also dragged several important ACSA stakeholders into the process, e.g. the government, police service.

Hlahla had difficulty with changes in Board members, heists at the airport; and an incredible amount of expansion that involves building operations. But, despite all these she seems to have navigated her way through the maze of challenges and eventually moved into stages two and three where she has now been leading for some time. She too had her opportunities to give up and leave, but did not.

During her leadership career at this very challenging State Owned Enterprise, she has learned some valuable principles that can assist every leader to move effectively through the leadership impact stages:

1. Keep focusing on the core purpose of the organisation and its goal. When the difficult times arrive and counsel comes from all angles, one can listen sincerely and then make a decision that is good for the organisation and its purpose.
2. The ability and humility to hear all views.
3. Decisiveness is critical. Sometimes a situation needs someone to just make a call rather than someone to necessarily make the right call. What becomes more important then is one's ability to manage unintended consequences.
4. Guts or courage.

Monhla served as the Managing Director and Chief Executive Officer of Airports Company South Africa SOC Limited from 2001 to September 2011. Prior to that, she was with the Development Bank of Southern Africa (DBSA), having joined in 1994 and successfully managed several large infrastructure projects. In 2005, she received the Business Women Association's (BWA) Business Woman of the Year award and the *Black Business Quarterly* (BBQ) Magazine's Woman of the Year award.

Good Leaders Stand or Fall by Their Principles

Hendrik du Toit

Article published in Sake Beeld on 17 September 2015.
Translated from Afrikaans. Used with permission

The current era is characterised by a paucity of political leaders, both nationally and internationally. It seems apt to label this the 'post-Mandela' era. Could this perhaps be attributed to social media, or the spineless politics of 'opinion polls'? Locally, citizens are faced with a surplus of Party apparatchiks in positions of power, and very few inspiring leaders. Europe has a surfeit of bureaucrats and professional politicians, but very few leaders.

What can we learn from leaders who make a difference? Ordinary people across Europe are frustrated by the handling of the economic melt-down in Greece, the volatile situation in the Ukraine and the chaos of the migrant crisis in the Mediterranean. Pope Francis, President Xi Jinping of China and Premier Narendra Modi of India offer glimmers of hope, but their respective tenures have thus far not been lengthy enough to merit a considered opinion.

Despite widespread optimism at the start of his historical election to the most powerful position on earth, President Barack Obama has not managed to sway America from its destructive path of petty politics, and has failed to pave the way for international cooperation in the post-Bush era. He was overly ambitious, and sadly did little to form the right coalitions. Leadership is about much more than making rousing speeches.

What can we learn from those leaders who truly made a difference through the ages? What do Alexander the Great, Admiral Nelson, Mohandas Gandhi, Winston Churchill, Deng Xiaoping, and our own Albert Luthuli, Nelson Mandela and FW de Klerk have in common?

Leadership is the ability to make a real difference by motivating people, rather than forcing them to work together towards a common goal. The concept of single-mindedness explains why certain leaders were so successful. Good leadership is not a popularity contest. In fact, Churchill was extremely unpopular when he vetoed any form of compromise with Hitler. Gandhi and Mandela were incarcerated; De Klerk was branded a traitor.

Good leaders do not change their tune at the drop of a hat. The have faith in the courage of their convictions, follow their own path and act in a consistent manner. They stand and fall by what they believe in. They are authentic, rather than the creations of spin-doctors. They step up to the plate in high-pressure situations. Cricket supporters who saw cricketer Clive Rice in action in his heyday will recall many instances where he shouldered the burden of responsibility, rather than expecting his team to follow instructions. Richie McCaw did the same during a game at Ellis Park, against the Springboks, where his unorthodox line-out calls soon swung the game in the All Blacks' favour.

True leaders are credible, be they politicians, businessmen or sporting heroes, because they are goal-oriented in their approach and have a clear vision. Why else would people walk through fire for them? Most successful leaders are authentic because they are comfortable in their own skins. That is one aspect of leadership which nobody can teach you.

Although leadership can be defined quite narrowly, leadership styles tend to be divergent. I usually encourage leaders to adopt the leadership style they are comfortable with. The literature outlines and analyses numerous leadership styles, but in my view those theories are not as important as this basic truth: no movement or organisation that works towards a common goal, can effectively channel the energy and talents of its people, without effective leadership at all levels. Those who underestimate the impact of good leadership or leadership development, do so at their peril.

Hendrik du Toit is Executive Head of Investec Asset Management and a Director of Investec plc and Investec Ltd. In 1991 he joined the group as Portfolio Manager and founding member of Investec Asset Management, before leading the company to become a multinational specialist asset management firm with assets in excess of R1 400 billion. In 2008 he was named *Global Investor's* Asset Manager of the Year. In 2011 *Financial News* named him one of the world's ten most influential asset managers. In 2012 he was *Financial News'* Executive Head of the Year.

Leader Excellence Asks for a Distinct, Shared Leadership Philosophy

GT Ferreira, Laurie Dippenaar and Paul Harris

Christel Fourie, based on her doctorate on the leadership philosophies
of GT Ferreira, Laurie Dippenaar and Paul Harris

GT Ferreira, Laurie Dippenaar and Paul Harris were the founders of the FirstRand Group. They had a remarkable partnership that endured for more than 30 years whilst providing executive co-leadership to the Group they founded. A partnership like the FirstRand founders' one is not born. It develops. At times they battled together, but the end game was always more important than who got the credit. The cohesion was stronger than the conflict. It did not fragment on the back of personalities.

The founders' leadership philosophy is intricately linked to their business philosophy. The essence of their shared leadership philosophy pivoted on ten distinct axes.

Be who you are

As a leader, be who you are. It has to be how you are naturally. The founders applied a leadership style that was natural to them. A lot came about intuitively; from a real honest place. They did not copy from textbooks. They are quick to point out that there are different strategies that can bring about success. The important thing is to know which team you are playing on.

Love what you do and have fun

Do something you love and have fun along the way. A shared perspective is that if you enjoy what you do, it takes you further. Financial results are important. But of greater importance is whether people want to come to work. It links to what keeps exceptional leaders engaged. When they enjoy what they do, when they grow in their roles, when you let them get on with things and pay them well, that is when they stay. What is hard to achieve, is made to sound simple.

The right partners

Handpick partners: like-minded people and future leaders who are similar, but also different. How GT handpicked his business partners initially, set the scene. Look for someone you trust, who is honest and works hard. All three were inherently entrepreneurs; were equally hungry and keen; and, importantly, did not take themselves too seriously.

The three partners are also very different. In a nutshell, GT is a strategist, a diplomat, a world-class negotiator and a people's person. Laurie is the numbers man, embodies strong values, is a big thinker and excels at follow-through. Paul is a risk taker, a creative thinker, brings passion, a dealmaker at heart, and new ideas make his antennae go up. The biggest success factor of their partnership was that they complemented one another. GT thinks they were very lucky that their skills and temperaments complemented each other so much so that it landed them in the fast stream.

The founders made it known that they look for a certain kind of person. Like-minded does not mean sameness. What matters greatly is attitude and performance. Essentially, it has to do with 'Do you fit in?' They surrounded themselves with the strongest people and were not intimidated by this. FirstRand's leaders are typically picked young, picked on merit and do not 'run' for short stretches (= stable leadership). GT, Laurie and Paul were able to spot talent a mile away.

Being an architect

A leader is an architect. The founders brought a specific approach to business, rooted in empowerment and innovation that turned out to be highly effective in starting new businesses. A crucial mindset is that you do not have to be dishonest to be competitive. Outsmart competitors with ingenuity. Also, work harder than your competition. No matter what you do, you will not achieve the pinnacle of success if you work from 8 to 5.

Furthermore, if you want to cultivate innovation, be prepared to tolerate mistakes. The founders were disruptors, and disrupted long before it had earned a 'name'. Then they actively encouraged others to disrupt. Making bankers and professional managers think like owners formed part of their considerable legacy. They lived the owner-manager philosophy one hundred per cent. It was rooted in the belief that if you treat the business as your own, you care more. It asks for high competence and maturity in leaders.

Model the organisational culture

A leader cannot fake culture. The values of an organisation stem from the way that senior leaders behave. It sends a message to others as to how they should react in certain situations. Values, or in FirstRand's language 'the things your mother taught you', are lived and practised. It comes through prominently in RMB's slogan that has not changed in 30 years: *Traditional values. Innovative ideas.* The founders maintained that if the organisation continued to choose its leaders in the same way, the Group's entrepreneurial culture will prevail. The word 'trust' permeated the founders' story and leadership. If you have trust in an organisation, it leads automatically to a good reputation.

It is about the 'We' not the 'I'

The role of a leader is not to make all the decisions, but to facilitate good decision-making. Leadership is not solo work. There is no 'I' in leadership, only 'We'. The message, 'We did not do this on our own; we have been surrounded by brilliant people', was reiterated time and again. In business, the egos can be bigger than a building. A leader has to work with that. If you can get the team focused more on the importance of scoring and winning as a team, and less about who gets the credit, it creates a 'We' mindset.

Being a talent magnet

The founders epitomised an ethos and a culture that attracted talented individuals to working with them. What people sensed around these three was: 'Here you make your own future'. Paul framed it as: "You are your own Pty Ltd. You make your own destiny." Due to humble beginnings, the founders were not into the hierarchy side of things. They just wanted to get things done. They always worked with people rather than ordering them around. Essentially, they created an environment that they wanted to work in.

Grow people

Be generous and commit to growing people. The founders spent a considerable proportion of their time developing potential. They were generous in sharing their knowledge and experience. They were incredibly happy about others' successes. They listened; asked questions to challenge; raised the bar; sparked ideas; offered intellectual support; and gave people wings. They inspired others through their example. The potent combination of youth and grey hair was not lost on them. They created an atmosphere of success.

Seamless succession

The most important responsibility of a leader is that when you leave, there should not even be a ripple. Aim for a seamless handover. Leadership succession can be compared to running a perpetual relay. As a leader you take the baton and you run your best round and then you hand over to the next runner in the best possible way. Give those runners who need to take over the baton time to establish themselves, and then get out of their way. If you get the right people on board, succession is not really an issue. Laurie maintains that in a succession race, there are more candidates who can be ministers than presidents. A statesman is a leader who can take the right decisions not for own gain, but puts a business or country's interests above their own.

Be humble, confident, courageous and passionate

In the founders, we have a fine example of leaders who had a natural humility combined with being confident leaders. They conducted themselves with chutzpah and demonstrated courage and a work ethic hard to equal. They have always wanted to make South Africa a better place. They are leaders who are not just passionate about business. They are passionate about life.

In 1977 GT Ferreira, Laurie Dippenaar and Paul Harris founded Rand Consolidated Investments Ltd (RCI) from which FirstRand Group and its offshoots developed. At present the Group owns well-known banking brands such as First National Bank, WesBank, Rand Merchant Bank and Ashburton Investments. The founders have since retired from the Group but still hold various Board chairmanships and directorships. They all have post-graduate qualifications.

SECTION 5

THE FUTURE OF LEADERSHIP

Chapter 10

LOOKING AHEAD

The Future of Leadership

Andrew J Johnson and Theo H Veldsman

In closing our brief excursion into *Leadership Dynamics and Wellbeing* it is worthwhile repeating some key assertions we made in the opening chapter:

- leadership is under severe scrutiny, and;
- leadership is in the overheating crucible of a reframed/reframing world that is in the throes of fundamental and radical transformation, hence; and
- the search is on for better and different leadership, in the present and going into the future.

Going into the future, the need for organisations to have an ongoing, deliberate, comprehensive and in-depth conversation about leadership is an imperative if they want not merely to survive but also to thrive sustainably.

In this chapter we would like to gaze into the crystal ball by posing the question: If there is a need for better and different leadership going into the future, what would it look like with the conditions attached to such future-fit leadership?

To this end we explore the features of the growing crisis around leadership; the unfolding, future contextual leadership challenges; profiling the "context fit" leadership of the future; effective leadership engagement with the future context through Skilful Improvisation; and finally, the implications of Skilful Improvisation for growing and developing future-fit leadership.

Features of the Growing Leadership Crisis

Some of the important features of the growing leadership crisis that will have a significant impact on future leadership are:

- *Leadership no longer has any place to hide.* Leaders are in the public eye and under public scrutiny constantly because of the power of social media, and more stringent and expanding corporate governance requirements and demands.
- *Accelerating mistrust, anger towards, suspicion of, disillusionment in, and sense of alienation from, institutional leadership*, whether in business, the public sector, or in politics. There is a growing general public perception that "they are in it for themselves and their own enrichment. People and institutions are merely the means to satisfy their ego-centric needs, wants and purposes."
- *Greater and unrealistic expectations for "leadership on steroids".* There is little patience with new leaders taking time to settle into and acclimatise to their new roles. The pressure is for instant delivery from the word "go", often against unreasonable deliverables, goals and standards. In many instances, the leadership role expectations from stakeholders are unclear and ambiguous, resulting in decreasing leadership tenures, and higher frequencies of derailment and burnout.
- The *emergence of more spontaneous leadership* in more places, at more times and by more people, the growing trend of "leaderless revolutions". These revolutions are fuelled

by the multiplication and mobilisation power of social media in the hands of everyone, everywhere, anytime. The spontaneous revolutions are blossoming around issues regarding globalisation, climatic warming, technological innovation, religious "holy wars", and demographic displacements like the European refugee crisis. Recent examples of such "leaderless" movements include the #arabspring movements of the Middle East; the #occupy movements in North America and Europe; and #mustfall movements in the South African higher education sector.

- The ***growing cancer of toxic leaders, followers and organisations*** because of the fanatical worshipping of unfettered individualism and egocentricity to the detriment of the pursuit common good; the rampant growth in personal self-interest and self-love (in other words, narcissism); putting "Me Pty Ltd" at the centre; the weakening of the overarching authority of commonly accepted ethical values and norms, also because of value clashes resulting from increasing multicultural settings; and weak followers unable and unwilling to challenge toxic leadership courageously and fiercely.

Unfolding Future Leadership Contextual Challenges

Against the backdrop of the above features of the growing leadership crisis, what are the most apparent unfolding future contextual leadership challenges? We would like to explore these challenges in terms of the conceptual framework given in Figure 10.1, constructed around the relationships in which a leader is embedded.

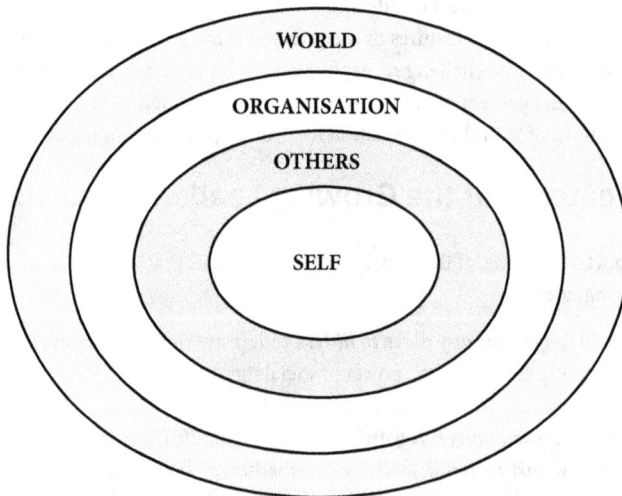

Figure 10.1 Leadership in relationship with the World, Organisation, Others and Self

According to the framework given in Figure 10.1, the leader's success resides in successfully connecting, nurturing and maintaining four interdependent, critical relationships – each with their unique interacting leadership challenges, demands and requirements – with the World; one's Organisation; Others; and Self. Each of the four relationship of leadership will be discussed in turn from a futuristic perspective. Though discussed separately and sequentially, the four relationships form an organic, systemic whole; are in constant reciprocal interaction; and form dynamic patterns, whether vicious or virtuous.

World

Much has been written and spoken about the VUCA World context of Volatility, Uncertainty, Complexity and Ambiguity, expanded here by ourselves to VICCAS: a World of increasing Variety, Interdependence (that is, connectivity), Complexity, Change, Ambiguity, Seamlessness and Sustainability. The counter, "dark" side of the above VICCAS features must also be considered: Over-standardisation, Over-dependency, Over-simplification, Over-formalisation, Over-control, Over-specialisation and Over-concentration. Going forward, the expectation is that the VICCAS Context will intensify.

The key challenges of the VICCAS Context are:

- Pressures arising from **macro destructive and threatening global, socio-economic dynamics invading the global village,** such as wealth concentration in the hands of a few "Haves"; the significantly growing income gap; the relative impoverishment of the middle class; growing structural unemployment because of the Fourth Industrial Revolution (see below); and population displacement because of climatic change and value clashes (see below). The sensitive, interwoven fabric and tapestry of the World – the playing field of leadership – is being torn apart.

- Social media **fragmenting the world into "e-suburbs" of vast global (radicalised) interest groups** talking only to themselves in self-referential ways in self-created echo chambers; radical group recruitment via the Internet; the global tsunami waves of fads and fashions, uninformed opinions and views engulfing the world; the snowballing generation of vast amounts of unvalidated data, information and knowledge feeding and swaying public opinion; parochial, selective views fed by search engines, for example, Google's search engines defining siloed realities for people. Those who have to be led are "disappearing" and becoming faceless in cyberspace through virtualisation and digitisation.

- **Vast technological innovation,** characterised by an exponential rate of change in and merging of multiple technologies across diverse domains such as the physical, digital, and biological manifested in, for example, Artificial Intelligence (AI), robotics, DNA sequencing, the Internet of Things (iot), driverless vehicles, 3D-printing, nanotechnology, biotechnology, big data, materials science, energy storage, and quantum computing. Digitisation and emails are replacing direct face-to-face leadership. It is believed that machines and systems are taking over, replacing people. Against the backdrop of keeping up with technological innovation, future leadership will have to align effectively in real-time technology, people, and working mode continuously relative to the strategic intent they are pursuing.

- Global fundamental **value system clashes and tensions** creating deep fault lines and schisms in communities, organisations and societies. Future leadership will need to build common, shared value spaces enabling diverse people to collaborate for the benefit and common good of all.

- The increasing **untrammelled power of big global corporates** – some bigger than states – leveraged from their control over vast resources globally, pressurising governments, institutions and stakeholders to "toe their line" in order to suit their parochial, narrow, corporate interests. The resources can be moved at the click of a mouse. The challenge to leadership is to move beyond narrow corporate self-interest and adopt a corporate social investment, common good, and a perspective infusing all of the corporate's thinking, decisions and actions.

- The growing **mismatch of global institutions** such as the United Nations (UN), World Bank, IMF, the International Court of Justice, International Criminal Court, and Interpol to oversee and deal in globally representative ways with the increasing contextual complexity of the World. Increasingly these institutions are becoming too simple for, and too unrepresentative of, the complexifying World. The leadership challenge is the re-creation of the existing, and the setting up of newly conceived, institutions matched to the requisite contextual complexity of the VICCAS Context.

Organisation

Against the features of the VICCAS Context, organisations (including institutions) to be led in the future will be facing at least the following challenges:

- The heightened *vulnerability of the organisation's reputation and brand* to social media used for mobilisation against organisations by lobby/interest/pressure groups. Future leadership will have to be a master of the social media, and dominate this communication in space-time.
- The *disruption of traditional business models* because of virtualisation and digitalisation, for example, Amazon, e-Bay, and the on-demand economy driven by the emergence of applications (apps)-based organisations, for example, Uber and airbnb. Future leadership will have to question their existing business model on a continuous basis from first principles.
- The *deconstruction of big corporates* into smaller, highly autonomous, network-based business units in order to instil corporates with nimbleness, agility, client centricity, and responsiveness. The leadership of the future will have to be a networker and alliance and partner builder. He/she will have to be outstanding at building deep and robust relationships.
- Increasing pressure for *demographic representivity* regarding race, gender and culture at all leadership levels from board-level down the organisation, reflective of the organisation's chosen operating arena. Diversity sensitivity will be essential for future leadership.
- Globalisation, enabled by digitisation and virtualisation, will force organisations and leadership to adopt a *global mindset* manifested in thinking globally but acting locally.
- Organisations and their leadership will need to be *future centric* by visiting the future in order to create previously unimaginable, desirable futures. They will then have to return to the present to realise that future. Merely extrapolating from the present into the future, and applying past success recipes, will be a cause of certain extinction for organisations.
- *Disruptive innovation* because of the Fourth Industrial Revolution will necessitate the ongoing re-invention of organisations in terms of client needs, products/services, markets, and modes of delivery. Organisations will be in a constant state of flux. Future leadership will have to be relentless innovators, entrepreneurs and risk takers.
- The *increasing "algorithmisation" of professional knowledge, expertise and decision-making*, enabling para-professionals and users to take over work previously reserved for and claimed by professionals such as medical doctors, lawyers, chartered accounts, and psychologists.
- The *global demand for talent* appropriate to the VICCAS Context will lead to quicker promotion of leaders, resulting in less "intelligent" and mature leaders (see below) in senior and executive positions.
- The VICCAS Context will impose the imperative to shift from *the all-knowing, all-powerful single leader* to *shared (or distributive) leadership and the creation of leadership communities* in organisations, operating beyond hierarchy and function. This will enable the organisation to address more effectively the "wicked" challenges, problems and issues of the VICCAS Context.

Others

Some of the more important future challenges with respect to others are:

- The *range and diversity of stakeholders* of organisations and leaders will grow by leaps and bounds, also because of some of the above discussed trends and leadership challenges, such as the power of social media. Leadership will have to be knowledgeable about the diverse and conflicting needs of multiple stakeholders, including shareholders, the board, employees, suppliers, customers, regulators, competitors and the communities in which they operate, as well as the dynamics infusing each and among one another.

- In the VICCAS context there will be a *growing sense of disempowerment among stakeholders*, and consequently growing feelings among them of being helpless, threatened, anxious and angry. There will be a fervent, mounting, search for "the leader who can save us", creating the potential for followers to be vulnerable to leader exploitation and toxicity.

- The growing ambiguity with regard to *commonly accepted ethical values and norms*, also because of value clashes arising out of the growth in multicultural settings, giving rise to a greater need for value-based leadership, and to build on the "should" and "right". This leadership will need to focus not only on ethical leadership but also on creating a better society and world for present and future generations. Future leadership will have to be imbued by a moral consciousness, compass and courage leveraged from a transcendental leadership stance, namely "why?" leadership.

- The *growing power of public opinion*, solicited by ongoing surveys and referenda, and resulting in the *rise of opportunistic leadership* playing to the grandstand without a firm point of view, and acting without integrity. The need would be for future leadership acting with integrity from a clearly selected position.

- The employee base of organisations shifting to a *significant number of temporary/part time/contract workers* – many merely linked to the organisation through the Internet or an app – who have no real stake in and long-term commitment to the organisation. The challenge to future leadership would be how to engender high levels of engagement from these employees who in many cases have highly sought-after specialist skills.

Self

The challenges emerging from the above will require the future leader to dig much deeper into him-/herself, even though already being overstretched. Specific to the leader, at least the following major future challenges can be distinguished:

- The *constant onslaught on the leader's identity*: who and what am I?; what do I stand for?; what do I want to achieve?; to what end, and for whose benefit?

- The *rapid unlearning of a fixation on past success recipes*; being seduced by transient fads and fashions, and/or the fervent search for "silver bullets" propagated by snake-oil salespersons.

- More *frequent and widespread leadership transitions* requiring constant transitional adjustments by the leader. Leaders will have to be equipped with strong transition strategies and capabilities.

- A *tuned-in-ness to the vulnerability to succumb to toxic leadership*, arising out of the worshipping of individualism and giving rise to self-love; unclear, ambiguous, and conflicting values; the greying of ethics; and toxic friendly followers.

- Leaders running the risk of falling into the trap of *self-protective, "spin-doctoring" conduct* to protect themselves against relentless, merciless public exposure.

- A significantly greater likelihood and frequency of **burnout and organisational derailment** because of contextual pressures and unclear/unrealistic leadership expectations and demands by stakeholders. Leadership resilience will be a key future capability.

"Context Fit"-Leadership for the Future

A cursory scan of the contextual challenges discussed above, highlights the sizeable and seemingly overwhelming contextual demands on leaders going into the future. Leading in this unfolding new world is somewhat, in the words of Hixonia Nyasulu, Chairman of the women-controlled Ayavuna Women's Investments, "like playing tennis in the dark with unknown opponents, unexpected balls, unclear tennis court lines, and unpredictable weather". Equally, there are the possibly bewildering myriad leadership capabilities seemingly necessary to navigate and lead in the VICCAS Context, as elucidated above.

This situation could potentially leave an existing and/or aspiring leader deeply discouraged, with the natural, spontaneous response to withdraw, succumb or fight, instead of engaging positively. Going into the future, we submit that what is required is not a "silver bullet" set of specific capabilities, all needed at the same time in order to produce the "super" leader, able to be fully in charge at all times and under all circumstances; instead, the need will be rather to appreciate situation-specific leadership requirements and in this way identify, grow and develop context-fit leadership. Additionally, a community of leaders should be established, people who are able to lead effectively in a given/expected context through complementary, shared leadership, supplying collectively all of the necessary capabilities within and across situations.

Furthermore, in going into the future, a long-term, complex, and not short-term, mechanistic, vantage point to leadership should be adopted. Such a vantage point will enable us to re-imagine in a holistic, organic, integrated and dynamic way at a truly deep level a leader as a whole person embedded in his/her fourfold relationships with the World, Organisation, Others and Self, which will have to be dynamically and simultaneously aligned in real time.

Going Wide: Future-fit Leadership Capabilities Domains

Based on the above "design criteria", we would like to submit that contextual future-fit leadership will consist of five interdependent capability domains:

- *Able:* The hard and soft capabilities necessary to perform competently relative to contextual demands. The deployment of the required capabilities needs to be infused with the necessary qualities that will bring about hope, passion, caring, harmony, faith, confidence efficacy, courage and perseverance among followers, the psychosocial capital essential for followers to deal with the VICCAS Context effectively.
- *Intelligent:* Leadership who can observe, think, judge, act, learn and reflect with a growing understanding as they engage – conceptually and practically – with the VICCAS Context through converting experiences into information, information into knowledge, and knowledge into wisdom. The total "intelligence" (or meta-intelligence) of an excellent leader will consist of the five interdependent intelligence modes of Intra- and Interpersonal, Systemic, Ideation, Action, and Contextual Intelligence.
- *Mature:* Leadership able to engage consistently in relevant, productive, meaningful and constructive and uplifting ways with Self, Others, the Organisation, and the World.
- *Ethical:* Leaders and leadership who do the right thing for the right reasons in the right way in the right place and the right time with the right persons, that is, the "Should Do", the "Right thing".

- **Authentic:** Leaders and leadership which nurture and affirm the dignity, worth and efficacy of an individual(s), concurrently creating enabling, empowering, and meaningful work experiences.

Specific Future-fit Leadership Capabilities

Given the need for able, intelligent, mature, ethical and authentic leadership, required by the VICCAS Context, Figure 10.2 provides summarised clusters of suggested, more important capabilities ("Can Dos") for future-fit leadership, as per the leadership relationship dimensions discussed above – World, Organisation, Others, and Self. All of these capabilities are infused by the five capability domains of ability, intelligence, maturity, ethics and authenticity, as outlined above.

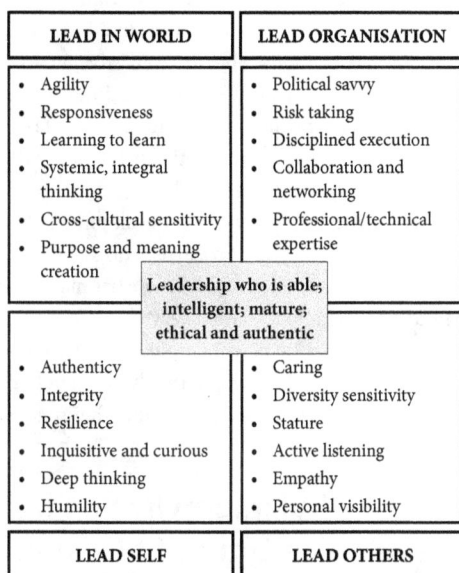

LEAD IN WORLD	LEAD ORGANISATION
• Agility • Responsiveness • Learning to learn • Systemic, integral thinking • Cross-cultural sensitivity • Purpose and meaning creation	• Political savvy • Risk taking • Disciplined execution • Collaboration and networking • Professional/technical expertise
Leadership who is able; intelligent; mature; ethical and authentic	
• Authenticy • Integrity • Resilience • Inquisitive and curious • Deep thinking • Humility	• Caring • Diversity sensitivity • Stature • Active listening • Empathy • Personal visibility
LEAD SELF	LEAD OTHERS

Figure 10.2 Clusters of suggested, more important capabilities for future-fit leadership

Effective Leadership Engagement with the Future Context through Skilful Improvisation

It should be clear that even when one distils the future-fit capabilities required by leaders – as per Figure 10.2 – to respond effectively to the VICCAS challenges, the list is daunting and intimidating. Therefore, as suggested earlier, one should rather adopt a situational appreciation for the contextual, relevant application of particular capabilities. Such an approach may then lead one to think of effective leadership as an act of "Skilful Improvisation". Perhaps as the futurist, Alvin Toffler, points out, a "new" type of leader is called for, one who depends less on his/her intellectual and technical skills, and is instead one who is open to learning new things, unlearning old things that no longer serve, and relearning some things of value that have been forgotten. In this case, "effectiveness" can be defined as the extent to which a leader is able to achieve his/her intended consequences in a certain context. If leadership is action, it implies that such action can be effective or ineffective relative to the context concerned. Skilful Improvisation entails enabling and empowering leadership to re-invent him-/herself continuously in real time as contextual leadership challenges, demands and requirements shift, expectedly and unexpectedly.

Conceiving of leadership as Skilful Improvisation accepts certain future-fit capabilities will be required to lead effectively in the unfolding Context. In order to do so, leadership will have to develop – holistically and organically – deep capabilities with regard to all of the relationships he/she is embedded in across the five critical capability domains discussed above: ability, intelligence, maturity, ethics, and authenticity. The development of such deep capabilities will require fundamentally deep self-introspection and reflection because the barriers to true leadership effectiveness, organisational change, and excellence reside fundamentally inside the individual leader.

We contend that the VICCAS Context faced by leadership we have sketched in *Leadership Dynamics and Wellbeing* will only become worse. It is quite possible that by the time we have developed our leaders in what we consider the "necessary" capabilities, they will already have become outdated. Skilful Improvisation appears to be best suited to address the chaotic VICCAS Context adequately: the insight and will to be able to "read" the situation as a leader correctly; to exercise the right judgement; to choose from a set of capabilities such as those given in Figure 10.2 those that are situationally relevant skills as demanded by the task, people, organisational and contextual requirements; reflecting-in-action both on his/her own state of mind and the backtalk[1] of the situation, in order to perform effectively.

Impossible? Then perhaps leadership growth and development should be informed by the approach of artists. The above is precisely what jazz artists do so well.[2] Leaders know very well that life more often than not does not turn out in the way one has planned it. What if our thinking and doing are agile enough to bend with what we get served, analogous to the way in which jazz artists think and act. The jazz band may be playing a piece that they have rehearsed well, then unexpectedly someone makes a mistake. Now what if the thinking in that moment is: "There are no mistakes"; certainly not a "mistake" by someone else. Only the "mistake" of an inadequate in-the-moment response to the backtalk of the situation.[3]

Implications of Skilful Improvisation for Growing and Developing Future-fit Leadership

Skilful improvisation requires very deep personal development. Because leaders have little control over their external (chaotic) context, and quite likely become drained by its demands, it stands to reason that leaders will have to find resources internally in themselves. Such growth and development will include capacity growth and development in respect of the capability range indicated earlier (see Figure 10.2) but first and foremost in his/her relationship to him-/herself.

Going deep

This is essential because there is a blindness in all human beings through years of socialisation that necessitates that such growth and development drill deeper into the deepest layers of leaders' lived world if they are to be capacitated for the intensifying VICCAS Context. Figure 10.3 depicts the respective layers making up the leader's lived world, from "deep" to "shallow".

Visible, tangible

Action learning

Layer 6: Everyday Lived
Experiences and Actions

Layer 5: Capabilities

Layer 4: Style and Attitude

Layer 3: Decision Making

Framework

Layer 2: Value

Orientation

Layer 1: Worldview

Invisible, intangible
Double-loop learning, learning to learn

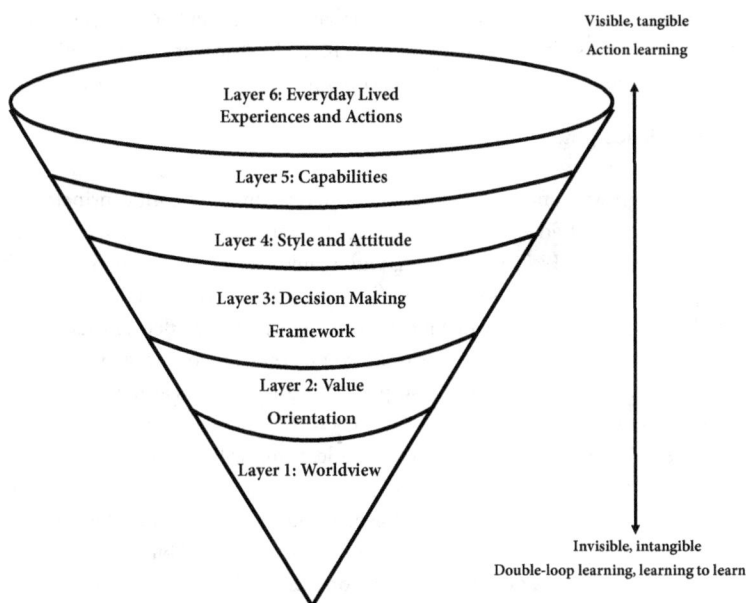

Figure 10.3 Layers making up the leader's lived world

Analogous to the building of a house, future-fit leadership growth and development have to commence with the deep Layer 1: Worldview (or Mental Model), and then proceed progressively to the more shallow layers in a "building onto" manner. Learning in this way will help the leader to bring his socially programmed blindness to conscious reflection, and develop new pathways towards effective leadership, including purposefulness: an authentic balanced disposition to the needs of others (= all stakeholders), the organisation, and the world. Learning approaches and methods will have to be employed by organisations that elicit valid information and knowledge about what individuals think and do at deep layers, because the default pattern of individuals is to employ defensive reasoning. We espouse leadership effectiveness, but as human beings we lack the ability to produce such holistic inside-out development. In addition, we are unaware of this serious, future-compromising limitation.

Bringing about deep learning

How do we effect this deep learning? As indicated earlier, one cannot simply focus on changing Layers 6: Everyday lived experiences and 5: Capabilities (see Figure 10.3). Layers 5 and 6 learning tend to break down when people experience stress because stress triggers default conduct. One has to change the underlying layers, in particular Layers 1 to 3, that drive the conduct, to Layer 6. Skilful improvisation requires drawing on deep, internal personal resources that this type of development endeavours to develop.

The knowledge organisations produce in our leadership growth and development programmes must be in the service of enabling leadership action with regard to Layer 6. Two expressions of such learning are (i) *double-loop learning*, aimed at getting to the mental models comprising underlying beliefs, values and attitudes (Layers 1 to 4) that perpetuate ineffective leadership action, in conjunction with (ii) *action learning*, focusing on conduct change through reflection on real stakeholder and organisational challenges (in other words, Layers 5 and 6) (see Figure 10.3). In the words of Argyris, Putnam, and McLain Smith,[4] methods will have to be employed "to make known what is known so well that we no longer know it, … so that it might be critiqued, … and to make known what is unknown, … the discovery of alternatives so that they too might be critiqued". Skilful improvisation contains such reflexive qualities.

Bridging the science-practice gap

Such leadership growth and development, based on sound scientific principles, will have the potential to respond adequately to bridging the perennial, ongoing science–practice gap. *Leadership Dynamics and Wellbeing* abounds with many such exemplars. In practice, this growth and development in organisations can be self-driven, technology-enabled, classroom- based, experiential and/or coaching, provided it conforms to its purposes: deep, inside-out growth and development from Layer 1 "upwards" towards Layer 6. Then and only then will organisations be preparing and delivering the right leadership in the right numbers at the right time and place, able, willing and empowered to perform effectively within the VICCAS Context.

Fundamental to this leadership growth and learning will be the need for academics and development practitioners to do less "esoteric", practice-estranged work that results in the growing gap between theory – the proverbial ivory tower – and practice. Within the VICCAS Context, real action research partnerships between academic institutions and business/non-governmental institutions/public sector are essential, focusing on leadership growth and development that is useful to leadership in the moment of action where it matters and will make a real difference. In other words, leadership growth and development that is characteristic of reflective practice, reflecting-in- and -on-action. Given financial pressures, organisations need to place a much greater emphasis on evidence-based, actionable knowledge to drive their change efforts. The speed of practice-referenced and -informed research delivery by academics will have to match the speed of change in the practical world. Otherwise, academics and academic institutions will rapidly become irrelevant to a VICCAS Context "running away" from them. They will become the extinct dinosaurs going into the future.

Conclusion

Having explored tomorrow's VICCAS Leadership Context with its features resulting in "wicked" leadership challenges, issues and problem, answering the remaining ultimate question posed in the Introduction is: "Is there a future for leadership?" Yes, there is a future for leadership, but it is conditional on:

- A *deep understanding of the unfolding VICCAS Context* going into the future in terms of leadership's fourfold relationships with the World, Organisation, Others and Self;
- *Adoption of a complexity vantage point* to leadership;
- From this complexity perspective, *re-imagine at a deep level leaders in a holistic, organic, integrated and dynamic way as a whole person,* in terms of their ability, intelligence, maturity, ethics and authenticity, as embedded in their fourfold relationships, all of which have to be dynamically aligned simultaneously in real time;
- Enabling and empowering leaders to engage with the Context through *Skilful Improvisation*;
- *Growing and developing leadership from the inside-out,* commencing with the deeper layers of leadership's lived world: Layer 1: Worldview through double-loop learning, progressing through action learning towards Layer 6: Everyday Lived Experiences and Actions; and
- *Forming vibrant two-way interactions between the academic and practice worlds,* producing just-in-time, evidence-based, actionable knowledge to drive change efforts to make leaders future-fit.

What a challenge lies ahead of all of us to make it happen in a world that is in desperate need of Leadership Dynamics and Wellbeing in order to ensure a sustainable, flourishing future for all.

Endnotes

1   "The situation talks back, the [leader] listens, and as he appreciates what he hears, he reframes the situation once again": *cf.* Schön, DA. 1983. *The reflective practitioner*. New York, NY: Basic Books.

2   *cf.* Also (a) Warren Bennis on jazz and leadership: "I used to think that running an organization was equivalent to conducting a symphony orchestra. But I don't think that's quite it; it's more like jazz. There is more improvisation"; (b) the leadership development training, styled on UK Channel 4s "Whose line is it anyway?", *Workplace IMPROV*, designed by stand-up comedian, Nadiem Solomon. The fundamental rule in this training is "pay attention".

3   Harris, S. 2011. *There are no mistakes on the bandstand*. TEDSalon NY2011.

4   Argyris, C, Putnam, R & McLain Smith, D. 1985. *Action science: concepts, methods, and skills for research and intervention*. San Francisco, CA: Jossey-Bass Inc. 237.

INDEX